VIETNAM AND THE WORLD

Vietnam and the World

Marxist-Leninist Doctrine and the Changes in International Relations, 1975–93

Eero Palmujoki
Assistant Professor
Department of Political Science and International Relations
University of Tampere
Finland

First published in Great Britain 1997 by
MACMILLAN PRESS LTD
Houndmills, Basingstoke, Hampshire RG21 6XS and London
Companies and representatives throughout the world

A catalogue record for this book is available from the British Library.

ISBN 0–333–69100–8

First published in the United States of America 1997 by
ST. MARTIN'S PRESS, INC.,
Scholarly and Reference Division,
175 Fifth Avenue, New York, N.Y. 10010

ISBN 0–312–17240–0

Library of Congress Cataloging-in-Publication Data
Palmujoki, Eero.
Vietnam and the world : Marxist-Leninist doctrine and the changes
in international relations, 1975–93 / Eero Palmujoki.
    p.   cm.
Includes bibliographical references and index.
ISBN 0–312–17240–0 (cloth)
    1. Vietnam—Politics and government—1975– 2. Vietnam—Foreign
relations.   3. Communism—Vietnam.   I. Title.
DS559.912.P34   1997
327.597'09'04—dc20   96–46359
                                                               CIP

This book is printed on paper suitable for recycling and made from fully managed and
sustained forest sources.

10   9   8   7   6   5   4   3   2   1
06   05   04   03   02   01   00   99   98   97

Printed in Great Britain by
Ipswich Book Company, Ipswich, Suffolk

To Silja, Lassi and Sauli

Contents

Acknowledgments

Over the past decade, I have enjoyed intellectual, practical and material help from my colleagues, friends and relatives. As this book grew out of a doctoral dissertation, I am indebted above all to my mentor, Osmo Apunen, the University of Tampere, for his guidance. Carlyle A. Thayer and Ilmari Susiluoto did painstaking work reading and commenting on the manuscript, and I am deeply grateful for their support in improving it. Harto Hakovirta, Pertti Lappalainen, Markku Peltonen, Stein Tønnesson, Pekka Virtanen and Raimo Väyrynen offered valuable comments on its drafts. I also wish to thank Jari Aro, Joan Löfgren, Jalil Miswardi and Tran Minh Canh for their assistance during the different phases of my research.

It has been a pleasure to delve into Asian studies and international relations. My colleagues on the staff of the Department of Political Science and International Relations at the University of Tampere have given me important support in my studies. I also immensely enjoyed working at the Institute of Southeast Asian Studies and in its library in Singapore, where the Vietnamese materials proved of utmost value to my study. I am indebted to various scholars and the staff of the institute and the library for their help and guidance. I also wish to extend thanks to my colleagues and the staff at the Nordic Institute of Asian Studies in Copenhagen for their assistance during my visits there. The Institute of International Relations in Hanoi was very helpful in arranging my visit to Vietnam.

I received important support in rewriting and publishing the manuscript. In this, I am particularly grateful to Harto Hakovirta, Markku Peltonen and Carlyle A. Thayer for their encouragement. I received invaluable help with the English, which is not my native language, from Paul Sjöblom, who did great deal of work putting the text into more readable form. I would also like to thank Marita Alanko for preparing the manuscript for the publishers. The comments and suggestions of the publishers have provided necessary editorial advice in the final stages of this project.

Many people have given assistance and moral support during the performance of my studies and the writing of this book – a larger number than I can possibly name here. I can only mention my mother and, finally, thank my wife Sirkku for her understanding, particularly during the final laborious years of the study.

Abbreviations

APEC	Asia-Pacific Economic Cooperation
ASEAN	Association of Southeast Asian Nations
CPSU	Communist Party of the Soviet Union
CGDK	Coalition Government of Democratic Kampuchea
CPV	Communist Party of Vietnam
CMEA	Council for Mutual Economic Assistance
DRV	Democratic Republic of Vietnam
FLPH	Foreign Language Publishing House
FRETILIN	Frente Revolucionária de Timor Leste Independente
ICK	International Conference on Kampuchea
ICP	Indochinese Communist Party
KNUFNS	Kampuchean National United Front for National Salvation
KPP	Khmer People's Party
LPDR	Lao People's Democratic Republic
NCLS	Nghien Cuu Lich Su
NLF	National Liberation Front
PRC	People's Republic of China
PRK	People's Republic of Kampuchea
SEATO	Southeast Asia Treaty Organization
SRV	Socialist Republic of Vietnam
TCCS	Tap Chi Cong San
TCTH	Tap Chi Triet Hoc
UN	United Nations
UNGA	United Nations' General Assembly
U.S.	United States
USSR	Union of Soviet Socialist Republics
VNA	Vietnam News Agency
VNC	Viet Nam Courier
ZOPFAN	Zone of Peace, Freedom and Neutrality

1 Introduction: Marxism-Leninism and Global Change

FOCUSING ON THE VIETNAMESE MARXIST-LENINIST DOCTRINE

The radical changes that have taken place in the global political landscape in general and in that of the Asia–Pacific region in particular in the past few years have challenged many established assumptions about political developments and international relations. The development of Vietnam's political thinking in response to these changes is extremely interesting in this respect. This book deals with Vietnam's international relations and foreign policy from the end of the Second Indochina War, in the spring of 1975, to the beginning of the 1990s from the point of view of Vietnamese political doctrine. The fall of Saigon and the defeat of the United States in Indochina in the spring of 1975 marked the high tide of "the world revolutionary forces" and in the influence of Soviet global foreign policy. By 1993, however, the two camps structure had been demolished, the radical Third World movement had simmered down, and the Asia-Pacific region was boosting its status in the global framework. Nevertheless, although the Soviet Union and other Marxist-Leninist state systems in East Europe have collapsed, totalitarian Marxist state systems have maintained at least their façades in the Far East, North Korea, the People's Republic of China (PRC), Laos and Vietnam up to the 1990s.

During the two decades following the Second Indochina War, Vietnam assumed an important role in both regional and global terms. After its victorious military struggle against U.S. forces, Vietnam took a crucial place in the Third World movement and held the key position in the delicate balance of power between the Soviet Union and China in Southeast Asia. Although its role changed radically during subsequent political developments in Indochina, which culminated in Vietnam's occupation of Kampuchea and in the Sino–Vietnamese war at the beginning of 1979, Vietnam remained a factor of undiminished importance in the region. Now it both enjoyed a close relationship with the Soviet Union and represented the Soviet bloc's global interests in Southeast Asia.

Despite the fact that Vietnam also lost this role when the structures of the Cold War started to break down during the late 1980s, Hanoi's adaptation to the new situation has been most interesting: it has striven to integrate into the regional system of Southeast Asia and simultaneously uphold the old political power of the Communist Party.

As the focus of the book is on the development of the political doctrine, its emphasis is not on the foreign-policy process or the decision-making level. Rather does this book concentrate on political ideas and how they have been used in political rhetoric. However, the study involves three established and, in fact, interrelated approaches in the field of political research, namely, comparative Communist studies, doctrine studies and cultural studies.

The aim of the first-mentioned studies is to compare the socialist systems and the Marxist-Leninist regimes with respect to their political doctrine, political culture and national particularities, their governmental structures and their Communist Party organizations. According to the most far-reaching premises, "Communist phenomena are not distinguished from non-Communist ones by any particular characteristics."[1] An interesting discussion has taken place on the comparative aspects of Asian Communism, one that is also relevant in the context of the present study.[2] However, the present study does not aim at such broad generalizations because its main attention is focused on the characteristics of the Vietnamese political doctrine and its development, particularly in the field of international relations. There is a specific reason for this more limited point of view. As far as I know, there exists no broader study based on original Vietnamese material that has tried to trace the development of Vietnamese Marxist-Leninist discussion among party cadres and that of Vietnam's foreign policy. Thus the systematic comparative aspect encompassing a larger strata of socialist countries lies beyond its scope. The comparisons involving the Soviet Union and China are made only with the main theses of Marxism-Leninism and, whenever the connection with the development of the political doctrine is evident, with the political choices of the Communist Party. Similarly, apart from the most obvious similarities, I have not carried out any systematic comparison of the political culture between Vietnam and its Asian neighbors.

There are two somewhat more specific ways of approaching the development of Vietnam's political doctrine. On the one hand, one might pay special attention to the relationship between the theoretical constructions of Marxist-Leninist doctrine and political behavior. On the other hand, the political behavior of a Communist government might also be explained by the traditional political culture: the Marxist terms only produce a new vocabulary to describe traditional behavior patterns. By studying Soviet Marxist-Leninist ideology in the light of the writings of Soviet leaders, Nathan Leites's pioneer work, *A Study of Bolshevism* (1953), tried to discover a political strategy pursued by the Bolshevik leaders, "an operational code," as Leites called it. He also examined the cultural aspects of Russia and thus inspired the birth of studies of political culture in general. Leites was looking for the cognitive elements behind Soviet Marxist-Leninist texts. Proof that the textual elements were also cognitive was given, according to Leites, by the abundant appearance of these elements in different texts and situations. In this, he managed to formulate some of the main characteristics of Soviet Marxism-Leninism, which could be generalized as permanent components of Marxist-Leninist doctrine. They include politics as a struggle between two opposite poles, a vision of future and past as a concomitant to this struggle, and justification of the means employed in relation to the ends, together with a number of minor epithets of Marxism-Leninism. Nevertheless, Leites and his followers were unable to solve the problem of whether these elements were really present in decision-making or were mere propaganda and served as a justification for the decisions made. In order to prove that these elements were cognitive and were driving Soviet politics, their validity had to be tested by comparing them with the political actions of the Soviet leaders.[3]

The concept of the operational code was established in Communist studies,[4] studies on political culture[5] and some general foreign-policy studies[6] in order to refer to those cognitive elements which give meaning to (decode) the political experience. Similarly, it gives the prediction for the most probable orientations of the decision-makers to the future's situations. In summary, these studies define doctrine as a set of beliefs which tries to explain reality and gives the goals for political action. The doctrine is thus a particular form of broader ideology on a concrete decision-making level. They include a number of different approaches the common denominator of which could be found in such concepts as doctrine, ideology, world view, belief-system and operational code.[7]

The doctrine studies often include the idea of rationalistic behavior. Hence the starting point is the individual decision-maker, and it was endeavored to make the analytical construction by proceeding from his cognitive intentions to the official statement or vice versa. The analytical schema of these doctrine studies was divided into the world-view, the policy goals, and the instruments used, and it is widely employed by the decision-makers and policy planners themselves when they describe their decision-making process.[8] However, as these analyses were valid only at the official and public levels, the connection between the world offered by the doctrine and the actual decision remained relatively vague.[9] The doctrine studies did not manage to connect the two levels, the individual and cognitive and the official and public; this derivation could not be done completely, owing to the singular character of foreign-policy decisions.[10] The operationalization of the cognitive approach has been more successful in the projects where the singular cognitive models have been tested by specific interviews.[11] Thus the constraining function of the official doctrine remains largely on its restrictive character for future decision-making. This constraining character is not due to the cognitive properties, but once the doctrine is issued, changing or replacing it is difficult because of its public character.[12]

These studies could not answer the question of whether those elements that have been seen as a cognitive basis for political action were in fact the real reasons for action or merely its ex post rationalization.[13] In fact, at one point in his work, Nathan Leites entertains the idea that the operational code provides nothing more than the peculiarities of Marxist-Leninist language and that this code has no connections to decision-makers' cognitive structures.[14]

Obviously, the particular characteristics of the parlance of Marxist-Leninist governments have complicated the attempts to connect the decision-makers' world-views and cognition to actual foreign-policy statements. In the Soviet case, the most interesting study would be to examine how Leites's idea of operational code and his theses on the cognitive basis of Soviet leadership tally with the material now available from the archives of the former Soviet Union. In the present work, however, I want to focus within doctrine studies on analyses of political language. This is not to deny its cognitive basis, but the problems that have not been solved in the foregoing doctrine studies are avoided. Therefore the aim here is to concentrate on certain regularities in the Vietnamese political language and on the expressions used in the actual application of foreign policy. This approach is also better supported by the available data, drawn from Vietnamese political texts, in which such regularities are quite apparent, but the individual side is totally ignored.

The Vietnamese political texts, like the Soviet ones, depend heavily on Marxist-Leninist terminology and theory, which thereby give an overall point of departure for an interpretative enterprise. Thus special attention is drawn to the Marxist-Leninist language and its relation to Vietnam's foreign policy. Moreover, there is a particular justification for limiting the examination of these texts more to the Marxist-Leninist language and to the manner of argumentation with this language rather than relying on the "deeper structures" of natural language. If this study were to deal with, for example, the mobilization of peasants or other popular segments to raise production or to participate in a national liberation movement, the sociolinguistic meanings of certain Vietnamese words would be important, and the "deep structures" of the cultural derivation of Vietnamese words would take on key significance. However, the data used here do not support this kind of exercise.

The crucial part of the Vietnamese data used here concentrates on ideology, politics and foreign policy and deals with the communication among cadres. The persons involved in this discussion were deeply attached to Marxist-Leninist theory and to its ways of reasoning. Moreover, Marxist-Leninist parlance is quite distinct from natural speech, as its structure is controlled and the crucial words have been introduced quite recently and sometimes by Party decisions. In addition, there is little doubt that Vietnam, unlike many other Asian Marxist states (the People's Republic of China, North Korea and Democratic Kampuchea under the Khmer Rouge, in particular), has never emphasized the national colors in its Marxist doctrine. The foregoing facts are even more salient in Vietnamese foreign policy. It comes therefore as no surprise that the most serious attempts to study present Vietnamese foreign policy have dealt mainly with doctrinal issues. These studies have shown the rise of Soviet concepts in the Vietnamese vocabulary, and they have examined their application in certain specific areas.[15] Hence the present study deals mainly with the relationship between Marxist-Leninist doctrine and Vietnamese parlance concerning international relations.

The development of Marxist thinking in Vietnam supports, to a certain extent, the cultural emphasis found in some interpretations of Vietnamese Marxism. The early stage of the anti-colonial movement emerged from the class of literati, whose intellectual origins lay in Confucian education and who then turned through nationalist movements to the Marxist revolutionary movement. When the old Confucian scholar-gentry began to disappear, owing to the colonial administration, which started to restructure the educational system, the nucleus of the nationalist and Marxist movements was formed by the intelligentsia, who were already drawn to Western ideas of freedom and equality as well as, ultimately, the Marxist conception of class. Members of this intelligentsia held key positions when the Indochinese Communist party (ICP) was founded in 1930, and some of these founding members and activists from the 1930s remained in the Party leadership up to the late 1980s.[16] The obvious similarities between Confucian thinking and Marxism stimulated an examination of Vietnamese Marxism as a new form of Confucianist social thinking from the functionalist point of view.[17] However, as David G. Marr, for example, has emphasized, Vietnamese thinking underwent remarkable changes during the colonial period and this can not be attributed simply to Confucianism.[18] And as far as political vocabulary is concerned, Marxist-Leninist concepts, expressions and way of arguing became dominant among the Party cadres because of the close contacts of Vietnamese Communists with the international Communist movement and, particularly, with the Comintern during the 1930s. Only after the resistance against Japanese occupation in the Second World War, which then continued as a war against French domination, the national aspects appeared in the ICP's policy. This was due to the tactics adopted by the Communists to broaden the resistance by having other national forces join in the Vietnamese anti-colonial movement, Viet Minh, according to which the cultural elements were introduced on purpose.[19]

Although the role of the cultural elements is not systematically examined in this study, the notion of culturally coded understanding must be emphasized. Trinh Van Thao (1990) has traced the interesting lineages of the political rhetoric between the Vietnamese Communist leadership and the intellectuals of the anticolonial literati class of the late nineteenth and early twentieth centuries. In his broad sociological study, he examines the intellectual history of 222 Vietnamese intellectuals and political leaders across three generations in order to follow the continuity and change of politico-philosophical thinking during the last hundred years. Apart from showing how the leading Vietnamese Communists came from families of the literati class, which were attached to Confucian education,[20] he points out how certain rhetorical expressions and semiotic modes prevailed in the political language during the period covered by his scrutinity.

It is another question, however, what place the cultural elements occupy. The main problem in the culturalist approach has been that they expect continuity and are unable to deal with political change and cultural interaction.[21] This is particularly important in the present study as the time period under scrutiny involves dramatic changes in international relations and therefore the changes in the development of political doctrine must be analyzed. I suggest that cultural aspects of politics should be looked upon as dynamic. As far as the Vietnamese political doctrine is concerned, it may contain several different vocabularies. In the present study attention is paid to two most obvious vocabularies: that of pragmatic approach introduced by the traditional literati class and formal Marxism-Leninism, which the Vietnamese revolutionaries adopted in rather orthodox form from the Soviet Union. Although in the Vietnamese political texts the place of the cultural elements is somewhat imprecise, it seems reasonable to assume that a careful study would show resemblances between the cultural modes of expression and Vietnamese Marxist-Leninist parlance. In the late 1980s and early 1990s, a new foreign-policy vocabulary is again becoming established, but the important question is: what is the relationship between the old vocabularies and the emerging political language?

In the research data of the present study, the traditional characteristics of Vietnamese political language do not, however, stand out in relief from the general discussion of Marxism-Leninism and international relations. This is largely due to the data analyzed in the present study. The study is based on two kinds of material, both of which emphasize the doctrinal point of departure. First, there are the more theoretical data, which include Vietnamese leaders' writings, the books and articles by high-ranking and theoretically oriented Party cadres as well as the textbooks used in political education. The main sources of the Party cadres' discussion are the Communist Party's theoretical and political review *Hoc Tap* (Studies), its successor, *Tap Chi Cong San* (Communist Review), and *Tap Chi Triet Hoc* (Review of Philosophy). Two other Vietnamese reviews, *Tap Chi Quan Doi Nhan Dan* (Peoples' Army Review) and *Nghien Cuu Lich Su* (Historical Research), are also relevant in this respect.[22] Second, there is the material that deals more with day-to-day politics, including statements by Vietnamese leaders and authorities on current foreign-policy and international issues. This comprises reports from the Vietnamese media as well as the Vietnamese leaders' speeches and comments at home, on their visits abroad and at international organizations. Important sources for this material have been the BBC's World Broadcast Service, as well as documents of the United Nations, the documents relating to the Non-Aligned Movement and various other documentary series.

This study focuses on two aspects of Vietnamese texts. First, attention is paid to the more permanent characteristics of the texts. These include, primarily, the meanings of individual words as well as sentences (Marxist-Leninist concepts in particular) and established phrases. Second, and more importantly, they include general rules on how a political text should be composed, i.e., how political parlance should be structured so as to give the words their proper signification in Vietnamese Marxism-Leninism. The second aspect of the texts is a practical one. This refers to the active use of language, to the communication of political messages. Nevertheless, certain elements, especially those dealing with international relations, were introduced into the Vietnamese political language under heavy international pressure, reminding us of the dynamics of the Vietnamese political vocabulary. The adoption of certain political concepts cannot be understood except in a broader political framework. Therefore the practical function of texts is naturally dealt with in the Party cadres' "theoretical" discussion as well.

THE MARXIST-LENINIST DOCTRINAL CODE

Communication and argumentation are on the main focus of the present study. Since political language plays a central role in it, I am bound to employ two research approaches – rhetorical and semiotic. Although the main weight of rhetoric is on the active side of language, while semiotics is concerned more with the permanent characteristics of language (language as a sign system), their borders overlap. In both approaches, the communication process occupies a central area.[23] The rhetorical approach to political language is concerned with argumentation, which is used in particular situations of communication. The central issues are the role of addresser and audience and the ways in which argumentation develops and changes according to the audience and the situations. This involves the questions of the role of addresser, the contents of argumentation and the way in which the argumentation proceeds.[24]

In this study, however, the crucial question is: how are political arguments constructed with special reference to the political doctrine? And, how do they develop in the case of political change?

Although rhetoric is concerned with the particular situation of argumentation, it comes closer to semiotics when it is dealing with constant modalities in the expression of thought.[25] In fact, an approach called "new rhetoric" clearly distinguishes between the structures of languages and the use of the varieties of language in argumentation.[26] It points out that "every linguistic system involves formal structural rules, which bind those who use it, but the practical application of the system can be reconciled with various styles, with particular formulas, characterizing a milieu, the speaker's place in it, a particular cultural atmosphere."[27] As these structural rules are the objects of semiotics, they are also the common denominators between these two research orientations of rhetoric and semiotics.

In semiotics, these structural rules are focused on the concept of code. The code is not a grammar in a linguistic sense, but a system having a central role in communication in a particular discourse. In order to emphasize the role of code in Marxist-Leninist parlance, I propose the term "doctrinal code."

The concept of code has been utilized in various studies of social semiotics and social linguistics. The role of code in these studies is that the codes "transmit the culture and so constrain behavior."[28] The code is a system where the speaker and the auditor have a variety of choices to interpret what is said.[29] This approach emphasizes that a speech or a dialogue is not conducted according to a set of rules, which both a speaker and an auditor share in order to respond to the speech act as intended. Both the speaker and the listener are free to interpret what is said according to a variety of choices.[30] However, opposite to this "systemic" approach to code, I am inclined to emphasize the view that the natural language may include several codes among which some might be much more restrictive than others. It depends on both the nature of the language as analyzed and the point of view applied in examining the language. In the present study, where the emphasis is on Marxist-Leninist language, it is assumed that the Marxist-Leninist doctrine provides the particular rules of argumentation. These rules may amount to such a restrictive code.

The role of code may vary in different types of message and different situations of communication. In his famous article, Roman Jakobson pointed out out six different elements and functions of the message. In ordinary communication, the context, of which function Jakobson calls referential, is usually regarded as the predominant function of communication.[31] Unlike normal communication, where this communicative function is predominant, I argue that in the political texts and in Marxist-Leninist texts in particular, the function, which Jakobson calls "the code," is often predominant. The code performs the metalingual function, giving an answer to the question, "What did you mean?" When this function dominates communication, the purpose of this kind of message is not to add information, but to repeat what is already known.

A single Vietnamese political text may include several codes, but our interest here focuses on the Marxist-Leninist language code, specifically the more or less permanent structure of the rules of Marxist-Leninist argumentation, the doctrinal code. Nevertheless, when natural languages are dealt with, it is important to ask whether the addresser and the addressee have the same code. The decoding problem is minimized in artificial languages (e.g., mathematics), where the transmitter and the receiver of the message have the same code.[32] A completely opposite situation prevails in an artistic text, as, for example, in a translation situation where the identity of the codes cannot be guaranteed. Translation is usually done by resorting to conventional equivalencies used by different cultures and which overlap and even have different connotations. The problem is still more acute in case the original text has several codes, some of which are lost in the translation process.[33]

It is no exaggeration to state that Vietnamese Marxist-Leninist texts lie somewhere between the purely artistic and the artificial. They are composed of natural language and highly sophisticated concepts, which are based, if not always on Party resolutions, at least on some kind of political decisions. Together with the doctrinal code, such concepts form the Vietnamese political language. Political texts are also delineated by concepts that have a highly artificial nature and that have an exact place in Marxist-Leninist argumentation. This all simplifies the decoding process.[34]

The "imported" political vocabulary – Marxism-Leninism – and the original natural language, Vietnamese, also raised questions different from the code understood as the structural rules of argumentation. Nearly all the Marxist-Leninist terms have been translated into Vietnamese using words already existing in the language, which thus had relations to other code systems. Consequently, this level of contact between the new code and old meanings can serve as a point of departure for examining the interaction between cultural codes and new terminology. This aspect of code bore a distinct affinity with the question of culture's role in the political change.

Several elements, which stand out in relief from the Vietnamese Marxist-Leninist doctrinal code, were already formulated by Leites when studying the Soviet operational code. The tendency to examine political reality according to two opposite poles and to examine the future and the past according to these poles is an obvious characteristic of Vietnamese Marxist-Leninist argumentation. The third element is the ritualistic pattern of arguing established in Marxism-Leninism particularly by Stalin.[35] This, i.e., the texts do not focus on new information but on the repetitions of words and phrases and other textual organizations that are unnecessary for a general communicational pattern, is clearly seen also in Vietnamese Marxist-Leninist language.

This "mantra content" which does not aim at normal communication but at "autocommunication," as Yuri Lotman calls it, is an important part of the Marxist-Leninist doctrinal code. The meaning of this kind of communication opens only to persons who already know the premises of communication.[36] For example, the widely used phrase in Vietnam's foreign policy during the 1970s, "the offensive posture of world revolutionary forces" *(the tien cong cua luc luong cach mang)* did not any concrete state of affairs; but it did strengthen autocommunication and the doctrine, as Vietnam was viewed as an important part of these revolutionary forces. It also referred to the doctrinal system, the fundamental aim of which is to justify the Communist Party leadership. The task of this kind of communication is not to add information, but to enforce the motivation and mobilization of the masses.

In this, autocommunication has an important role. The notion of power and Marxist-Leninist language in the Soviet Union is particularly relevant in the context of power and ideology. The classical Marxist theories did not accord with the control of the revolutionary movement and construction of socialism, because this would have required the simplification of Marxism, turning it into everyday speech. This process was started by Lenin and fully developed by Stalin, whose political language created a kind of "pigdin-Marxism." Stalin's language included continuously repetitive syntagmas, the text forming into a dialogue sequence and a pattern of opposite poles. Its function was to mobilize the people for the task of building socialism.[37]

The idea that the task of ideology is to control and mobilize the masses is on the textual level leading to the structural rules of argumentation. The focus here lies on the concept of politics. The Marxist-Leninist definition of politics, which the Vietnamese also adopted, includes a general concept of politics originating from the writings of Marx and Engels, which refers to the class struggle. It also includes a more specific Leninist concept of politics, in which the emphasis is on the management and guidance of a movement or a state, and thus on the political struggle, involving party politics and the winning and maintaining of power.[38] As for management and guidance, the function of ideology is to serve as "the reason of society" *(ly luan xa hoi)*,[39] thus providing a guiding principle to political action; and in the case of political struggle and party politics, the role of ideology is to control the movement and the state. In semiotic terms, the guiding principle refers to the possibility to produce and adopt new information and the control aspect refers to the function of ideology to maintain autocommunication.

This twin role of ideology is also acknowledged in some Western studies. Besides guiding political and social action, ideology has to create coherence and control over the movement.[40] In spite of this common notion, a special trend has developed that examines the interplay between the two functions of ideology in totalitarian movements. This approach might be called the "totalitarian ideology" approach or "ideological project," and although the concept of the ideological project was originally coined in this specific meaning by Kenneth Minoque,[41] was originally coined in this specific meaning by Kenneth Minoque,[41] the idea could already be found in the writings of Hannah Arendt and Claude Lefort. In the works of Arendt and Lefort, this idea focuses on the totalitarian system and on its central role in organizing totalitarian society. The same idea can also be found in Herbert Marcuse's study, *Soviet Marxism*.[42] In dealing with Soviet Marxism, Marcuse refers more to the practices established under Stalin's regime than to the theoretical premises of Lenin. Minoque tends to connect ideology only to those parts of social movements that change from critical movements to totalitarian ones. He calls the theory of ideas that represents the world as a battleground of oppressor and oppressed a "pure theory of ideology."[43]

The main concern in these studies is to link together social theory, action and domination – i.e., to explain how a rational social project is transformed into a means of social control and domination. In this ideological project, rule combines the twin variables of action and domination. He who can organize and mobilize a society or a movement to pursue a given goal also acquires supreme social power. In this project, action is the main element aimed at mobilizing people to serve the general interest. This means that everything becomes political and public, and this penetrates into every sector of society.[44] But certain elements of this development, which the totalitarian movement has elaborated to perfection, can be found, according to Arendt and Lefort, in all political movements.[45]

PRAGMATISM AND FORMALISM IN VIETNAMESE MARXIST RHETORIC

In Vietnamese Marxism-Leninism, there seem to be two main approaches. The first rhetorical pattern is more practical, starting from the question of what kind of action is possible in an actual situation. The second is orthodox Marxist-Leninist rhetoric, where the conclusion is always drawn from the premises of doctrine. The connection of the latter approach to the established Soviet style of arguing is obvious. However, the origins of the first pattern are much more complicated. Despite the fact that this pragmatic point of view was presented by Lenin, it is emphasized far more in Vietnamese rhetoric. In fact, this pragmatic approach, which emphasizes political realities and ponders possible action in response to it, was very important according to the Confucian scholar-gentry's rhetoric when the methods of opposing French colonialism were contemplated at the turn of the century.[46] Naturally, in practical politics these argumentation patterns overlap, and even theoretical texts might include aspects from both of them. It can be argued that the existence of these two kinds of argumentation patterns is one of the central characteristics of radical Marxism.

In brief, formalist argumentation means that the nonformal character of natural language is turned into the formal reasoning of logic or mathematics. This pattern is quite evident in Marxist-Leninist formalism, which requires theoretical consistency in argumentation. However, the premises are very difficult to define explicitly and in an unequivocal way, as serious logical demonstration supposes. This is therefore rarely even attempted. The difference between more or less ambiguous premises and formal procedure leads to the problem of incompatibility. This problem arises in Marxist-Leninist reasoning, where it is very often difficult to fit political reality into the premises. In formal logic, when the premises are well defined, the system becomes independent of will and chance. In this quasi-logical argumentation, however, there exist no unequivocal premises, but the system is still represented as an independent one. This independent system has without doubt led to quasi-logical argumentation: the logical approach assumes that an independent formula can be derived from well-defined premises and that the logical problems can be solved by deduction. In the same vein, formalism assumes that practical problems can be solved by similar deduction. This means that the uncertainty of the future is eliminated and all questions can be solved technically.[47]

It must be emphasized that the question is not whether this kind of formalism is true or not; rather is it related to the other main type of argumentation, pragmatic argumentation and its connection with political developments in Vietnam. There, the formal Marxist-Leninist trend gained strength together with the development of the political power of the Communist Party. In the pragmatic rhetoric, which dominated at the early revolutionary stage in Vietnam, the arguments were based on the political reality of the revolutionary movement. This argumentation was developed in order to create a connection between the judgments presented and certain aspects of reality. Similarly, the word "reality" does not mean that these arguments are more correct than others. Thus the interest here lies in the question of how the reality is presented, and therefore the word "reality" does not refer to any ontological position.

This kind of argumentation based on the existing reality is typical in political action. It judges the action according to the consequences, and it can be used only if there is agreement on the value of the intended ends and consequences of the action. Moreover, pragmatic argument presupposes that a clear distinction is made between ends and means. However, in political action, there is a tendency for the means to turn into ends. When the means become ends, the options and practical thinking to which pragmatic argumentation appeals disappear.[48] As we shall see, this type of argumentation is quite common in Vietnam in general and in retrospective Vietnamese representations of the national independence struggle in particular.

Owing to this fusion of ends and means, pragmatic arguments are frequently used for political mobilization and propaganda. In fact, this is exactly what happened in our earlier examples of autocommunication. Furthermore, pragmatic argumentation attracts the practical man, who wants to keep his options open as far as possible and only act when the situation demands. But when the practical man prepares to encounter the unexpected future, the political ideologies in practice dispel his freedom of choice by fixed ends.[49] This ostensible pragmatism is clearly evident in totalitarian ideologies.

In retrospective examination, it is rather simple to outline the course of political development according to a rationalistic model. The results to which this development has led to can be considered as a goal of successful political action. At the same time, unsatisfactory results may be regarded as unsuccessful choices of the political means. The situation is, however, different when the question is of the future. In such a case, it is far more complicated to justify the political lines adopted. The addresser has in this kind of situation two choices: either to turn to formalism with the fixed premises of action or to justify the course adopted by the techniques of analogy widely used in pragmatic argumentation. In the field of politics, historical analogy is most common. Therefore the use of the past in pragmatic argumentation reflects the vision of the present and the future.

FOREIGN POLICY AND THE CHANGE OF THE DOCTRINE

It seems obvious that pragmatic and formalist approaches represent two different politico-cultural levels in Vietnamese Marxist doctrine. Accordingly, in a rhetorical approach, the doctrine involves two obvious components: the vocabulary and the code. Political vocabularies have an important task in the parlance of Marxist-Leninist governments. It is by the variety of the concepts that the audience is chosen, and it was by the different emphasis put on them that the socialist countries used to show their place in the socialist world system. Besides this, the vocabularies connected the arguments to the Marxist-Leninist doctrine and to the code.

On the basis of the foregoing discussion, three obvious questions suggest themselves: What are the structural rules of Marxist-Leninist argumentation, i.e., the doctrinal code, which is common to both pragmatic and formal patterns? How is the foreign-policy argumentation structured? And, what happens when the doctrine changes?

The emphasis here is on those functional tasks of ideology (mobilization and control) distinguishable as central characteristics of the doctrinal code of Marxism-Leninism. In Vietnamese political parlance, this concept of ideology can be identified by its functional tasks and its structural properties, which Arendt, Lefort, and Marcuse discuss at a general level. At the textual level, these functional tasks are included both in formal and pragmatic argumentation and in autocommunication. Therefore, ideology understood as a social project shares a common basis with rhetoric and semiotic approaches. Although Marxism-Leninism might also refer to the cognitive and mental side of ideology, political parlance in Marxist state systems and Marxist-Leninist revolutionary movements, when connected with political action, ideological education and cultural activities, emphasizes these functional tasks. In this respect, the way ideology constructs political language is crucial.[50]

The general characteristics of the Marxist-Leninist doctrinal code can be viewed from two different angles: from that of the ideology as a project and from rhetorical and semiotic standpoints. They share the common nominator: reality examined from a limited point of view. For Minoque, in the ideological project, the world is seen as a battleground, divided into the oppressed and the oppressor. For Lefort, it is a project aimed at modernization, which legitimates power and penetrates all social levels. And for Arendt, it is a pseudo-scientific phenomenon, which forces one to explain the movements of history from the past to the present as well as to the future in terms of the same premises; world history is something that can be predicted by means of it.

From the semiotic point of view, autocommunication includes at least the following characteristics: the repetition of certain textual elements and the division of the text into rhythmic segments, where the semantic connections are weakened and the emphasis is laid on the syntagmatic expressions. These expressions do not amplify information but represent an endeavor to create the idea of membership in a group that supports the implementation-oriented action.[51]

The doctrinal code of Marxism-Leninism thus includes the following elements: attempts a) to examine the reality according to opposite poles,

b) to extend this division to every segment of social strata, producing a common social endeavor, c) to set the goal of this endeavor in the future, and to explain the present and the past according to this goal, d) to repeat the constellation of opposition and the concept, syntagmas, and formal structures referring to this opposition.

The minimum condition for argumentation is that the addresser and the audience have a common language. This does not mean solely the natural language; both must understand the message in the same way; they must have the same code. Even more importantly, successful persuasion requires that the addresser start the argumentation from premises acceptable to the audience. This means that the starting point of argumentation presupposes agreement between the participants. The premises are a necessary condition of argumentation; premises are not rejected on account of any wrong conclusion derived from them, but because they have been unacceptable to the audience. It follows that in a situation where the identity of the audience is not obvious, the premises might suggest to whom the message has been addressed.[52]

In the case of Vietnamese material addressed to a broader domestic and foreign audience, determining the premises and the preliminary agreements of the argumentation is crucial to exact identification of the audience. There are certain ways to recognize the premises and preliminary agreements between the speaker and the audience in a political speech. In foreign policy, the preliminary agreement is made by using broad themes on international issues, which connect and separate different governments. The aim is not always to persuade different governments for the addresser's sake, but the themes reveal the main orientation of the foreign policy and the place of the country in the international system. In the Marxist-Leninist texts dealing with foreign policy, there is a limited range of legitimate topics. These topics are the starting points of argumentation in, first of all, multilateral diplomacy; and they awaken the interest of the potential audience and perhaps manage to convince this audience or a part of it. Similarly, the same themes could ignore a part of the potential audience. To summarize, the themes introduced in a text refer to its audience and the themes of a speech can be considered as preliminary agreements between speaker and audience.

According to the thesis presented here, the structure of argumentation remains rather constant in spite of the changes of audience and situations. Thus the basic presumption hypothesizes the stability of the doctrinal code. However, in the long run, three rival hypotheses on the nature of the doctrinal code and the change of the doctrine can be presented: first, the possible development of the doctrinal code, which means that a new element is introduced or an old one is rejected in the structure of argumentation; second, the possible disintegration of the doctrinal code, when a different kind of code system has appeared alongside the dominant code system. In this case, the substance presented by the addressers may be the same, but the structure of argumentation may be based more on a rival code system – for example, on another politically or culturally based structure of argumentation. And finally, a diminishing of the doctrinal code takes place in Vietnamese foreign-policy argumentation, which means that the structural rules of argumentation begin to disappear and other functions of communication become more important. These alternative presumptions characterize the nature of politico-cultural elements in the doctrinal change.

Contrary to the Marxist-Leninist doctrinal code, pragmatic and formal approaches are bound either to the argumentation situation and the audience or they can express Vietnam's choices in foreign policy or the political trend in Hanoi. Similarly, the themes and, to a certain extent, the concepts (depending on their importance in the doctrinal system and the prevailing political trend) can vary according to these factors. The addresser's argument includes four components, which have to be analyzed: (A) the doctrinal code of the argument and (B) the argumentation pattern; (C) the foreign-policy themes, which are important for maintaining the communication channel between the addresser and the audience; and finally, (D) the foreign-policy concepts, which, together with the code, refer to the passive side of the political language, although they can vary in argumentation. Their significance depends on what kind of reference is accepted for argumentation and how this reference, on the general level, is expressed. However, contrary to the doctrinal code, the foreign-policy concepts can also be applied as part of the active use of the language, owing to the connotative properties of the concepts.

The reference includes those foreign-policy issues that the Vietnamese should, and could, deal with publicly. As the context of the messages, these issues do not determine the arguments; but the addresser is bound to the code, concepts and themes selecting the issues dealt with publicly. However, there might arise international issues not determined by the code and which obviously make it difficult to deal with the Marxist-Leninist doctrinal code. In this kind of situation, a theme is chosen that is not contrary to the code. The audience, whether domestic or foreign, determines the choices of foreign-policy themes. As there exist a limited number of themes that are in full harmony with the code, the addresser is bound to certain kinds of expressions.

The present study is divided into three parts. The first part (Chapters

2 and 3) deals with the two Vietnamese Marxist-Leninist approaches in general and the place of the doctrinal code in these patterns in particular (Chapter 2). It also surveys the development of the foreign-policy vocabulary and themes and their place in these patterns (Chapter 3). The second part (Chapters 4 and 5) discusses the role of the doctrinal code and the development of Vietnamese foreign policy argumentation vis-à-vis concrete foreign policy issues. In Chapter 4, the focus is on the situation prevailing between 1975–1978, when Vietnam could rather freely choose the themes of its foreign policy. Chapter 5 examines the Party cadres' rhetoric and Vietnamese diplomatic parlance in 1979–1985, when the Kampuchean question dominated Vietnam's foreign policy. The last part of the study (Chapter 6) re-evaluates the pragmatic and formal approaches on international relations in the Party cadres' discussions during a period when the Soviet attempt to develop the Marxist-Leninist doctrine led to the collapse of both the socialist bloc and the Soviet Union itself.

Part I
Vietnamese Marxism-Leninism and Foreign Relations

2 Two Approaches of Vietnamese Marxism-Leninism

The coexistence of two different rhetorical modes can be identified clearly from Vietnamese Marxism-Leninism. The first, flexible action-oriented argumentation is based on the structure of political reality. I call it revolutionary pragmatism. The other, formal Marxism, is based on theoretical premises, and it employs an orthodox Marxist-Leninist vocabulary. Although these two approaches seem to be opposite to each other, they are not mutually exclusive. They do not necessarily focus on any given factions in the Communist Party, nor are they identified purely with particular Vietnamese leaders. Rather are they an integral part of Vietnamese Marxism-Leninism and, depending on the situation, one can rise to a dominant position. Although different persons emphasize different sides of the Marxist teachings, they usually stress, on the one hand, the need for rational calculation, depending on the balance of forces in an uncertain political environment; and, on the other hand, they point up the need for organization on theoretical grounds, as justified by the historical task and the necessity of revolution. Marxism-Leninism would call this relationship dialectical; mutual contradictions may be created, but they are also prerequisites of each other.[1]

In this chapter, I will analyze these two patterns, particularly to show how the Marxist-Leninist doctrinal code is structured in Vietnamese political argumentation and how it appears in these two lines.

Although this division is obvious in Vietnamese Marxist political texts, I hesitate to distinguish two codes. In social linguistic studies, the different structural rules of language, which belong to different social strata, are separated into different codes of the language. However, with respect to Vietnamese Marxism-Leninism, I am inclined to speak of only one code, especially because the two sides can be presented in the same text and by the same person. Therefore the terms of argumentation describe this division better. They share the same doctrinal code of argumentation, but the argumentation patterns are different. The writings produced in the active phase of the revolutionary movement emphasized the arguments based on the political goals related to prevailing political reality, as opposed to the more orthodox Marxist-Leninist writings that present quasi-logical reasoning based on the theoretical premises of Marxist thinking.

This division is evident in the writings of General Vo Nguyen Giap, where the ABCs of the revolution are connected to the organization and the control of the revolutionary movement. His outline of three-stage revolutionary guerrilla warfare was indeed of Chinese origin, and he was economical with orthodox Marxist-Leninist vocabulary in his texts during the 1950s and 1960s. Giap's manuals on revolution did not contradict the guidelines laid down by Lenin and Stalin, although he did not deal with the contents and theory of Marxism and their application to Vietnamese society. In this respect, the Vietnamese leaders maintained some kind of division of labor. Ho Chi Minh's activities and writings concentrated on the general awakening of Vietnamese society to oppose colonial rule, and Vo Nguyen Giap dealt with revolutionary theory and practice, emphasizing a pragmatic approach. The works of Truong Chinh and Le Duan[2] dealt mainly with Marxist-Leninist theory, its premises and their ideological application inside the revolutionary movement and in a post-revolutionary situation applying more dogmatic vocabulary and argumentation. However, this division is not categorical, but their writings thus reflect their position inside the Vietnamese revolutionary movement at a certain moment. If these approaches are put within an epochal frame, the texts based on action-oriented thinking dated from the early revolutionary period in the mid-1940s up to the beginning of the 1970s; and the orthodox Marxist-Leninist approach prevailed from the establishment of the DRV in the mid-1950s up to the latter part of the 1980s, exerting its strongest influence between the 4th and 5th Party Congresses, that is, between 1976 and 1982.

"THE ENEMY AND US" IN THE PRAGMATIC APPROACH

One of the main theses of revolutionary pragmatism emphasized that the success of a movement depends on the subjective and objective conditions of the situation. The subjective conditions *(chu quan)* were the combination of the lessons of early revolutionary experiences, which the Party leadership could apply with the help of theory in a new situation, while the objective conditions *(khac quan)* refer to the balance of forces between the revolutionaries and their enemies.[3] The point is how the subjective factors are able to take advantage of the possibilities lying in objective conditions. The ability to seize the opportunity *(thoi co)* or opportune moment *(dung luc)* in rapidly changing situations points up the decisive role of subjective factors.[4]

In this respect, the principle of distinguishing friend from foe *(phan biet ban thu)* is crucial. There were several expressions for this idea, such as *dich va ta* (the enemy and us, them and us) and *biet dich, biet ta* (recognizing the enemy, knowing us). Identifying the enemy leads to several options and consequences in politics. According to the Party history, "the origin and the existence of the contradictions among the ranks of the enemy of the proletarian class are an objective reality."[5] The recognition of friend and foe, which is by all counts more Chinese and Vietnamese than Soviet, amounted to a tool for benefiting from these contradictions. Although Lenin discussed this matter in his *Left Wing Communism – an Infantile Disorder*, it never gained the same position in Soviet Marxism-Leninism as in Vietnam. In China, Mao Zedong referred to this in his conception of contradictions, which was an application of dialectical materialism and Chinese naturalism.[6] In Vietnam, the tactic of taking advantage of the contradictions in the enemy ranks was "a leading strategic principle" *(nguyen tac chi dao chien luoc)* of revolution, as the Party history puts it. It includes a clear identification of the principal enemy *(ke thu chinh)* in order to "concentrate the sharp point of the struggle against the most dangerous enemy."[7] Truong Chinh pointed out that "revolutionary strategy is the science of discerning the enemy," a task that has to be done at every revolutionary stage. At each stage, besides recognition of the principal enemy, identifying the concrete enemy *(xac dinh ke thu cu the)* is a matter of survival. In regard to this, the Party must, first of all, "constantly have in view the concrete, present enemy rather than the enemy in general, and distinguish the principal from the secondary enemies."[8]

Distinguishing friend from foe had thus three aims. The first aim was the concentration of forces in a situation where the Vietnamese communist had many potential enemies. The second aim was to mobilize as strong as possible political force in any given situation. And third, by identification of the principal enemy, the revolutionaries tried to create and promote contradictions among all potential and concrete enemies.[9] The foundation of the National United Front included these aims: This front "was to be a vast assembly of all the forces capable of being united, neutralizing all those which could be neutralized, dividing all those it was possible to divide in order to direct the spearhead at the chief enemy of the revolution, invading imperialism."[10]

Vo Nguyen Giap's accounts about how the distinction between friend and foe was made during the early stages of the Vietnamese independence struggle are illustrative. According to Giap, the structure of the political reality of Vietnamese revolutionaries is composed of three potential opponents: the French, the Americans together with the British, and the forces of Chiang Kai-shek. The French strove to preserve their declining status, the British and the Americans aspired to gain a foothold in Indochina, and the Kuomingtang aimed to extend its authority to North Vietnam. But as the objectives of these foreign powers were in part contradictory, and as the French threat appeared to be the greatest and most immediate, it was decided that the French colonialist aggressor (as the Vietnamese saying went) was the most imminent and concrete enemy, against whom a popular uprising and guerrilla warfare were to be organized. However, since France and Vietnam reached an agreement on March 6, 1946, concerning the status of Vietnam, the principal enemy was seen to consist of those who opposed the treaty and who wanted to push Vietnam back to its former position. These were, in the terminology of the politburo of the Communist Party, the French "reactionaries." This called for a reassessment of policies, and it was the cause of Ho Chi Minh's journey to France in 1946. When the situation changed once more, on account of open conflict between French troops and Viet Minh, it was decided yet again that the principal enemy was the French colonial aggressor, which called for an armed struggle.[11]

The differentiation between friend and enemy, as Giap put it, deals with the external reality purely on the horizontal level. In politics, this means that the different contending political parties are always identified according to concrete situations and not against a background of class. Giap's argumentation refers constantly to the political ends and practical consequences of politics in a real situation. The interaction of the political ends and reality is here interesting. Whenever changes take place in the political environment, the means employed, as well as possibly also part of the ends, may change. Similarly, the changes in political ends lead to a re-examination of the political reality. This horizontal analysis is at variance with the original Marxist theory, in which political struggle is examined vertically, as a symptom of class struggle.

Consequently, deciding who are one's friends and foes also involves selecting the political instruments to be used and determining the level of mobilization of the movement. The division between friend and enemy is a crucial part of the doctrinal code of Vietnamese Marxist-Leninist language.[12] It was the skeleton over which the language of revolution was woven, and it provided the base for political mobilization. The question of how accurately the enemy is identified determines who the political actors are and how strong their control is over the masses. The more concrete the identification, the larger is the participation in the political struggle and the stronger the control over the population.[13] Hence the friend/enemy conception serves both functions of ideology in two ways: 1) It provides a possibility for rational calculation, and 2) it effectively enables control of the masses by directing people's attention toward a common goal.

It is arguable that the ideological aspect of the doctrine, control over the masses, emerged as a by-product in the revolution's manual. On the one hand, educating, organizing and arming the revolutionary movement supplied its strength and, on the other hand, the mobilization of the peasantry was the countermove against the puppet administration of colonial power.[14] But although Vo Nguyen Giap emphasized the role of ideology and propaganda as a method of large-scale preparation for the people's war, he did not deal with the practical realization of this task. In his guidelines, he did not try to argue in favor of the Party power over the movement as an orthodox Marxist-Leninist, but rather did he examine mobilization and control as necessary in the long-term resistance struggle.[15]

Insofar as Giap is dealing with decision-making in a concrete revolutionary process, he emphasizes the uncertain environment, in which the decisions are made. Although the doctrine provides certain tools, such as the division between friend and foe, in a real situation there might still be several options to consider. This situation underlines the competence of leaders.[16] In an uncertain environment, the task of this concept is to simplify things in order to make rational calculation feasible. In spite of the ultimate goal of action, the concrete goal must be defined in such a way that a sufficiently concrete friend/enemy division is possible. Giap was thus resorting to the pragmatic argumentation in which the concrete goals always refer to the prevailing reality and the options are kept open as far as possible.

Evidently Vietnamese revolutionary pragmatism refers to the same naturalism that can be found in Mao Zhedong's writings and in Lenin's discussion on the tactics of the Communist Party in its pursuit of power. But within the doctrinal code and on the side of this argumentation there developed in Vietnamese Marxism-Leninism a more orthodox vocabulary, which connects it to the ideological side of the doctrine. *Within* refers to the fact that the ABCs of revolution include the rudiments of mechanism of totalitarian control. *On the side* refers to the fact that the Vietnamese directly incorporated a great deal of Soviet practices and vocabulary in their doctrine, which remained in a highly orthodox form up to the mid-1980s.[17]

Inevitably, the Vietnamese revolutionary process had to create a motivation system to support its action. Thus the ideological side of the doctrine tended to examine Vietnamese culture and history according to the aims of the revolution. The moulding of ideology to serve these aims was done purposefully and according to elaborate plans, as the Viet Minh front's *Theses on Vietnamese Culture* proved. The *Theses* defined the development of Vietnamese culture as having taken place in two stages. First, it was necessary to build the national democratic culture toward mobilizing a whole social stratum for national liberation and only after that to start to establish a socialist culture in Vietnam.[18] Truong Chinh, who further developed these *Theses*, encouraged taking advantage of traditional culture for propaganda purposes, particularly "the forms most effective in influencing," to the broad masses in case "a new content and new artistic spirit" is provided. Thus the method of the selection and filtration of traditional culture, forms an essential part of the code. By the appplication of ideology, the future subordinates the past with the selective utilization of traditional culture and the reality is examined from this perspective.[19]

The order of this logic is that the ideology is created first, and that this is followed by the political organization, which then realizes the objectives set by the ideology. Similarly, in the examination of political organization and ideology, the control function of ideology becomes emphasized. Le Duan points out that it is not possible to refer to ideology without referring to organization. Ideological purity is guaranteed by the unity of organization. Consequently, this calls for a tightly organized party, which allows no hesitation or opposition to its defined line.[20] The task of organization is to realize the ideology, and the task of ideology is to provide the organization with direction. "If we want to practice anything, we must *make ideology one with organization*" (Le Duan's italics).[21] The organization represents the standard of measurement in the realization of the ideological line, and through its supervision it is possible to verify whether society is on the desired course. The correct line is enforced by continuous training. Therefore, within the context of the control function of ideology, the individual cadres share the crucial task of drawing the masses behind the goals and in support of the ideology.[22]

The strict organization of the Communist Party and its emphasis on the importance of organization reflect as well on the acceptance of the harsh realities of clandestine political work during French colonization and as well on the mobilization of the masses for the war of liberation. Vo Nguyen Giap puts the question of the goals and organization simply: "For a people's war, *the entire nation must be mobilized. ... The mobilization and organization of the entire nation for insurrection and war is a continuous process of mass education and organization carried out by our Party, passing from lower to higher forms pursuant to a correct revolutionary line*" (italics by Vo Nguyen Giap).[23] Consequently, the necessity for mobilization strongly supports the establishment of Marxist-Leninist rule.[24]

The direction and competence of organization are assessed in relation to the ideological plan, which lays out the political course.[25] In relation to the organization, ideology thus forms the project, which has both a control and a power function. The criticism *(phe binh)* and self-criticism *(tu phe binh)* campaigns, determining the manner of control of Party unanimity, were launched. This method was aimed to increase the cadres' capabilities and to purge the Party of disloyal and corrupt members. Similarly, the heightening of motivation among the masses was realized through the emulation *(thi dua)* and remoulding *(duc lai)* campaigns. Thus these campaigns became a crucial method of maintaining control over the masses and the cadres. The remoulding process involved "nothing else than propaganda and educational work, criticism and self-criticism" in order to drive socialist society forward. Referring to Zdanov, Le Duan pointed this out as a necessity for the development of the socialist state and Communist Party. The purpose of remoulding is the construction and the deconstruction of old practices and the cultural heritage – "but construction constitutes its principal object."[26]

According to the definition derived from Stalin, which also occurred in Vietnamese in the *Dictionary of Philosophy*, "socialist emulation *(thi dua xa hoi chu nghia)* is a Communist method of building socialism, a method based primarily on the highly positive character of the ranks composed of millions of working people."[27] Moreover, this definition includes the idea of a positive example which the masses should follow.[28] Although the original Vietnamese idea on emulation was not Stahanovism as understood in the Soviet Union during the period of rapid industrialization, the political purposes involving the masses were the same.

Basically, emulation in the Vietnamese revolutionary movement signified the binding of all social activity to given political and social objectives; and this involved old women and children just as much as the soldiers of the liberation front.[29] In this manner, social and political objectives served as the instruments of control over all public activities. The objective of emulation and ideological training was to produce new socialist individuals, whose characteristic was that they had become indoctrinated with the role of communist organization, discipline, work and "their struggle for the common cause."[30]

The ulterior idea of the project is that the control function would be realized by the movement itself. This happens when the members of the new society share a consciousness sufficiently in line with the ideological project. This consciousness guarantees unity of action, which is further emphasized by the activity of the Communist Party. The Vietnamese Communist Party History sets as a prime condition for the success of Marxism-Leninism in Vietnam and as the first lesson for the future cadres that they "closely combine Party action relating to politics, ideology and organization."[31] This leads to other lessons on how the Party, penetrating through social levels, could enforce and construct itself.[32] The Party is the ideal toward which the entire social organization in Vietnamese Marxist-Leninist thought aspires. The Party forms an ideological totality, which signifies "that the Party is a monolithic bloc not only in ideology but also in organization. And this serves as a guarantee of action."[33] Thus the doctrinal code in pragmatic argumentation is structured by using different elements: The premise, the goal, is examined on the basis of opposing poles, from which different cultural and social phenomena as well as time periods are surveyed. The formation of these opposing poles directs and enforces political mobilization – the essence of Marxist-Leninist rule and its different concrete methods. This is all further emphasized by the claim of unity in action and in organization, which finally secures power for the one party.

"TWO ROADS OF DEVELOPMENT" AND FORMAL MARXISM-LENINISM

Examination of the relationship between the structural rules in pragmatic argumentation and the control mechanism emphasizes the view that the ideology is an artificial product moulded from the doctrine by the revolutionary leaders. But on the side of the practical, instrumental function of ideology in the Vietnamese revolutionary ABCs, there was a stronger Stalinist emphasis. The statements on Marxism-Leninism claiming it to be the most scientific and revolutionary of ideologies allude to this more monolithic conception of science in relation to ideology than Lenin's pronouncement in, for example, *What is to be done?* The logic of these statements is that, because ideology is an indispensable element in political action, the results of political action reveal which ideology is closest to objective truth. The outcome of political action is determined by the social struggle for power. Thus the revolutionaries' justification of the power of the Communist Party signifies that they are practicing the most scientific politics. The Party is the most concrete expression of this scientific consciousness.[34] The argumentation advocating action and justifying Communist Party power is put into the mode of formal deduction.

These views refer to that part of Vietnamese Marxist-Leninist ideology which developed on the side of Vietnamese action-oriented thinking. Originally, this side was not concerned much with the struggle against foreign powers but with the building of the socialist state in Vietnam. This justification of the power and the politics of the Communist Party emerged after it had established its power in the North at the beginning of the 1950s, and it was elaborated to perfection during the period after the fall of Saigon. Whereas in the previous chapter I dealt with the elements of the doctrine formulated during the revolutionary movement against the foreign powers, the present examination deals with the elements adopted toward justifying the power of the Communist Party and fitting Marxist theory into Vietnamese conditions. This orthodox Marxist-Leninist tradition is clearly evident in the Vietnamese Party cadres' textbooks, where Stalin appears as an equal authority alongside Marx and Lenin.[35] Besides the theoretical reasoning borrowed from the Soviet Union, also Soviet Marxist-Leninist concepts were consolidated and "vietnamized" more in accordance with Vietnamese vocabulary. Its characteristics lie in an attempt to extract the present social and political situation from Marxist premises and give political action a formally correct basis.

The point of departure in formal argumentation is the theoretical premises of Marxism, incorporating the particular characteristics of Marxism-Leninism. Accordingly, the society is following the objective laws of the development from feudalism via capitalism to socialism and communism. The key factor in this evolutionary process is the struggle between the social classes, particularly between the bourgeois class and the proletarian class. The crucial question was how to fit the development toward socialism into Marxist theory in the framework of Vietnam's colonial and feudal conditions. This stirred up sophisticated discussion among the Party Cadres, heavily dependent as they were on Soviet Marxism-Leninism. The Vietnamese answer was – as Soviet counterparts – to advance to socialism bypassing the stage of capitalist development *(tien len chu nghia xa hoi, bo qua giai doan phat trien tu ban chu nghia).*[36]

As this revolution took place in an agrarian society with weak capitalist and workers' classes, in contrast to the thinking of Marx and Engels, who based their theory on socialist revolution in the capitalist countries, certain adjustments had to be made. First, the main struggle did not happen in an armed uprising as such, but afterward. Second, the struggle is not between the working class and the bourgeoisie as such, but what is involved is a wider class struggle waged between two roads – the capitalist and the socialist roads. The struggle is focused on the question "who will win over whom between the two roads" *(ai thang ai giua hai con duong)* or, to put it more briefly, "who wins, who loses" *(ai thang ai thua)* or simply "who will win over whom" *(ai thang ai)*. This concept appeared already in Stalin's writings and was established in Soviet Marxism-Leninism,[37] becoming further emphasized in Vietnamese Marxism-Leninism. The time during which this struggle is completed is called the transitional period to socialism *(thoi ky qua do len chu nghia xa hoi)*, or simply transitional period *(thoi ky qua do)*.[38]

This formal reasoning was clearly evident in the politico-philosophical contemplation of two cadres, Tran Con and Ho Van Thong. Tran Con, affiliated with the Philosophical Institute, and Ho Van Thong, who worked at the Nguyen Ai Quoc Higher Party School, both followed the established Soviet formula. Dealing with the relation between the concept of class struggle *(dau tranh giai cap)* and the struggle waged between two roads *(dau tranh giua hai con duong)*, Tran Con argued that, owing to their essence, they could be considered synonymous. He rejected the argument that the concept of *dau tranh giua hai con duong* is a supplement, developed from the concept of the class struggle between the proletariat and the bourgeoisie in the transitional period. Tran Con's critique focuses on the idea that in this situation the question is not one of winning the political power or maintaining it, but of turning the struggle in the home country to the orbit *(quy dao)* or off the orbit of socialism. He argued that in a situation where there is the danger of veering off the course of socialism, the proletarian class does not hesitate in deciding whether or not to seize political power in order to guide the country back to the socialist orbit. In the second place, the struggle taking place between two roads is a wider form of class struggle, because those who travel the socialist road include not only the working class but also the peasants and the members of the progressive intelligentsia, taken collectively, when the travelers on the capitalist road are not only the bourgeoisie but also other reactionary elements and agents of the imperialist clique, together with all the forces of spontaneous capitalism *(tu phat tu ban chu nghia)*. Thus, during the transitional period, the concept of class struggle and the concept of the struggle between two roads cannot be separated.[39]

Ho Van Thong stated that "the transitional period is the period which advances by leaps and bounds from the old social substances to socialism,"[40] and its main characteristic is the struggle between the capitalist and socialist roads of development. During the transitional period, there also exist two different economic systems. They are represented by large-scale socialist mass production and small-scale commodity production based on spontaneous capitalism, according to Stalin as cited by the Vietnamese.[41] Because the capitalist class is weak, spontaneous capitalism refers in Vietnam mainly to persons engaged in commerce and in the handicraft sector. Still, according to this reasoning, in spite of the weakness of the spontaneous capitalist class, the *ai thang ai* struggle is fierce and burning hot, because there is always a possibility that capitalism is going to recover. If the rudiments of the capitalist class are not swept away completely, socialism will gradually become a battlefield and "the road of socialism is going to be a tortuous stage of development, with even the danger of going back to the starting point."[42]

The above reasoning leads to the following conclusions. First, it justifies the proletarian dictatorship *(chuyen chinh vo san)*, which in practice means the absolute sovereignty of the Communist Party. Second, during the transitional period, three revolutions have to be carried out to sweep away the rudiments of the capitalist class and to lay the foundations of the socialist system. These are the revolution bearing on the means of production, the scientific-technological revolution and the ideological and cultural revolution.[43] The first revolution means replacing private ownership of the means of production with collective ownership and simultaneously eliminating small-scale production in order to create a system of mass production. The scientific-technological revolution is needed to introduce this system of socialist mass production, while the ideological and cultural revolution is needed to support the socialist system at the individual level.

Consequently, the *ai thang ai* struggle should be waged through all these revolutions. According to the Communist Party ideologist, owing to Vietnam's uncertain international position after unification, the significance of this concept is further emphasized. The way he puts it is that, during the transitional period, "if we speak of socialist revolution with respect to its political character and system of rule *(chi phoi)*, this [*ai thang ai* struggle] is the special trait of Vietnam's socialist revolution."[44]

In this respect, there are similarities between *ai thang ai* and the concept of discriminating friend from foe *(phan biet ban thu)*. With a certain reservation, *ai thang ai* could be regarded as a special form of the friend/foe conception. As far as the ideological aspect of the doctrine is concerned, *ai thang ai* works like the friend/foe conception in mobilizing the masses in the struggle to achieve a common goal. Simultaneously, it gives to the Party a leading role as an organizer of the struggle. But this concept does not have operational value similar to the friend/enemy concept. It is bound to the concept of the struggle between two roads, and it is not bound to any actual situation like the friend/enemy concept. And as one purpose of the friend/enemy concept was to divide and neutralize all other potential opponents, the *ai thang ai* concept is in this respect more dogmatic: it recognizes only friend or enemy. *Ai thang ai* thus enforces the two-bloc structure, giving no chance to the third force. When emphasizing the class struggle as its theoretical justification, it is dealing with the political struggle more on a vertical than on a horizontal level, contrary to the friend/enemy concept. Owing to this concept, which does not identify the enemy in advance but in an actual situation, the doctrinal code at the phase of the national revolutionary movement seemed to be more open, tolerating and accepting more new information than in the later period, when the orthodox Marxist-Leninist language was established. The *ai thang ai* concept seemed only to reinforce the code, having no informational role at all. *Ai thang ai* operates solely on the publicity level and is not based on separate Party leadership resolutions, such as the discrimination between friend and foe. But it has a curious relationship with the continuation of the system of rule developed during the anticolonial struggle. The *ai thang ai* concept was intended to replace the ideological role of the friend/enemy concept at the new phase.

The role of ideology was to cover the gap that occurred in the system of rule when the goal of mass mobilization, independence and unity was reached. Without explicit expression, it seems that the Vietnamese authors consider the friend/enemy concept as belonging to the national democratic revolution *(cach mang dan toc dan chu)* and *ai thang ai* to the socialist revolution *(cach mang xa hoi chu nghia)*. The former refers in established Vietnamese parlance to the time extending from the August revolution of 1945 up to the Geneva agreement of 1954 and the latter from 1954 (in the North) up to the present. In the new situation after the spring of 1975, when the enemy was no longer on Vietnamese soil, another kind of motivation was needed. This called for an ideological system that reaches all the social levels and sectors so as to keep the masses toeing the line of the Communist Party. This task is given to Marxist-Leninist theory.[45] This ideological system forms the doctrinal code of Vietnamese Marxist-Leninist language. In brief, its essence lies in the mobilization of the masses, which is based on a clear recognition of the adversary, whether *phan biet ban thu* or *ai thang ai* is used. However, in formal argumentation, the adversary is derived from Marxist-Leninist theory and is staying rather constant as opposite to revolutionary pragmatism, in which concrete goals determine the distinction between friend and enemy.

The purpose of the ideology now, at the mature stage of Marxism-Leninism, is to show the difference between two roads in all spheres of social life. This was put into practice in all social discourse; and it received concrete manifestations in the emulation campaigns, already familiar in the North and inside the liberation movement. The aim was to create and maintain "a new socialist man" *(con nguoi moi xa hoi chu nghia)*, which had started to emerge in the North after the year 1954; and now the intention was to produce it in the South as well. The new Vietnamese socialist man possesses a sense of patriotism *(chu nghia yeu nuoc)*, revolutionary heroism *(chu nghia anh hung cach mang)*, communist humanism *(chu nghia nhan dao cong san)* and collectivism *(chu nghia tap the)*. The new socialist man is drawn voluntarily toward socialism and possesses a conciousness of the superiority of his system over capitalism.[46]

FOREIGN RELATIONS AND IDEOLOGICAL MOTIVATION

Despite the fact that both the pragmatic and the formal approach include the same doctrinal code, I argue that foreign policy and foreign relations played different roles in the argumentation involving these patterns. Two different kinds of texts shed more light on this question from a more particular point of view. First, it can be asked: What are the premises that link the Vietnamese Communists' struggle to that of foreign relations in pragmatic and formalist patterns? How is the doctrinal code reflected in these arguments? Finally, a still more particular question: What are the roles of communication and autocommunication in these texts? In order to give answers to these questions, I shall analyze the pragmatic argumentation of the study group of the Military Institute that it presented in the November and December 1972 issues of the Communist Party's theoretical journal *Hoc Tap* and the formalist rhetoric of one high-ranking Party cadre at the beginning of the 1980s.

The title of the Military Institute's study, *Tai thao luoc kiet xuat cua ong cha ta* (The talent and pre-eminent art of war of our ancestors), seems evidently more of a historical study than one of political argumentation. Similarly, its general vocabulary, which lacks nearly all the conventional Marxist-Leninist concepts, refers more to the other code systems than to the Marxist-Leninist doctrinal code. In this sense, the question of the different, simultaneous code system in this text is legitimate. Nevertheless, the general structure of this essay reveals the rationalist structure of revolutionary pragmatism. Its ostensible nature as a historical study is even more questionable, when placed against the general political situation where it was published. The main denominator in the situation vis-à-vis this study was the peace talks between the U.S. and North Vietnam, at which the latter tried to get the Americans to abandon the war on

Vietnamese soil, while it intended simultaneously to intensify its offensive against South Vietnam's government. The study emphasizes the significance of peace talks *(nghi hoa)* – the principle of negotiating combined with simultaneous warfare.[47] In this way, the Military Institute's study represented a justification of this policy by using historical analogy, a method that is quite common in argumentation referring to present reality. This context is emphasized even more when China's negative attitude is connected to this policy, similar to China's general trend of foreign policy in its approach to the United States. Therefore, the historical examples – the Vietnamese warfare against the Northern Power – that the essay deals with may be intrepreted in the light of both the context of Vietnam's present struggle and the circumstance of their serving as a notice to China.

The premise of this approach is the goal, and it is in reference to this goal that the arguments are developed. Accordingly, the study group argues that the goal of ancient military art was to win and maintain Vietnam's independence. In line with this denominator, the Vietnamese wars were just wars and those waged by the enemy, unjust wars. With respect to this goal, the ancient Vietnamese tried to fit their strategy of survival among China's other tributary states and southwestern neighbors.[48] The study group outlines eight crucial points that characterized the traditional military art. Certainly, it is not purely by chance that these points followed the rationalistic pattern evident in, for example, Vo Nguyen Giap's writings. They include: 1) *Biet dich biet ta,* 2) armed uprising and warfare, 3) the building up of armed forces, 4) establishing the rear areas, 5) certain methods of military tactics, 6) an ideology supplying concrete guidance in the conduct of the war, 7) striking against the enemy by dealing directly with persons in the enemy's ranks and, 8) finally, combining offensive military action with the foreign-policy (diplomatic) offensive.[49] With respect to the questions put forward in the foregoing, the main interest here lies in the first, sixth and eighth points as well as in the relationship between them.

According to the theses laid down by the study group, the idea of *biet dich biet ta* can be found from the period of the Tran dynasty at the end of the 13th century as established in Vietnamese thinking over the centuries. The study group emphasizes the connection of the concept to the attempt at estimating the relation of the forces on both sides: "In estimating the relation of the forces between the enemy and us, our forefathers' method of examining things is the national way of examining. It fits both the valiant struggle and the views of 'grasp widely, know deeply *(hieu rong biet sau),*' and has thus 'the ability of envisaging the events *(tinh duoc viec tu truoc khi co viec xay ra)*'."[50]

Pursuing revolutionary pragmatism further, the study group argues in favor of the decisive role of the subjective side of the traditional Vietnamese military art, which emphasized "an ideology supplying the concrete guidance for fighting against the foreign aggressor." The way the study discusses the role of ideology reveals a basic starting point for rationalist thinking: ideology is used to support the action and not vice versa. According to the theses presented in the study, a particular line of thinking developed in Vietnam, being "first of all, an active thought process taking the initiative in an offensive to wipe out the enemy and expressing a deep understanding of strategy and tactics gained from many armed uprisings, wars of defense, and wars of liberation."[51] Not surprisingly, but interestingly enough, the study group views Marxism-Leninism as continuing this tradition of offensive ideology in order to mobilize the masses for war and for a concrete analysis of the power relations in Vietnam's present situation.[52]

The central role selected for foreign affairs in this essay is rather extraordinary in the field of Vietnamese revolutionary pragmatism, but it corresponds well to its basic premises. In every case, the emphasis on diplomacy refers to the actual negotiations conducted between Hanoi and Washington in Paris. In these negotiations, the peace pact with the U.S. was not an objective in itself but a means to weaken the position of the Saigon government. The study argues that this amounted to an essential part of traditional Vietnamese military art. By historical analogies the conclusion is drawn that "the way to end a war is to combine military action and struggle on the foreign-policy front toward achieving complete victory."[53] Owing to its instrumental role, foreign relations do not enforce as such the doctrinal code in pragmatic contemplation. The role of autocommunication in enhancing the spirit of the national and revolutionary movements was given to ideology, which supplies the "concrete guidance" and enforces mobilization by aiming at the goals, leaving the realm of foreign policy to the discretion of the political leaders. Accordingly, foreign relations are not viewed through prefixed dogma but from the point of view of the political goals related to the current political situation.

The instrumental role that the study group gives to foreign policy is rather distinct in formal argumentation. Owing to its role as a part of Marxist-Leninist rule, the formal vocabulary, which became established in Vietnamese Marxism-Leninism during the 1950s and -60s, and emerged dominant during the 1970s, dealt more with the ideological aspect than the action-orientated calculations of the doctrine. But when dealing with foreign relations, it gave some principles for conducting foreign policy. This gave a specific relationship to foreign policy and Marxist-Leninist rule. Evidently, it led to the examination in which foreign policy is viewed as a part of ideology. Therefore, this excursion into formalist argumentation highlights foreign relations as an important part of autocommunication in the political argumentation in the form proposed by Lotman.

The connection between foreign policy and Marxist-Leninist rule was emphasized in essays that Hoang Tung, a member of the secretariat of the central committee of the Communist Party and editor-in-chief of the Party's daily *Nhan Dan*, presented between the years 1980–1983 on various occasions to the Party's cadres and officers. Hoang Tung's position as the Party ideologist just under the top leadership is not of special interest here except for the evident formalism in his argumentation, which he presented on solemn occasions and in publications up to 1986. The essays cited here were published under the title *May van de ve cong tac chinh tri va tu tuong trong chang duong hien nay cua cach mang xa hoi chu nghia* (Some questions concerning political and ideological work at the present stage of the socialist revolution). Hoang Tung's aim was to prepare and then justify the resolutions of the 5th Party Congress in 1982 concerning the guidelines of the Party's political tasks and ideological work. During this period, Vietnam's dependence on the Soviet bloc was on the increase, as it was isolated from the rest of the world on account of the Kampuchean question. Similarly, relations with China formed an immediate military threat to Vietnam at that juncture. Simultaneously and partly because of the blockade, Vietnam's economy performed badly, offering poor prospects for the country. This was roughly the background of Hoang Tung's discussion of the relationship between external factors and internal rule.

The point of departure in Hoang Tung's lectures is clearly the theoretical premises of Marxism-Leninism. In almost every lecture, the arguments are derived from the struggle between revolutionary and reactionary forces on both domestic and international levels. In each of the ten lectures, reference is made to this struggle. The crucial point in Hoang Tung's arguments is connecting the international situation to Vietnam's internal situation.[54] Internationally, according to this formalist argumentation, the whole world is in a transitional period from capitalism to socialism. Following this, he emphasizes that the Communist Party of Vietnam has realized the objective laws underlying the trend of world development. This trend, as he argues, is leading toward the socialist system and in the current situation is introducing the preconditions also to the capitalist countries.[55] This period began with the Russian October Revolution and has progressed by ups and downs to the final stage.

Thus with Vietnam's having been drawn into the global trend of developments, Hoang Tung grants legitimacy to Communist Party rule in Vietnam. However, by emphasizing the fact that the *ai thang ai* struggle is not yet over, he connects the international relations organically to Vietnam's domestic rule. He therefore emphasizes that, despite the fact that it had lost its superiority to socialism, imperialism remained very dangerous. "The relation of the forces *(so sanh luc luong)* operating between socialism and capitalism has reached a point highly important to the question of death and survival *(van de mot mat con)* between two social systems in the world sphere... The *'ai thang ai'* struggle accelerates every day and hour in politics, economics, culture, belief-systems *(he y thuc)*, and international life as a whole is governed by the rules of this struggle."[56] Thus this struggle exerts an influence on the Communists all over the world and it may manifest itself in the Communist movements as nationalism, petit bourgeois Communism and various different negative forms. After stating this, he warns: "If we do not go deeply into our economic matters and if we do not examine the influence of the *'ai thang ai'* struggle on our Communists, it would be very difficult to understand sufficiently the issues of revolutionary struggle in our own country."[57]

For this reason, the Vietnamese people and, first of all, the Party cadres have to be fully aware of these international connections in their country. On the side of education, industrialization and economic tasks, Hoang Tung emphasizes turning attention to the international problems confronting the Vietnamese Communists, which primarily means identifying the external aspects of the *ai thang ai* struggle in their country. According to Hoang Tung's analysis, the struggle has to be waged in the areas mentioned above; but the special emphasis is laid on the culture in general, along with the political thinking among the cadres and Party members. The old cultural vestiges offer the possibility of propagating new colonialist thinking among the masses and eraditing Maoist thinking from the ranks of the cadres and Party members.[58] Therefore, as Hoang Tung concludes, ideological education must instill in the cadres a readiness to identify the enemy and an ability to build and maintain an organization fit to struggle against it. "Involved is not only the issue of peace and war, but also the *'ai thang ai'* question, which occurs in very drastic guise on the Peninsula of Indochina. It is an extremely important leitmotiv *(chu de)* in our ideological work."[59] The intensity of the *ai thang ai* struggle can not abate before the proletarian dictatorship is firmly secured and "the Marxist-Leninist ideological system has succeeded in dominating *(thong tri)* the whole society."[60]

The following conclusion can be drawn from the Military Institute's study and Hoang Tung's lectures. Ideology signifies for Hoang Tung, first of all, a control system, in which the *ai thang ai* concept is raised to a very high abstract level, offering an extremely vague guide to concrete action. In orthodox Marxism, *ai thang ai* is an objective fact in social and international relations. It thus presents a striking difference from the friend/enemy concept of pragmatism. According to the Military Institute's study group, the correct use of *biet dich biet ta* reveals the proficiency of the national leaders. It is therefore a skill associated with political calculation. On the other hand, *ai thang ai* refers clearly to the connection between the control system and international relations in the Marxist-Leninist doctrine. The *ai thang ai* concept does not seek to take advantage of possible rifts inside the two-bloc system, but to strengthen it internationally and nationally. As Hoang Tung's essays proved, the *ai thang ai* concept took advantage of the two-bloc system for the benefit of Vietnam's internal rule. First of all, the *ai thang ai* concept has turned to a phrase, the task of which is to enforce the code. This means also that, as a text dealing with foreign policy, the role of the essays is more in autocommunication than communication in the traditional sense. Typical of Marxist-Leninist parlance, the task of these lectures was to enforce the code at the cost of actual information. However, when we look at the audience to which they are addressed, we also see an informational aspect. This aspect is intended to instruct the party cadres to emphasize the role of international relations in their propaganda work.

Although Vietnamese concepts concerning foreign policy do not have any obvious and direct relation to the ideological control system, the doctrinal code forms the connection to it. Therefore, in the formal rhetoric, the foreign policy concepts also reflect the domestic rule. Evidently, in pragmatic argumentation, the doctrinal code is weaker than in formal argumentation. In the Military Institute's study, foreign relations do not play the same role of enforcing the code as in Hoang Tung's essays. On the contrary, foreign relations are considered to be one instrument of political power, similar to political mobilization as another. The mutually complementary nature of these argumentation patterns explains the general practice of using both of them in the same political texts.

3 Vietnam and the World's Revolutionary Forces

THE CONCEPTS AND THEMES OF INTERNATIONAL RELATIONS 1960–86

Pragmatic and formal rhetoric reflected the politico-cultural influences of Vietnamese Marxism-Leninism adopted from traditional politico-cultural thinking and from Soviet Marxism-Leninism as well as from Chinese Marxism. Nevertheless, since the Marxist-Leninist concepts on international relations are, at least in theory, based on Marxist-Leninist premises, an examination of these concepts brings emphatically into view a formalist pattern. The formal premises became evident as early as the Third National Congress of the Lao dong (Workers') Party in 1960; and particularly the 9th session of the Party's Central Committee, held in December 1963, strengthened the formalist trend.

However, in the Party cadres' texts, in the Party documents and in diplomatic argumentation, both patterns coexist very often in the same passages. The difference lies in the premises of the argumentation, but these are not always easy to distinguish. For example, the goal of foreign policy might be chosen to serve as the premise of argumentation, but the goal itself could be deduced from the Marxist-Leninist doctrine. It is therefore asked first what kind of position the concepts and themes dealing with foreign policy have in the Marxist-Leninist doctrine and what their actual significance is with respect to Vietnam's international situation. After that, the foreign-policy texts are examined with respect to the argumentation patterns and the code imposed by the Marxist doctrine.

Hoang Tung's essays represented the developmental phase of Vietnam's Marxist-Leninist doctrine during the 5th Party Congress at the beginning of the 1980s. They represented a sophisticated discussion on the relationship between ideology and foreign policy, and they partly reflected the result of developments, involving the Marxist-Leninist doctrinal code, formalist argumentation and foreign policy. But they still contained elements that already existed when Vietnam's Communist Party started to establish its foreign-policy orientation during the 1950s and 1960s.[1] The stability and coherence of these elements and concepts were so obvious during the period between the 3rd and the 6th Party Congresses, 1960–1986, that, although Vietnam's foreign-policy environment changed dramatically during these years, the theoretical evaluation of the foreign policy underwent only minor changes. Therefore its importance lies in ostensibly small changes made in the concepts and in the introduction of new concepts formally derived from the old doctrine.

Ever since the outbreak of the dispute between the Soviet Union and the People's Republic of China, considerable attention was paid to Vietnam's stances on the conflict and its attitude toward the differences in the political and ideological emphases of the Soviet Union and China. Despite varying interpretations, a common conclusion has been drawn: The Vietnamese made a practice of promoting views that better supported their current dual goal: building socialism in the North and reunifying the whole country. The Vietnamese did not try to maintain absolute neutrality, but they pursued an independent line whenever the DRV's vital interests were involved.[2]

During this period, up to the spring of 1975, several questions arose where the views on international relations of Vietnam and its great allies differed. In spite of the fact that Vietnam, by emphasizing its own stance, most probably seemed to step on one side against another, it did manifest its view with consideration but nevertheless clearly. Vietnam revealed its doubts about Khrushchev's emphasis on peaceful coexistence and the possibility of avoiding war between the superpowers. Similarly, the Vietnamese leaders could not agree wholeheartedly on Khrushchev's view of a peaceful transition to socialism, while they were intensifying their campaign for reuniting South Vietnam with the DRV.[3] Although these postures seemed to indicate a shift by Vietnam toward China's orbit at the beginning of the dispute, and certain matters, such as Vietnam's critical stance toward the Test Ban Treaty of 1963, supported this view, it was not the big picture. Vietnam's policies were bound to its special position, which at that moment was determined by its struggle to reunite South Vietnam with the DRV. After Vietnam became convinced that the Soviet Union was not going to abandon the DRV's vital interests and after the American attack on the DRV's territory, which resulted in the granting of Soviet military aid to the North, the Vietnamese and Soviet policies were harmonized. But this did not mean that the Vietnamese had needed to change their views.[4]

Correspondingly, there existed important differences between the DRV leadership and China on the diplomacy and conduct of the war in Vietnam, especially in its latter phase. Similarly, the DRV leadership did not hail the cultural revolution and personal cult in China and, finally, they disagreed with China's outlook on the global situation. This was expressed first in Vietnam's vehement emphasis on the unity of the socialist world and then in its bitter criticism of China's rapprochement with the U.S. in the late 1960s.[5]

The Sino–Soviet conflict, which reached its climax in 1969, when border clashes occurred, and the U.S.–China rapprochement, together with the American troop withdrawal from South Vietnam, constitute the brief international context in which the Vietnamese evaluated their Marxist-Leninist doctrine as fitting their international position before the fall of Saigon. After the spring of 1975, the doctrine had to adjust to the new situation. The rise in importance of the formalist pattern in foreign policy evidently has its basis in the changes in Vietnam's position both with respect to Soviet–Chinese–American relations since the beginning of the 1970s and then with respect to the unified socialist Vietnam after the spring of 1975.

Interestingly enough, the Vietnamese Marxist-Leninist political texts, viewed even in a pragmatic light, seem, when dealing with the internal struggle, to examine the political arena at the horizontal level; but when they turn to deal with international relations, they emphasize the class structure of international relations. While the victory of the Vietnamese revolution has been described as the result of skilful tactical and strategic moves, it has been connected internationally to the class struggle on a world scale.[6] Thus the two modes of argumentation, revolutionary pragmatism and theoretically orientated Marxism-Leninism, appeared side by side in Vietnamese texts.[7] There existed arguments based on the friend/enemy concept referring to different states, but the general way to describe Vietnam's international relations has taken place along vertical lines, starting from more or less orthodox Marxist-Leninist premises.

Thus class theory occupies an important place in Vietnamese analysis of international relations. Although it deals with certain theoretical viewpoints, an important element in the writings on international relations deals with action. As the Vietnamese tend to emphasize a rationalistic model for their conduct of politics, accompanied by quasi-logical deduction in international relations, the following analysis of the Vietnamese discussion of foreign relations includes: A) A theory of international relations, the main elements of which are the question of international class relations and the issue of national versus international; B) an appraisal of the international situation; C) the question of the foreign-policy goal(s) and the themes that the Vietnamese apply in their foreign-policy argumentation.

The question of national versus international

There was obviously a lack of theoretical discussion on international relations and foreign policy in Vietnam up to the 1980s. For example, there were no theoretically oriented articles on purely foreign relations in the Communist Party's theoretical journal *Hoc Tap* between 1970 and 1975, except Le Duan's formulation of theoretical viewpoints on international relations[8], and hardly any article in which Vietnam's foreign policy and international relations were the main issue. After the fall of Saigon, from May 1975 up to December 1976, there appeared in *Hoc Tap* only two articles in which Vietnam's foreign policy was examined.[9] There did appear articles that connected Vietnam's situation to the general world situation, and some of them included theoretically and politically important evaluations.[10] In these evaluations, the ideas on international relations were represented as part of the total structure of Marxist-Leninist doctrine, and foreign policy was connected to the other activities of the Communist Party. Thus international relations and foreign policy seemed to have no separate forum for theoretical and evaluating discussion. Characteristically, the *Dictionary of Philosophy* mentioned foreign policy in one sentence in its definition of politics. According to it, "politics *(chinh tri)* is a manifestation of the interests of social classes and the relations between these classes. Politics also manifests the relations between nations and states (foreign policy) *(chinh sach doi ngoai)*."[11] The other way around, on both national and international levels, every class struggle is a political struggle.[12] But, owing to the uneven development of class relations on the global level, the class struggle is carried on between two orientations, the socialist road of development and the capitalist road. The struggle is fought between world revolutionary forces *(luc luong cach mang the gioi)* and imperialism *(chu nghia de quoc)*, which later, according to the Vietnamese definition, gained the support of the world's reactionary forces *(luc luong phan dong tren the gioi)*. The world's revolutionary forces include the socialist countries, the national liberation movements *(phong trao giai phong dan toc)* in the Third World and the workers' movements in the developed capitalist countries. Imperialism refers first of all to the United States as well as to the old colonial powers, but the meaning of the world's reactionary forces is far more obscure. It means the anti-communist parties in the capitalist countries or the anti-communist governments in the Third World and refers, after the disruption of Sino–Vietnamese relations, also to China.

The theoretical premises of Vietnamese Marxism-Leninism with regard to international relations can be figured out from these theoretically orientated essays and studies on Vietnam's general situation. The premises appeared clearly in Le Duan's two articles published in 1970 – one a longer essay on the history of Vietnam's revolution in the February issue and the other a more condensed theoretical article dealing with the Marxist-Leninist premises on political conduct in the present international situation, which appeared in the June issue of *Hoc Tap*.[13] These articles include theoretical formulations and, particularly, appraisals of the world situation, which meant that Vietnam was turning more decidedly to the Soviet Union's lines in its foreign policy and distancing itself from China.

Le Duan argued that the revolutionary line that Vietnam's Communist Party (Workers' Party, *Lao dong* at that time) was following under the leadership of Ho Chi Minh was Leninist and had adhered to Lenin's theoretical and political premises. The point of departure is dialectical materialism and historical materialism, from which the analysis of both national and international developments is derived. The crucial element in this analysis is distinguishing the fundamental contradictions in the world. According to this definition, which was based on the 1963 resolution of the Lao Dong Party's central committee,[14] there exist four fundamental contradictions, the resolution of which determines the world's development: the contradiction between proletriat and bourgeois; the contradiction between the colonies and the imperialist powers; the contradiction between these imperialist countries; and, after the October Revolution, the contradiction between the socialist and capitalist systems.[15] This analysis forms the nucleus of the Vietnamese Marxist-Leninist doctrine, which has not been basically changed during the evaluations of the doctrine during the 1970s and early 1980s. Le Duan specified the contents of these contradictions by adding (or replacing) the contradiction between the colonies and imperialism to the contradiction between national liberation movements and imperialism.[16] The analysis of one contradiction is therefore connected in Le Duan's formalism to the analysis of another contradiction, thus joining national analysis to international analysis of class relations.

According to these formulations, a strong interaction exists between national and international questions. Although the *ai thang ai*-struggle is resolved both nationally and internationally, the main factor is the working class in each country, which has to resolve this question nationally and take over the power with all the other segments of the proletariat. The developmental driving force has turned to the old colonies, where the victories of the national liberation movement energize the proletarian revolutionary movement in the mother country.[17] But the most important factor is the emergence of the socialist camp, the "support area" of the revolutionary movements.[18]

Consequently, with regard to the questions concerning class, nation and international relations, the Vietnamese were reluctant, at least theoretically, to make distinctions. The revolutionary forces in old colonies, when vanquishing the old feudal lords and liberating their lands from colonial rule, also advance the cause of revolution internationally. The question is one of combining patriotism *(chu nghia yeu nuoc)* with socialist revolution, of exploiting patriotic feelings for the sake of liberation and socialist revolution. "Independence *(doc lap)* is the motive force that legitimates the state" and "the idea of the state leads more and more to a class standpoint. And, on the other hand, the question of the state can be grasped only with a serious concept of the proletariat." According to this reasoning, the proletarian class combines the idea that the struggle in one's own country connects to the proletarian class in all other countries in order to pursue common goals. Thus class and state, like patriotism and proletarian internationalism, cannot be separated. Therefore the relationship between national emancipation and socialist emancipation is close, and international cooperation between Communist parties offers a guarantee of revolution in each country.[19] This is called, in Marxist-Leninist terms, "the dialectical relationship between national and international factors" *(quan he bien chung giua nhan to dan toc va nhan to quoc te)*, where the Vietnamese national liberation struggle, and the national liberation struggles in the rest of the world constitute part of the international class struggle.[20]

Although this vertical theory combines domestic and international struggle, the emergence of the concepts dealing with international relations proved that foreign policy and international relations formed an independent realm also for the Vietnamese. Later developments and the application of Vietnam's foreign-policy concepts confirmed this. So far, the Vietnamese vocabulary did not refer to any political choice between Soviet and Chinese lines, as the idea of class struggle and the significance of national movements was generally accepted in both the Soviet Union and China. On the conceptual level, uniformity prevailed up to the 1970s, that is, until both China and the Soviet Union developed further their concepts of international relations. Naturally, the vertical class concept is too general for it to be, in Marxist thinking, itself the subject of any dispute. The problems arose when the Soviet and Chinese modifications of the class-struggle concept started to differ in their appraisal of the world situation.

Sino–Soviet dispute and revolutionary currents

Although the Vietnamese appraisal of the world situation tolerates some changes in the actual estimation of world politics, its foundation lies in more or less fixed concepts. The point of departure also here was the fierce *ai thang ai* -struggle, which is carried on between the revolutionary forces of the world and imperialism during the transitional period from capitalism to socialism. The *world revolutionary forces* is the term that Le Duan used in his report from the Communist and Workers' Parties Meeting in Moscow in 1960.[21] The expression that appeared in the documents of the 3rd Congress of the Lao dong Party was the *forces of socialism, national independence, peace and democracy in the world*, which are "driving ahead the process of the inevitable collapse of imperialism."[22] However, the wording of the concept was not important; so far, it did not appear as a symptom of the Sino–Soviet dispute. It was essential to create this kind of concept, since the *ai thang ai* -concept had risen to the international level. Developments in the world had proceeded so unevenly that the pure class-struggle concept of international relations was even more unsuitable than the class-struggle concept at the national level. Therefore support for the socialist road was drawn from three different sources: the socialist camp, the national liberation movements, and the workers' and democratic movements in the capitalist countries. But after the socialist camp, the Vietnamese put special emphasis on the national liberation movements in the Third World at the expense of the workers' and democratic movements in the capitalist countries. This was due to the current phase of the transitional period, when the struggle is focused on "the life and death struggle between imperialism and the anti-imperialist forces."[23] The aims of the revolutionary forces in this struggle "are peace, national independence, democracy and socialism" and thus "the struggle for their realization is a resolute anti-imperialist struggle."[24] The political purity of the national liberation movement in this struggle was not the most crucial question, because the demolition of the colonialist system, as a result of the national liberation struggles, has drastically weakened the imperialist countries. After that, the Vietnamese recognize the role of the workers' movement, owing to its task of giving a lethal blow to the already debilitated imperialist system in the mother country.[25]

For the DRV's leaders, the development of the concept of revolutionary forces during the 1960s and the 1970s turned the concept into a political matter, at the very center of which was the question of leadership inside the socialist camp and then the appraisal of the international situation. In the vocabulary of the Soviet and pro-Moscow Communist Parties, the revolutionary forces included three elements, namely, the world socialist system, the Communist and working-class movement in the capitalist countries and the national liberation movement. The point here is that the emphasis was laid on the socialist system, the content of which was the socialist camp, headed by the Soviet Union. The pro-Moscow parties concluded: "The world socialist system is the decisive force in the anti-imperialist struggle. Each liberation struggle receives indispensable aid from the world socialist system, above all the Soviet Union."[26] Under the leadership of the socialist camp, the three revolutionary forces form a mainstream leading to the world transition from capitalism to socialism. The problem here was China, which was difficult to fit into this definition. The most common explanation was that China went against this mainstream, pursuing its own interests at the expense of the unity of the socialist camp.[27] But the concept itself ignores the conflict between the socialist countries, just as does the *ai thang ai* -concept. Thus the concept, which includes these three components, expressed, first of all, loyalty to the Soviet leadership in the international Communist movement.

Consequently, on account of their international position, the Chinese developed further their terminology until the emergence of the three worlds theory in the mid-1970s. Although it appeared as a relatively short period (1974–1979), it dramatically distinguished Chinese foreign-policy thinking from that of Soviet-based Marxist-Leninist theory.[28] Like the world's revolutionary forces, the division between the international proletariat, the socialist countries and the oppressed nations constitutes a central part of the theory. But as Chinese rationale points out, these parts are not monolithic entities, since, for example, the international working-class is divided, besides which the socialist and the Third World countries carry mutual contradictions.[29] However, the main challenge to the Soviet-based concept of *revolutionary forces* lies in the Chinese emphasis on the Third World as a major force in the revolutionary struggle. The reason for this is twofold: The oppressed people of the Third World make up the absolute majority of the world population and they are directly subject to imperialist exploitation.[30] And, for another thing, the mother country of socialist revolution, the Soviet Union, had turned its highly centralized socialist economy into a state-monopoly capitalist economy. Owing to the decline of U.S. global power, the Soviet Union was able to exert its own global influence both politically and economically as well as in military terms. During this process, the Soviet Union lost its revolutionary character and became transformed into a hegemonist power, which struggled for world domination with the United States. This is the reason for the re-estimation of the Soviet and socialist camp's significance in the anti-imperialist struggle. Therefore, as regards the Soviet influence on the workers' movements in the developed capitalist countries, it was split into different ranks and remained as a residual and potential force in the anti-imperialist struggle.[31]

The world's anti-imperialist movement should, according to this Chinese view, consider the world situation from a practical and not abstract point of view. This calls for differentiation between friend and foe in horizontal (state to state) terms. Accordingly, in a practical situation involving the anti-imperialist forces, the world is divided into three camps: The First World consists of the two superpowers, the United States and the Soviet Union. Their competition for world power is the main global problem. Between them, the Soviet Union is the more dangerous, because economically it is weaker than the U.S. and therefore tries to compensate for this by means of military power. The socialist countries and the proletariat in the imperialist countries, insofar as they can resist Soviet influence, form the Third World together with the oppressed underdeveloped countries. The developed capitalist countries between these two worlds constitute the Second World. The position of the Second World allows the anti-imperialist forces, that is, the Third World, to exploit it in opposing the First World in certain situations.[32]

Certain similarities appeared between Chinese reasoning and the early Vietnamese definition of revolutionary forces. Both emphasized the significance of the national liberation struggle in the Third World, and the friend/enemy concept emerged in Mao's three worlds theory in the way it occurred also in Vietnamese political thinking. The workers' movement in the capitalist countries is, as in the Chinese definition, residual, and sometimes the Vietnamese failed to connect it at all to the world revolutionary forces.[33] But the differences were even more definite. In the Vietnamese definition, the socialist camp, under the leadership of the Soviet Union, was the most decisive factor in the anti-imperialist struggle. It was supported by national liberation struggles, which are going to converge so as to culminate in socialist revolution, transforming the world capitalist system into a socialist system. China was included in the world socialist system, its dispute with the Soviet Union being considered as temporary.

The changes that took place in Vietnam's foreign-policy environment at the beginning of the 1970s were followed by certain redefinitions of the central concepts. The most important of these changes was the Sino–US rapprochement in the late 1960s and early 1970s, without which the Vietnamese doctrinal redefinitions cannot be fully understood. The concept of revolutionary forces was replaced partly by the concept of three revolutionary currents (streams) *(ba dong thac cach mang)* or three revolutionary trends *(ba trao luu cach mang)* in the world, which clearly distinguished the Vietnamese definition from the Chinese. There appeared to be no practical difference between this concept and the formulation of revolutionary forces, which the International Meeting of Communist and Workers' Parties adopted in Moscow in June 1969. Le Duan applied the concept in both of his 1970 *Hoc Tap* articles – factually, it was identical to Moscow's formulation;[34] and Pham Van Dong placed the Vietnamese appraisal of their enemies into the context of the present era, "the era of the three revolutionary currents, which are repulsing, step by step, and defeating, part by part, U.S.-led imperialism."[35] The Vietnamese confirmed this definition in the joint statement on Podgorny's visit to North Vietnam in October 1971,[36] and they repeated it later, during Premier Pham Van Dong's visit to China in November 1971.[37] The concept of three revolutionary currents had emerged earlier in the Vietnamese press,[38] but now it seemed to have become established in the diplomatic and political vocabulary.[39] The concept appeared in documents of the 4th Party Congress in 1976 where, for the first time, it formed a coherent world appraisal; and when connected to the *ai thang ai* -struggle, it raised the themes of proletarian internationalism and the anti-imperialist struggle against imperialism.[40] The concept was emphasized even more in documents of the 5th Party Congress of 1982. Thus it turned into the central foreign-policy concept in the Vietnamese Marxist-Leninist doctrine up to the mid-1980s and disappeared only after the 6th Party Congress, held in 1986.[41]

The concept of three revolutionary currents formed a part of the Marxist-Leninist vocabulary in the appraisal of international relations, which emphasized the massive social forces turning the direction of the world's development and not allowing much room for horizontal analysis of world politics. In his *Hoc Tap* article, Le Duan put the concept into the broader theoretical outlines of Marxism-Leninism, including the four fundamental contradictions and the development of the world's revolutionary forces. He underlined this development by using the expression depicting the offensive posture of the revolutionary forces *(the tien cong cua luc luong cach mang),*[42] an expression that was also established in Vietnamese vocabulary during the 1970s. This was further connected to the relations of the forces at work on a world scale, which the Vietnamese estimated to be turning in favor of socialism.[43]

The meaning of three revolutionary currents in Vietnam's policy involving the Soviet Union and China was obvious: it revealed Vietnam's pro-Soviet stance. Insofar as Sino–Vietnamese relations were formally correct, China was included in the concept as a part of the socialist system.[44] But the concept was also an important part of the Marxist-Leninist doctrinal system in postwar Socialist Vietnam. Its function was to connect the *ai thang ai* -struggle between two roads to the tasks of Vietnam's foreign policy, giving a positive prospect to the outcome of the struggle.[45] This closer connection to domestic mobilization meant that the concept also gained a stronger ideological connotation. At the 5th Party Congress, Le Duan demanded including the concept in social-science research; and thus it stayed not only at the political level but also penetrated the discourse in the social sciences. Its real referent was obscured and its task was turned to enforce the code in the texts dealing with international relations.[46] The concept has thus a double role: as part of the doctrinal code to connect the lines of domestic and foreign policy and as a foreign-policy concept showing Vietnam's orientation toward the socialist powers.

At the same time, it emphasizes an active attitude toward foreign policy. According to one analysis, the connection of the concept to the *ai thang ai* -struggle is described as follows: "Just now is the period of three revolutionary trends, originating from the October Revolution, which have rapidly developed into the three great revolutionary currents of the era, launching continuous offensives against imperialism."[47] Vietnam plays a twin role in these currents. On the one hand, it is a member of the world socialist system and, on the other hand, it represents the national liberation movements in the Third World. The Vietnamese did not hesitate to assert their importance in both currents: Vietnam has the task of spreading and defending socialism, especially in Southeast Asia.[48] In the enthusiastic revolutionary mood of the 1970s, the Vietnamese believed that their victory supports and has shown the way of success to the revolutions of Africa, Asia and Latin America.[49]

The term offensive posture refers to the active role that the Communist Parties in each country had to adopt in order to take advantage of the world's general trends. Consequently, the more skilfully the Communist Party can take advantage of these trends, the stronger these trends will develop further. The Vietnamese did not underestimate their role in the world situation after the spring of 1975: "Clearly, the complete defeat of U.S. imperialism in the face of the violent offensive posture of Vietnam's revolution has 'marked a downward step' for the imperialist chieftain, turned upside down its global anti-revolutionary strategy and consequently pulled together the whole imperialist system toward a new period in the general crises."[50] Similarly, when the concept of three revolutionary currents become a significant element in the doctrinal code of Vietnamese political parlance, another important point should be made. The three revolutionary currents determine the themes and the audience, the subject matter that the code is allowed to deal with, and to whom Vietnamese foreign-policy texts are addressed. This took place especially in the multilateral situations where the allies and more or less permanent supporters have to be brought together. Consequently, the concept determines the audience: the socialist countries, the Third World countries and the national liberation movements as well as the "progressive forces" in the capitalist countries.

The goals and themes of foreign policy

So far as Marxism-Leninism is considered as a guide to action, the question of foreign-policy goals is crucial. This is emphasized in pragmatic rhetoric, where the goals serve as the premises. However, in the light of the study of Vietnamese views on international relations and appraisal of the world situation, it can be observed that these aforementioned elements seem to overlap with goals. There also seems to be some obscurity about the goals and the foreign-policy themes, which are bound to the Marxist-Leninist doctrine. In fact, this fusion of ends and means is one of the characteristics of pragmatic argumentation and this holds true also of Vietnamese Marxism-Leninism. The reason for the obvious proximity of the appraisal of the world situation, the goals of the socialist states and the foreign-policy themes is the multiple role of Marxism-Leninism: as much as it serves as the guide to action, it is an ideology, the task of which is to justify the system of rule, proletarian dictatorship, in each country; and the ostensible or real pursuit of the given goal has a crucial role in it. This aspect seemed to be strengthened when Vietnam adopted its more orthodox vocabulary from the Soviet Union.

According to Marxist-Leninist theory in general, the goal of foreign relations was clear also to Vietnam's Communist Party: "The ultimate goal of all the Communist and workers' parties is the establishment of socialism and Communism all over the world."[51] This general aim laid the groundwork for the Marxist-Leninist ideological project also at the level of international relations. In practice, however, the aims of foreign policy were far more modest. These aims were related to the actual situation of the Vietnamese revolutionary struggle. Thus the foreign policy during the period before the fall of Saigon was aimed to support actively the struggle for the independence and unity of Vietnam.[52] After the unification, its task was to assist and enforce the construction of a socialist system in Vietnam. Thus these two goals, the ultimate objective of all Communist Parties and the practical goal of the Vietnamese Communist Party, are both serving the ideological project. The changes in practical aims are acceptable when they are connected to the purpose of achieving the ultimate goal. Therefore, the leaders need not reject the ultimate goal, which would be drastic for pragmatic argumentation, but should turn the practical means into objectives themselves.[53]

Even so, there were expressions that extended the Vietnamese goals beyond national limits. These goals derived directly from the doctrine's appraisal of the world situation, which connected these goals to a formal argumentation pattern. Accordingly, Vietnam's construction of socialism is part of the process taking place in the period of transition to socialism on a global scale. Thus Vietnam is part of the larger trend and its foreign policy should actively encourage it. Vietnam's natural arena for this is its immediate surroundings in Southeast Asia, where it should help "the national struggle in the Southeast Asian countries toward peace, independence and genuine neutrality, and to support the forces of national liberation and the independence movements in Asian, African and Latin-American countries."[54] Without going here deeper into the different elements of this foreign minister's statement, it clearly indicates Vietnam's postwar vision and points to the prospects that could be reached by an active foreign policy. This kind of confidence is shown, of course, by the Vietnamese appraisal of international relations during this period.

According to the rationalist model of pragmatism, the polical goals determine the means employed in practicing foreign policy. Vietnamese pragmatism introduced such a method as the friend/foe concept and the use of negotiations while fighting. The friend/foe concept connecting rational calculation on the basis of the relation of forces offers the method of argumentation on the horizontal level. But as this survey proved, the friend/foe concept, the art of manipulating the contradictions between potential enemies, had to make room gradually for the vertical class analysis. The friend/foe concept provided a setting that offers several options, but *ai thang ai* gives a rigid premise to foreign policy. In formal terms, the contemplation on ends and means is not crucial to argumentation, whereas the themes sometimes presented as methods of foreign policy are.

The mature Soviet tradition introduced its own concepts as the themes of Marxist-Leninist foreign policy. Proletarian internationalism *(chu nghia quoc te vo san)* and peaceful coexistence *(cung ton tai hoa binh* or *chung song hoa binh)* were by all means much older than the concepts the Vietnamese used in their appraisal of the world situation, but their position in the doctrine did not stabilize until the 1970s.

Naturally, this instability of the doctrinal system, combined with the conjunction of two Vietnamese approaches, must be placed in a wider political context – first in Vietnam's position in the Sino–Soviet dispute, and then in the development of the external environment of unified Vietnam. This is due especially to the concept of peaceful coexistence, but also to proletarian internationalism. This latter concept, which has a long historical background in Marxist thinking, was essential when the Vietnamese were confronted with the Sino–Soviet dispute and in view of Vietnam's attitude toward these countries.

Owing to early Vietnamese contacts with the Soviet Union and with the Comintern during the colonial period, the concept of proletarian internationalism was firmly rooted in the Vietnamese vocabulary.[55] The concept has its roots in the class analysis of international relations, according to which the struggle of the proletariat in each country is linked to the success of the proletarian struggle in other countries. The working class in each country should support every national struggle led by the proletarian party. Simultaneously with its national duty, the proletarian class has international tasks to carry out. Therefore, as the Vietnamese argued, following established Marxist-Leninist reasoning, proletarian internationalism must oppose bourgeois nationalism *(chu nghia dan toc tu san)*, which is a source of war.[56] Thus "proletarian internationalism originates from the basic qualities and the historic mission of the proletarian class all over the world," but the Vietnamese connected it also to the long-term existence of independent states.[57] Proletarian internationalism is a principle *(nguyen tac)* bound to the class idea and emphasizing the vertical nature of international relations;[58] but it is also a political concept *(lap truong chinh tri)*, one that refers to the cooperation between socialist states and Communist Parties.[59] Yet, first of all, as later defined by one Vietnamese author, it is a basic principle on how to draw the borderline between the foreign policy of socialist countries and that of the countries belonging to other systems.[60]

With the development of the socialist camp, the meaning of proletarian internationalism shifted from the class point of view more toward describing the relationships between socialist states. This leads to its innovation, the concept of socialist internationalism *(chu nghia quoc te xa hoi chu nghia)* used as a synonym for proletarian internationalism. This, also a Soviet term, became in focus an instrument of maintaining cohesion between the socialist countries. Its content was connected to what was later known as the "Brezhnev Doctrine." Indeed, the Soviet interpretation of proletarian internationalism between socialist states, socialist internationalism, had a strong control function. Besides its emphasis on Soviet leadership in the socialist camp, it called for an internal division of labor, common political and economic goals and a common ideology.[61] The term was used to some extent in Vietnam as early as 1960, but it never replaced the concept of proletarian internationalism. The meaning of socialist internationalism lay better in the Vietnamese vocabulary in the early 1960s as an expression of unity between the socialist countries rather than as the Soviet Union's right to intervene in the fraternal countries' internal affairs. Although the Soviet leadership among the socialist countries was acknowledged, the emphasis on unanimity required that the interests of China were also to be recognized.[62]

The reason for the adoption of proletarian internationalism in lieu of socialist internationalism into the Vietnamese vocabulary was its broader usage. This concept could cover, besides the party contacts with the socialist countries, the support given by the socialist countries to the national liberation movements, which in Vietnamese thinking is of central importance.[63] But even despite the long tradition of proletarian internationalism in Vietnamese political usage, the modern meaning of the concept was bound to the two camps theory. Its primary significance was connecting Vietnam's foreign relations with the socialist countries, at both the governmental and party levels. Thus, notwithstanding the fact that the Vietnamese had embraced the Soviet more than the Chinese interpretation of international relations, by the concept of proletarian internationalism Vietnam regarded China as a part of the socialist world system. Up to the 1970s, the concept referred to – and was – an organic part of the theme of the unity of the world's socialist system.

Similarly, the concept of peaceful coexistence received its Vietnamese content from the two camps theory. In contrast to proletarian internationalism, it did not take root in the Vietnamese vocabulary during the period of anti-colonial struggle, but was adopted more or less reluctantly from the Soviet Union in the late 1950s and early 1960s. In fact, the concept had no real place as a theme in Vietnam's foreign-policy argumentation before the late 1970s. Khrushchev brought the term to the 20th Congress of the Soviet Communist Party in 1956 with new emphasis, which was against the actual interests of the Vietnamese communist leaders.[64] But the real problem arose when China took a stand against the Soviet approach. This forced the Vietnamese, who did not want to become involved in the Sino–Soviet dispute, to search out an interpretation that was not against either side, and yet expressed Vietnam's own interests.

Le Duan discussed peaceful coexistence thoroughly in his report from the 1960 meeting in Moscow of the Communist and Workers' Parties. In this report, Le Duan did not reject the concept, but gave it an emphasis that supported Vietnam's position. The point of departure was that peaceful coexistence is a form of class struggle in a world of two opposing systems. The precondition of peaceful coexistence was the growth of the forces of socialism, which prevents imperialism from starting a war against the socialist system. Vice versa, peace gives a favorable condition for building socialism. However, as Le Duan emphasized the Vietnamese point of view, although peace was accepted as a practical goal, the final victory over imperialism requires violent revolutionary struggle. This called for active resistance to imperialism in a way in which armed struggle was not rejected. Despite the fact that the national liberation movements played the key role in this struggle, Le Duan pointed out that "lopsided emphasis on the defense of peace and peaceful coexistence and lack of concern in the stepping up of the revolutionary movement in the capitalist countries or restriction of this latter for the sake of peace and peaceful coexistence" will damage the revolutionary movement and anti-imperialist struggle in the capitalist countries.[65] The function of peaceful coexistence in the strategy of the world's revolutionary forces is to force the imperialist system "into a stalemate in which neither side can destroy the other." The complete destruction of the imperialist system is carried out by the national liberation forces and the working class, first breaking it up piecemeal in the Third World, after which the revolution in the capitalist countries will finally lead the world from capitalism to socialism.[66]

Consequently, peaceful coexistence was accepted as the Soviet policy toward the capitalist countries; but for Vietnam, owing to its role among the world's revolutionary forces, it was not a practical matter. It was mentioned in the documents relating to the Third Party Congress as a means of isolating the United States and as a principle for achieving relations between different political and social systems; but no concrete areas where it should be implemented were designated.[67] Le Duan mentioned the concept in his important article of 1970, but restricted its use to a far more limited realm than that governed by Soviet practice.[68] Although the concept was associated with Vietnam's policy toward the capitalist countries of Southeast Asia after the spring of 1975,[69] it was given short shrift at the Fourth Party Congress held in December 1976, where it was mentioned in the political report only once. Similarly, according to the Party documents at the 5th Party Congress in 1982, the emphasis given to it was no stronger. Evaluation of the concept did not start until the 6th Party Congress, at a time when the Soviet Union was reviewing the position of the concept. The long disregard of peaceful coexistence pointed also to the fact that the DRV had real contacts with neither the developed capitalist countries nor the capitalist countries of Asia in the two blocs' structure. Therefore the relations with the capitalist countries failed to rise as a theme in Vietnam's foreign policy until the late 1970s.

Within these two concepts, proletarian internationalism and peaceful coexistence, there was a doctrinal theme that had originated basically from the Vietnamese situation. In fact, it had been the most persistent among these concepts, having been emphasized by the Vietnamese from the 3rd Party Congress all the way up to the 5th Party Congress. It holds no special position in the vocabulary of Soviet-based Marxism-Leninism, like the previous concepts, but it can be derived directly from the revolutionary forces or from the three revolutionary currents. It is a manifestation of the struggle waged in the national independence movement *(phong trao dau tranh doc lap dan toc)*, or of the anti-imperialist struggle, which the Vietnamese claimed as their main role in the transitional period of this stage and as the main theme of their foreign policy. This distinguished Vietnamese thinking from Soviet Marxism-Leninism, although the Vietnamese were concerned to fit it into the Soviet-based vocabulary, especially in relation to the concept of three revolutionary currents. However, its origins could be traced more to Vietnam's own experience, which was in accord with the mainstream ideology of the new Third World countries, as exemplified by the Non-Aligned Movement. As in Vietnamese foreign policy, anti-imperialism occupied an important position in several radical and Marxist-oriented governments' foreign policy in the Third World.

The status of the newly independent nations and their role in the anti-imperialist struggle were not always, however, considered crucial, as Ho Chi Minh's presentation at the 3rd Party Congress proved. Here he refrained from describing the Non-Aligned Movement according to the Soviet terminology as a "Zone of Peace."[70] This cautious appraisal of the Non-Aligned's significance was changed to emphasis of its role in the sphere of Vietnam's foreign policy in the documents of the 4th Party Congress. In fact, it was rather simple to turn the anti-imperialism of the Non-Aligned Movement into part of the Vietnamese doctrine. According to one analysis, "the idea of anti-imperialism is more and more closely connected to the idea of anticapitalism, and the struggle against neo-colonialism is more and more closely connected to the struggle for the road of noncapitalist development..."[71] Although Vietnam's own struggle was simply considered as an important part of the global anti-imperialist struggle, the Vietnamese themselves stressed their role in intensifying it regionally and globally.[72]

Of course, in the Non-Aligned Movement, anti-imperialism referred more to the foreign-policy orientation of these countries than to their internal political, social and economic policies. In this respect, the emphasis laid on this theme brought with it a possibility to achieve a pragmatic stance, which was turned to advantage in Vietnam's policy toward the Sino–Soviet dispute. Moreover, the theme formed a uniform entity with Vietnam's own internal course and foreign policy. Thus the Vietnamese linked anti-imperialism and socialism together. Therefore this theme supported both Vietnamese foreign-policy goals, its appraisal of the world situation, and even Vietnam's domestic situation, as national independence was tightly connected to socialism. Accordingly, the theme of anti-imperialism fits well in both the formal and pragmatic reasoning. The Vietnamese claimed that their goals, independence and socialism, were also the goals for the majority of the national liberation movements in the Third World.[73] Thus this material force, comprising the socialist camp together with the national liberation movements and the newly liberated nations *(cac dan toc moi giai phong)*, constituted the main factor directing international developments during the transitional period. The Political Report of the 4th Party Congress went even so far as to declare that "the movement for national liberation and national independence plays a most important role in the realization of the transition to socialism on a global scale."[74] The task of Vietnam's foreign policy was set to use to advantage this force and to strengthen it so as to support the building of a developed socialist state in Vietnam. Consequently, the successful progress of socialism depended on the growth of the revolutionary forces both regionally and on a global scale.[75]

This Vietnamese notion of the role of the national liberation struggle combines the concept of proletarian internationalism as a link between the socialist system and the liberation struggle. The national liberation struggle is thus the main part of the anti-imperialist struggle and the crucial question in the *ai thang ai* -struggle between the two systems.[76] Owing to the direct connection to Vietnam's own experience and domestic rule, the role of the national liberation struggle was emphasized in the field of foreign policy in Vietnam's Marxist-Leninist doctrine. These two concepts thus pointed out Vietnam's main foreign-policy themes, the unity of the world's socialist system and the anti-imperialist struggle as well as the audience for its foreign-policy messages. Although the international setting laid down certain other themes that Vietnam has to deal with, they were treated so far as possible along the lines allowed by these themes and the code.

PRAGMATISM, FORMALISM AND FOREIGN RELATIONS

The foregoing concepts and foreign-policy themes were indisputable in Vietnamese Marxism-Leninism from the 1970s to the mid 1980s. During this period, they belonged to the official dogma and their use did not directly reveal either the premises of the arguments or, sometimes, their sophisticated political orientations. However, the particular emphasis laid on these concepts, or the disregard accorded some of them, gives the reference to the pattern and political orientation of the argumentation, if they are connected both to the textual context as a whole and the political context where the concepts are presented.

Despite the stability of the concepts, the changes in Vietnam's international status necessitated certain revisions in the definitions of foreign policy. But along with these changes, the crucial question arises: how have the two approaches of Vietnamese Marxism-Leninism, revolutionary pragmatism and formal Marxism-Leninism, occurred in foreign policy-discussion? Similarly, how has the more constant element of argumentation, the doctrinal code, appeared in these patterns? To shed light on these questions, I have examined some basic texts on international relations, and I have paid particular attention to two articles that appeared in the *Hoc Tap* October 1975 and September 1976 issues. In fact, these two articles are the isolated cases in *Hoc Tap* between 1970 and 1976 that deal exclusively with Vietnam's foreign policy. The interest generated by examination of these two articles, the arguments of which rest on rather different premises, depended also on the time of their appearance, i.e., the period between the fall of Saigon and the 4th Party Congress. During this period, the approach for the foreign policy of unified and socialist Vietnam was confirmed.

The general characteristics of Vietnamese foreign-policy argumentation appear in the coexistence of both pragmatism and formalism. The author can therefore on the same occasion lay claim to both pragmatic premises – the prevailing reality and the goal of action, as well as to the formal premises – Marxist-Leninist dogma on international relations. Owing to the importance of the Marxist-Leninist concepts in international relations, Vietnamese parlance tends to emphasize the formalist pattern. However, these theoretically deduced concepts also received other meanings in political practice that have nothing to do with the argumentation patterns. By the application of these concepts, the Vietnamese assert their position in the international system in general and in the socialist world system in particular.

In this respect, the approach of Foreign Minister Nguyen Duy Trinh's retrospective survey of Vietnam's foreign policy in the October 1975 issue of *Hoc Tap* is ambiguous. In fact, it includes both pragmatic and orthodox Marxist-Leninist vocabulary. Similarly, the premises of argumentation are less clear and consistent because his arguments are not drawn solely from policy goals or theoretical starting points. However, both the retrospective examination and the emphasis on rationalistic calculation refer to pragmatism. This calculation is not based as consistently on policy goals as was, for example, Vo Nguyen Giap's argumentation in his article that appeared ten months earlier in *Hoc Tap*.[77] Trinh does mention the Vietnamese goals, but his argumentation is not based on them. But he refers to the conditions of reality, which Vietnam's foreign policy had to cope with. In this sense, foreign policy has a purely instrumental role to play in order to support the national policy of the Vietnamese revolutionaries.[78] Reality lies in constant change, and each historical phase poses new challenges to foreign policy.

Nguyen Duy Trinh notes the simple setting of Vietnam's foreign policy in the past: The foreign policy focused on the relations between two countries, and it can be reduced to the relationship between two armies.[79] During the national struggle against French and American imperialism, the task of the foreign-policy makers was to secure the victories won on the battlefield. In this respect, when confronted by an overwhelmingly superior enemy, the foreign policy had to find a solution acceptable also to the enemy at the negotiation table, despite the enemy's defeat on the battleground.[80] However, the foreign policy dealt with in Nguyen Duy Trinh's article is not reduced solely to war diplomacy. In fact, the retrospective survey was an introduction to the approach the Vietnamese should take in dealing with the present conditions of international reality.

Trinh repeats the official appraisal of the international situation, including the offensive position of the three revolutionary currents.[81] However, this formalist vocabulary also contains pragmatic contemplation of Vietnam's new international status after the victory scored in the spring of 1975. The crucial issue here is Sino–Soviet relations and Vietnam's stand toward them. Here he falls back on both formalist and pragmatic vocabulary. He resorted, according to the established manner, to the theme of proletarian internationalism to conciliate the Sino–Soviet dispute, but turned to pragmatic vocabulary when defining Vietnam's approach to it. Trinh's reasoning was clearly based on a concrete power calculation involving the friend/enemy distinction the way it appeared in the old texts on revolutionary pragmatism. Following this, the socialist countries have become the strategic allies of Vietnam in its struggle against the U.S. in a situation where the Vietnamese strove to "increase the number of friends and decrease that of enemies" *(them ban, bot thu)*. Nguyen Duy Trinh uses the expression "win over allies and isolate the enemy" *(tranh thu dong minh, co lap ke thu)* to illustrate its principle of managing international relations. With respect to the socialist giants, he makes no exception.[82]

Vietnam's position between China and the Soviet Union is not argued by the friend/enemy distinction alone. Nguyen Duy Trinh's bold analysis of state to state relations in the current international system put a limit on the theme of proletarian internationalism vis-à-vis Vietnam's big socialist allies. Although he acknowledges the significance of their support, he recommends keeping a clear distance from these allies. Depending on historical lessons, he warns that too close partnership and collaboration would threat Vietnam's independence. Thus the Vietnamese must take their affairs into their own hands: "Only if we are strong will they take account of us. If we are weak, we would only be tools in the hands of others, no matter that the others could be friendly allies of ours."[83] Thus Trinh does not operate only at the level of friend and foe but "makes a difference between ourselves, our friends and our enemies" *(phan biet ta, ban, thu)*.[84] Obviously, this emphasis on self-reliance vis-à-vis other socialist countries reflects the reasons why Nguyen Duy Trinh was forced to leave his post, together with Vo Nguyen Giap, in the Party leadership when Hanoi turned toward a closer alliance with the Soviet Union.[85]

However, when dealing with national mobilization, foreign policy and international relations, pragmatic and formal patterns become tangled up in Trinh's rhetoric. Vietnam's struggle against the United States and its striving for unification and the construction of a Marxist system, as he argues, was not only national and anti-imperialist struggle but was in full harmony with the three revolutionary currents.[86] This followed well the doctrinal code as the Vietnamese must "take a correct revolutionary line, one capable of mobilizing the forces of the nation, and simultaneously pursue a correct foreign-policy line, making it possible to rely on the strength of the nation, win over the self-supporting strength *(suc manh ho tro)* of our era and form a great international front in support of the national struggle."[87] Consequently, these two patterns of argumentation sustained each other and the doctrinal code, as mobilization and rule are heightened by both formal and pragmatic reasoning.

The premises of formal Marxist-Leninist argumentation can be extracted from two of Le Duan's articles published in 1970 in *Hoc Tap*, particularly the June issue. Here he laid down the starting point of the four contradictions of the present era; and the three revolutionary currents of the world manifest the process of resolving these contradictions at the international level. From these premises, he derived the methods to be applied by Vietnamese foreign policy in its approach to proletarian internationalism, the anti-imperialist struggle and peaceful coexistence. Although this orthodox formula dominates Le Duan's rhetoric, on the side of it exists the argument concerning the political aims of the DRV. Le Duan pointed out three targets *(muc tieu)* at which the Vietnamese Communists are aiming. These are national independence, democracy and socialism. However, this does not change the formal character of his argumentation to the pragmatic approach. The targets are derived from the Marxist-Leninist theory of international relations, where national independence is the logical result of the anticolonial struggle and democracy represents the stage of the anti-imperialist struggle, which is followed by socialism.[88] This is emphasized by connecting these targets to the domestic projects, on top of which is socialism as both a foreign-policy and domestic goal, including large-scale mass industrialization and the establishment of a socialist economy.[89]

Huong Nam's article *Chinh sach doi ngoai cua Nuoc Cong Hoa Xa Hoi Chu Nghia Viet-nam* (the foreign policy of the Socialist Republic of Vietnam) in the September 1976 issue of *Hoc Tap* follows this formalist pattern. The author was not at the top of the Communist Party, and he was not thus leading Vietnamese discussion, a circumstance that shows the growing dominance of Marxist-Leninist orthodoxy as "official dogma." The article was published three months before the 4th Party Congress in December 1976, and therefore it most probably reflects the preparation of the foreign policy line adopted at the Party Congress.

Huong Nam binds Vietnam's foreign policy to the concept of the three revolutionary currents. This, he maintains, provides "the international background for the Vietnamese revolution, which we should fully understand when we are implementing our foreign policy."[90] Thus the three revolutionary currents serve as the premises and the condition for the foreign policy, the aim of which is to strengthen these currents. It is up to the policy to exploit this condition. Accordingly, decisive in the victorious Vietnamese, Laotian and Kampuchean revolutions is the fact that socialism is forcefully gaining ground in the global system. As a consequence, the national liberation movements, which constitute the other important current, are adopting the socialist path of development, thereby supporting and promoting Vietnam's orientation in foreign affairs. Consistently enough, Huong Nam concludes in line with the established Vietnamese world appraisal: "The offensive posture of the three revolutionary currents has ever greater capacity to develop more strength, while the global situation of imperialism declines."[91]

This appraisal of the world situation stands out in Huong Nam's analysis of Vietnam's foreign policy. The crucial idea here is that the "Vietnamese revolution is a deeply based part *(mot bo phan khang khit)* of the world revolution." It determines the fact that "our state is a proletarian dictatorship needing no pretext to refuse the task of supporting and helping the revolutionary struggle of the working class people and the oppressed nations in the capitalist world system."[92] Thus this argumentation gained a strong autocommunicative function: The Vietnamese are mobilized for the international revolutionary struggle, which supports the system of rule, proletarian dictatorship, in their country. The inevitable victory in this struggle is deduced from Marxist-Leninist theory and the reality is examined from this angle. The masses are mobilized by the premises of the theory, which are simultaneously considered as an objective reality, and not by concrete goals as in revolutionary pragmatism.

The revolutionary and anti-imperialist basic trend that Huong Nam deduced from the concept of the three revolutionary currents was then reflected in more detail in Vietnam's policy toward two other Indochinese and other Southeast Asian countries. His arguments regarding the policy toward these regions coincide with the Marxist-Leninist premises which he laid down. With respect to Vietnam's Indochinese neighbors, this quasi-logical argumentation includes the claims for limited sovereignty, or the Brezhnev Doctrine, and its application became an important issue when the Kampuchean–Vietnamese conflict came out into the open. However, the formal argumentation pattern does not lead to this case as such. Huong Nam did not refer to any "correct" way of implementing socialism, but he transferred the determinants that had been used in Vietnamese–Laotian dealings to cover all the relations involving Vietnam, Laos and Kampuchea. There are two determinants in the relations: the relations between socialist countries and the relations between neighboring countries that have had common historical experiences in the struggle against a common imperialist enemy. Thus the premises for this "special relationship" *(quan he dac biet)* are proletarian internationalism and the anti-imperialist struggle, in addition to the geographical factor. The first two are important for formal argumentation and the third is emphasized in pragmatic argumention referring to the structure of reality. This pragmatic premise is ignored in his article. As in the case of the other Southeast Asian countries, Huong Nam derives Vietnam's policy toward them from the formal premise. The determinant is the anti-imperialist struggle and is directed particularly against the policy pursued by the United States in Southeast Asia. He used the already established expression "national independence, peace and genuine neutrality," which refers to Vietnam's aim to cut the ties between the United States and the Southeast Asian countries. All this was in accord with the three revolutionary currents.[93]

The conformity of Huong Nam's arguments for Vietnam's foreign-policy orientation and the expressions that exist in the Political Report of the 4th Party Congress, held three months later, indicated that Huong Nam was acquainted with the draft resolutions of the Party Congress. The Central Committee's Political Report included the same world appraisal presented by his article on the general level and the same concrete policy orientation, particularly toward Southeast Asia.[94] If Nguyen Duy Trinh's article is compared with this, the dominance of formalist thinking can be clearly found in the Political Report. However, this does not conclusively prove any general shift away from pragmatism to the formalist approach. In retrospective examination, the pragmatic rhetoric tends toward emphasis, as probably was the case in Nguyen Duy Trinh's article, when formal and theoretical premises tend to be stressed under future-orientated scrutiny, as in the policy planning and political reports of the Communist Party. On the other hand, the independent line vis-à-vis the Socialist bloc, which Trinh's pragmatic arguments emphasized, differs from the formalism represented by Huong Nam's article and the Political Report of the 4th Party Congress. This also points to two distinct political orientations. Moreover, another difference existed also between Trinh's pragmatism and formalist argumentation. In Trinh's article, the doctrinal code is clearly bound to the general national mobilization, which is separated from foreign-policy deliberation. In formalist argumentation, the possibilities for such deliberation are limited and can not be separated from the doctrinal code, which is dominated by the autocommunicative nature of Marxist-Leninist theory. Therefore the argumentation proceeding from formal Marxist-Leninist premises could not deal with any question raised by the Sino–Soviet rift and Vietnam's stand toward it.

Part II
The "High Tide" of the World's Revolutionary Forces 1975–85

4 The Striving for Avant-garde Foreign Policy 1975–78

There were obvious trends that supported Vietnam's class analysis and formal reasoning on the development of international relations when the People's Army of Vietnam occupied Saigon on April 30, 1975. Simultaneously with the victory of the DRV over the U.S. and the American-backed regime in South Vietnam, several Marxist regimes, supported by the Soviet Union and its bloc or by China, came into power as a result of Cold War struggles and the decolonialization process during the years 1975–76. Besides the victories of the national Marxist movements in the Indochina Peninsula, the demolition of the Portuguese colonial system created new regimes and helped the Soviets gain more influence in the Third World. Coincidentally, Vietnam's archenemy, the United States or American imperialism *(de quoc My)*, as the Vietnamese put it, was reducing its military presence in Asia and losing its influence in the Asian Pacific area. The Watergate scandal, culminating in the resignation of President Nixon, was further understood to be a symptom of the general crisis of American imperialism. Similarly, the high tide of the Non-Aligned Movement, as a representative of the Third World, occurred in the latter part of the 1970s, giving proof of the progress of the world's national liberation movement.

Notwithstanding this evidence of the "offensive posture of the world's revolutionary forces," there existed opposite tendencies, a circumstance very difficult to fit into Vietnam's evaluation of the world situation. Contradicting the class analysis of international relations, the Sino–Soviet dispute remained unsettled and entered a new phase when the U.S. forces withdrew from Indochina. Nine months before the fall of Saigon, China tried to strengthen its grasp on Indochina by occupying the Paracel Islands in the South China Sea, which belonged to South Vietnam at that time, and by opposing Soviet policy toward Southeast Asia. The conflict over the islands in the South China Sea forced Vietnam to abandon partially its established Marxist vocabulary on foreign relations. Even more difficult to fit into rhetoric based on the quasi-logical deductions of Marxism-Leninism was the conflict between Vietnam and Democratic

Kampuchea, which broke out immediately after the end of the struggle against the U.S. and the U.S.-backed governments in Indochina. Although this conflict started as a territorial dispute between two neighbors, it soon turned into part of the Sino–Soviet and Sino–Vietnamese conflicts. The chief way to keep all these troubles under control and in harmony with the Vietnamese doctrine was to pass over them in silence. Excepting the question of the South China Sea islands, where both countries, China and Vietnam, published their own official and contradictory views, Vietnam did not officially make public any of the problems with its socialist neighbors before late 1977.[1]

In the previous chapter, I examined Vietnamese discussion on international relations as it has appeared in the Party cadres' theoretical publications apart from the actual foreign-policy context. In this chapter, particular interest is turned to the way the Vietnamese arguments develop in foreign-political and diplomatic practice. The change from study with a theoretical orientation to a scrutiny of actual foreign-policy parlance also implies a certain change in the research material. The analysis in the previous chapters is based on the Party cadres' discussion of foreign relations, as it appears in studies with a theoretical orientation in Party journals and other publications. Now the special concern is on statements and documents created in concrete foreign-policy situations as well as on Party cadres' articles dealing with actual foreign-policy issues.

The crucial questions in the following three chapters are: How are the two major lines of Vietnam's foreign policy, proletarian internationalism and anti-imperialist struggle, pursued in these problematic areas of Vietnam's international relations – particularly in Vietnam's policy concerning the Soviet Union and China, as well as its neighbors in Southeast Asia? Similarly, how did the pragmatic and formalist approaches develop in response to the trend of international affairs? After examination of these particular areas, it would be pertinent to deal with Vietnam's rhetoric at the two main arenas of Vietnam's multilateral diplomacy, the Non-Aligned Movement and the United Nations.

VIETNAM AS A PART OF THE SOCIALIST WORLD SYSTEM

The question of the Sino–Soviet rift was not a new one for Vietnamese diplomacy in the spring of 1975. However, Vietnam's international situation had dramatically changed after the withdrawal of the American troops and the fall of the Saigon regime. This did not immediately bring about any change in the vocabulary used by Hanoi since the first half of the 1970s. The theme of proletarian internationalism was addressed to both the Soviet bloc and China as well as to the Vietnamese themselves in their own internal discussion. The split between the two socialist giants was acknowledged in public, but the Vietnamese were operating with the terms of unity *(thong nhat)* and solidarity *(doan ket)* based on proletarian internationalism, thus emphasizing Vietnam's position between these rivals.

After the U.S. defeat in Indochina, the strategic basis of Vietnam's alliance with the Soviet Union and China appeared in a new context. During the war, Vietnam derived even some advantages from the Sino-Soviet rivalry, but after the withdrawal of the U.S. armed forces from Indochina, Vietnam turned into an issue of dispute in this rivalry. So far, excluding the Vietnamese and Laotian Communists, the Communist Parties in Southeast Asia had been more or less clearly pro-Chinese rather than pro-Soviet. At the end of the 1960s and the beginning of the 1970s, the Soviet Union started a new approach toward the Southeast Asian countries, where the state-to-state relations with the capitalist countries of this area were emphasized. Brezhnev introduced the idea of an Asian collective security system based on peaceful coexistence between the different social systems in Asia. The idea, which emerged from one sentence referring to the European security system in Brezhnev's speech at the conference of Communist and workers' parties held in June 1969 in Moscow, remained obscure despite certain clarifications.[2] This Soviet idea, as it later became obvious, was addressed directly to the capitalist countries of Asia, and no Asian Communist government was directly connected with it. This, together with the fact that during the first five years after the first mention of it none of these Asian Communist-ruled states responded positively to it, illustrated the Soviet Union's unstable position in Asian politics in those days. As Brezhnev's speech included criticism of Chinese anti-Soviet policy and its negative attitude to peaceful coexistence, the idea was interpreted as an attempt to isolate China from Asian politics.[3] Indeed, in the Chinese vocabulary, the Asian collective security system began to be viewed as synonymous with Soviet expansionism and pursuit of hegemony in Southeast Asia. The Soviet proposal of establishing a collective security system in the post-Indochina war situation in Southeast Asia was considered to be the Soviet Union's attempt to take the former place of the U.S. there.[4] Simultaneously with the victory of the Communists in the South Vietnam, China judged the Soviet Union to have turned into the most dangerous and expansionistic superpower, pointing to the Soviet attempt to extend its influence to Indochina.[5]

Despite China's overt attack on Soviet policy in Southeast Asia and its more or less direct warning to the Vietnamese for following the Soviet Union, Vietnam avoided a response, its tactic being to raise the Sino–Soviet dispute to a high abstract level. For this purpose, Hanoi fell back on highly theoretical formulation, which ignored the possibility of a power struggle between the socialist countries. This saved Vietnam from becoming involved concretely in this dispute, but it also exposed Vietnam's negative attitude to the Chinese appraisal of the Soviet role in Asian affairs. As the rift between the socialist countries did not even fit into the Vietnamese theory on international relations, Vietnam emphasized the temporary nature of the conflict. Thus the most important contradiction in the development of international relations was the contradiction between socialism and capitalism, for in the *ai thang ai* struggle "the restoration and consolidation of solidarity within the socialist system and the international Communist and workers' movement on the basis of Marxism-Leninism and proletarian internationalism is a question of utmost importance."[6] This Vietnamese policy of accepting the Soviet role on a general level was expressed clearly when, two days after the fall of Saigon, Vietnam's ambassador to China stressed that Vietnam's victory came from "the three revolutionary currents in the world," thereby giving the central role to this Soviet appraisal of global developments.[7]

This did not mean, however, Vietnam's acceptance of the Soviet proposal for a collective security system in Asia, as the concept of peaceful coexistence and détente did not appear in the Vietnamese vocabulary at that moment. It rather indicated Vietnam's reluctance to become involved directly in the Sino–Soviet power struggle in Asia and its intent to strive to keep the consistency of the doctrine at a domestic and foreign-policy level. In this language, the socialist system is a united world system, where Vietnam and China "are both comrades and brothers."[8] Nevertheless, this theme of the unity of the socialist world system was not manifested as an expression of loyalty to the Soviet approach to international politics. The Vietnamese did not, unlike China, attack détente as a general approach to the relations between the superpowers, but negated its application in Southeast Asia in a situation where there were hopes for the spread of revolution to the other countries of the region, which would sweep away the U.S. presence and influence there. In this respect, the other Vietnamese foreign-policy theme, the national liberation struggle, or anti-imperialist struggle, was given priority over détente. The Vietnamese argued that imperialism and colonialism are the origin of tension all over the world and therefore détente must be based on the recognition of the legitimacy of anti-imperialist struggle "by all the means."[9] Consequently, the Vietnamese theme of the unity of the socialist world system was taken advantage of when dealing with the Sino–Soviet conflict and did not necessarily include any other commitments by either power. Thus it included both rational power calculation, which took into consideration the danger of Vietnam's direct involvement in the Sino–Soviet dispute and, at the same time, it supported its own ideological project and rule system.

Besides the vocabulary's connection with Vietnamese doctrine, the concepts were also an obvious signal to both socialist giants. Ignoring peaceful coexistence exposed the distance between the policies of Vietnam and the Soviet Union. In fact, Vietnam persistently resisted the Soviet Union's bid to exert excessive influence over the country in the postwar situation. The Soviet Union tried to connect economic aid to closer coordination by Vietnam with Soviet policy and to press Vietnam to support détente more actively.[10] Correspondingly, the appearance of the concept of three revolutionary currents in the Vietnamese political language simultaneously with the rapprochement of China and the United States at the end of the 1960s and the beginning of the 1970s was both a Vietnamese protest to this development and a sign of Vietnam's rejection of China's appraisal of the world situation. Therefore, language based on class analysis suited Vietnam's need to deal with the Sino–Soviet dispute on a general level. However, its weakness and limitations became evident when Vietnam was confronted by the concrete issues involved in the Sino–Soviet dispute.

The issue of the offshore islands in the South China Sea directly challenged Vietnam's policy toward China. Two island groups, the Paracels *(Hoang Sa)*, in the north, near the Chinese Hainan island, and the Spratlys *(Truong Sa)* more to the south, between the southern part of Vietnam, Borneo and the Philippines, were brought under French control during the colonial period; and when France withdrew from Indochina, they came under the administration of South Vietnam. The government of National China had already occupied a part of the Paracel islands and one of the Spratly islands in 1946, but the situation changed drastically when PRC forces seized the rest of the Paracel islands from Saigon's troops in January 1974. The PRC had declared as early as 1958 that the Paracels and the Spratlys were located in China's territorial waters, and this was acknowledged also by the DRV. However, in the mid-1960s Hanoi ceased to recognize the PRC's right to these islands; and when the Paracels fell into Bejing's hands and Saigon secured its position in the Spratlys, the North Vietnamese kept silent. While the Saigon regime was falling, the DRV's navy busied itself by capturing the remaining island of the Spratly archipelago from South Vietnam's troops.[11]

The problems of the viability of vertical class analysis and orthodox language emerged when Vietnam had to operate on the state level instead of as an avant-garde of the world's revolutionary movement. Vietnam's approach was not made easier by public Soviet criticism of China's policy relating to the Paracels, which brought the Sino–Soviet aspect to this issue.[12] Vietnam could not accuse China of being a threat to its ownership of the islands either from the political point of view or on the basis of its doctrine. It nevertheless argued for its right to keep the islands. According to Vietnamese media, the islands had turned into "impregnable fortresses, which stand proudly in the fatherland's waters" and are "valiant forward guardians whom no force can subdue."[13] Interestingly, behind this defiant affirmation of absolute sovereignty over the islands, Vietnam tried to negotiate with China on the island question.[14]

Hanoi used both pragmatic and formal arguments when dealing with the island question and relations with China. Vietnam tried in public, on the one hand, to assert its sovereignty over the islands and, on the other hand, professed friendship with China. In May 1977, *Nhan Dan* made an extraordinarily strong claim on the islands, using an argument, where it referred to Vietnam's 4000-year history of struggle for sovereignty, connecting the question of territorial waters to this question. It did not mention China, although the reference to Vietnam's history was transparent. Simultaneously, *Nhan Dan* presented the principle of defending the country's independence, sovereignty and territorial integrity as being in full harmony with pure proletarian internationalism.[15] However, neither China nor Vietnam admitted officially any problems in their relationship. On the contrary, on his visit to China two weeks later, Vo Nguyen Giap turned to Marxist orthodoxy when proclaiming that Vietnam's and China's relationship was based on Marxism-Leninism and proletarian internationalism, and thus "the two countries, who share the same ideal of socialism and communism, will, as in the past, forever remain close comrades-in-arms, who are both comrades and brothers."[16]

The island and territorial waters issue forced Vietnam to introduce concepts such as sovereignty *(chu quyen)* and territorial integrity *(toan ven lanh tho)*, which were operating more horizontally on a state-to-state level than in the framework of the class analysis of international relations. These concepts did not have the same connection with Marxism-Leninism as the concepts that Vietnam used to employ in its relations with the socialist countries. Although these concepts have been the fundamental principles of international law for centuries, the context of Vietnam's reference was much younger. These terms were crucial in the vocabulary of the Non-Aligned Movement, in which Vietnam was increasing its activity after the fall of Saigon. The basic rights of the newly liberated countries in the language of the movement included self-determination, sovereignty and territorial integrity.[17] Thus the Vietnamese argued as if their audience comprised the whole international community, notably the countries in the Non-Aligned Movement. The references to Vietnam's history presented to this audience the idea of a particular threat to Vietnam. However, Vietnam had no desire to change the vocabulary as it concerned its relations with China, which would have happened if Vietnam had mentioned China. This would have nullified the option to prevent the Sino–Vietnamese conflict, which was still under control at that moment.

This examination of Vietnamese statements shows that, although Vietnam tried to employ in its relations with the Soviet Union and China Marxist-Leninist doctrine, the issues involving its maritime boundary and later also land borders forced it to introduce more conventional concepts of state-to-state relations. Naturally, this involves the fact that unified Vietnam had to deal with very different kinds of questions, in a situation where it had an enemy on its own soil. After the second Indochina war, it was directly faced with the old colonial border delineations and the Sino–Soviet dispute. The new concepts indicated that after unification there emerged in the sphere of foreign policy an area the connection of which to the code imposed by the doctrine and ideological project was not so strong as it was during the liberation struggle.

Nevertheless, also the public statements of both Vietnam and China revealed that they were following different courses. The whole content of Hanoi's argumentation was fully understood only after the outbreak of the Sino–Vietnamese and Vietnamese–Kampuchean conflicts at the beginning of 1978. In the spring of 1977, both Vietnam and China showed their hand in the power constellation in Asia by their public statements. In its resolution on the celebration of the 50th anniversary of the October Revolution the following autumn, the Vietnamese Communist Party leadership acknowledged the decisive role of the Soviet Union in the national liberation struggle and affirmed the need to step up the mobilization of the cadres and the entire people along the lines of "the great victories and precious experiences" of the Soviet Union. Particular emphasis was laid on the Soviet Union's role in the world developments.[18] Consequently, Vietnam no longer maintained that only its policies toward the Soviet Union and China differed, but it also gave a signal that its relations with the Soviet Union were given priority over its relations with China. Correspondingly, China emphasized its support of Democratic Kampuchea and its policy in Indochina. Just before Pham Van Dong's visit to Peking to start the negotiations for the islands, Chinese Foreign Minister Huang Hua praised the role of Kampuchea in opposing hegemony in the area and was confident that in the future their cooperation would be even closer.[19]

However, the Vietnamese preserved the illusion of reality by advancing formalist arguments to sustain the hope of the restoration of unity between the socialist powers up to the end of 1977. Similarly, up to that moment, the unified socialist world system prevailed as a historical necessity despite the fact that Kampuchea, which was receiving strong public support from China,[20] was already in a full, although secret, war with Vietnam. The territorial issue with China was wide open and there was hardly any common ground between the Vietnamese and Chinese appraisals of the world situation. This did not prevent the Vietnamese from arguing according to the theoretical premises of Marxism-Leninism, although the arguments had no real referent. In these arguments, the socialist countries, including China as a crucial factor, were represented as a unified force opposed to imperialism.[21]

On Le Duan's official visit to China at the end of November 1977, the different courses taken by these two countries were clearly recognized. The visit produced no joint communiqué or statement but two different kinds of world appraisals with different political vocabularies. The Chinese emphasized that they were "determined to act according to Chairman Mao's theory of the differentiation of the three worlds" and would ally themselves "with all countries subjected to imperialist and social-imperialist aggression, subversion, interference, control or bullying to form the broadest possible united front against superpower hegemonism."[22] Thus the Chinese both warned against a pro-Soviet policy and also advanced arguments in favor of support to Democratic Kampuchea. In their response, the Vietnamese clearly showed their commitment to the Soviet vocabulary, including the three revolutionary currents. The response included two dissident viewpoints as regards China's foreign policy, namely, affirmation of Vietnam's intent to stay on the Soviet side and delivery of a protest against China's policy of cooperation with the United States – both being based on formal premises.[23]

With respect to the strong Chinese anti-Soviet stance, the Vietnamese theme of the unity of the socialist world system turned from preliminary agreement among the discussants to symptoms of disagreement. However, the Vietnamese did not simply raise the points of dispute, for there did take place some kind of search for common ground. This was expressed in the references to the common struggle of Vietnam and China against feudalism and imperialism, the struggle against a common enemy, U.S. imperialism in the past, and Chinese aid to Vietnam in this struggle. The Vietnamese expected that this aid, now given for the building of socialism, would continue also in the future.[24] Despite the fact that these utterances can be also understood as criticism of the actual state of affairs between these countries in a situation where China was decreasing its aid to Vietnam, this was not necessarily the case. Similar reference to the past common struggle, in the hope that this might continue, was also made in Hua Guofeng's speech.[25] These utterances can be understood as autocommunication between two parties, the real referent of which might be found in the content of their mutual talks. In this respect, Le Duan's confidence that China "would decidedly not allow any exploiting class or reactionary force in the country to raise its head in an attempt to cause the new China to change its color" can be seen as a critical attack on China's orientation in the economic field and in its international relations.[26] However, when connected to Le Duan's recognition of China's modernization program, this statement takes on a more conventional tone. These pronouncements, which can be interpreted in many ways, possess in large measure the cryptic properties of Marxist-Leninist language, which gives several options for the future. Similarly, the formal approach embraces the troubles between Vietnam and China, but also conveys to Beijing Vietnam's stance toward Sino–Soviet relations.

Vietnam's situation changed dramatically in the Sino–Soviet power struggle when the conflict between Vietnam and Kampuchea came out into the open and China declared its support of the Khmer Rouge. An appeal by Vietnam for reconciliation between the two socialist giants would have been absurd in this situation and thus it disappeared from the Vietnamese vocabulary.

Formally, the concrete issues under dispute seemed to be separate from the Sino–Soviet power struggle. These issues involved territorial waters, the demarcation of land borders, and, especially, the status and treatment of Chinese residents (Hoa-people) in Vietnam. But soon after these issues had emerged, they became tangled up with the conflict between Vietnam and Kampuchea and the Sino–Soviet power struggle. There occurred a period between January and May 1978 when Vietnamese pronouncements represented the situation in an ambiguous manner, giving the impression that it might be possible to solve the border issue peacefully between Vietnam and Kampuchea.[27] Nevertheless, in its English broadcast of February 21, Hanoi Radio referred extraordinarily straight to China, giving to it the code name "international reactionaries," which had become established to mean China in relation to the Kampuchean question. The commentary wound up its broadcast with a wider reference to China's orientation in foreign policy by concluding that "those who have used Kampuchea to attack Vietnam have also made the wrong move and committed a blunder in their choice of allies and objectives."[28]

Vietnam did not openly challenge China for backing Pol Pot in the Kampuchean affair before May 1978. The situation changed, however, when the question of the ethnic Chinese in Vietnam was raised. The position of the Chinese in Vietnam involved difficult social, ethnic and political questions. Attention was focused on the mass exodus of these Hoa-people as refugees, first to China, but then also to neighboring Southeast Asian countries and finally to the U.S.A. and Canada, Australia and Europe.

In the spring of 1975, there lived approximately 1.2 million ethnic Chinese in Vietnam, nearly 85 per cent of them in the South. Traditionally, they were engaged in commerce, and according to one estimate, by 1961 they were controlling 80 per cent of the total retail trade and 75 per cent of all South Vietnam's commercial activities. Their importance to the economy of the South became clearly evident after the unsuccessful campaigns for the transformation of private industry and commerce into socialist economy in the late 1970s.[29] During the Indochina wars, Hanoi tried to control the political activities of the Overseas Chinese *(Hoa kieu)* through different organizations; in the North the Chinese population was introduced to the mainstream educational campaigns and in the South the Communists tried to stimulate revolutionary and anti-imperialist sentiment in the Hoa community.[30]

The interests of the Vietnamese Communists and the Chinese residents collided when the social transformation started in the South after the spring of 1975. The position of the Hoa population was in the kernel of the *ai thang ai* struggle in the period of transition to socialism, as Hoang Tung's essays proved. This campaign of social transformation was partly directed against small-scale trade capitalism, "the Hoa capitalism" *(chu nghia tu ban Hoa kieu)*, among the other collectivization measures taken in the South.[31] The first campaign against the compradore capitalists, which was in fact largely directed at the Hoa business interests in the Saigon–Cholon area, was implemented between September 1975 and December 1976.[32] During the spring of 1978, this ideological struggle became tangled with the relations between Vietnam and China. The question of social transformation was followed by a more ethnic issue, namely, Hanoi's policy of pressuring the Chinese population in the South to acknowledge only Vietnamese nationality from the beginning of 1976. In September 1976, all the Chinese newspapers in the South were ordered to shut down along with the Chinese schools.[33] When these domestic matters became linked to the growing tension between Vietnam and China, Vietnam started, after the first border clashes in April 1977, to remove the Chinese population out of the border areas near China.[34]

China started to take action in response to the Hoa people's exodus at the end of April, charging the Vietnamese authorities with maltreating Chinese residents in Vietnam, and finally sent ships to Vietnam's coast to evacuate the Chinese population.[35] This forced Hanoi to make a public issue of its relations with China. In its response to Chinese charges, Vietnam's Foreign Ministry continued to use traditional vocabulary. First, it emphasized that the anxiety among the ethnic Chinese was due very much to the socialist transformation campaign in the South, and that this anxiety was being exacerbated by China itself through its campaign of blaming Vietnam for bad treatment of the Chinese. Second, by emphasizing the elements of the three revolutionary currents, it contended that the problems with China could be resolved only on the basis of Vietnam's current foreign policy: this meant that China should accept Vietnam's relationship with the Soviet Union. Finally, the Vietnamese Foreign Ministry admitted for the first time the connection between the Kampuchean problem and Vietnam's relations with China.[36] However, on May 29, an article in the *Nhan Dan* put it more clearly, accusing China of using the Hoa people as a foreign-policy instrument and of threatening Vietnam's sovereignty. Simultaneously, the article sounded the note that a decisive reappraisal of China's position in Vietnam's foreign policy was taking place, as the Vietnamese "are not stupid when friends undergo a change of heart."[37]

After the dispute between China and Vietnam had come out into the open, the concepts of sovereignty, self-determination, and independence were crucial when Vietnam defined its relations with China. In fact, through these concepts, Vietnam attempted to connect its relations with China to the struggle for the unity of the Third World. The Vietnamese charged that this unity was threatened by the American imperialistic policy of promoting division in the national liberation movement. Accordingly, Hanoi radio argued that whenever national pride and the endeavor to make one's country prosperous and powerful, which – as it was pointed out – are legitimate aspirations, turn into nationalism and chauvinism, imperialism is ready to exploit and promote this tendency. This had happened to Cambodia and, first of all, as the Vietnamese code name for its northern neighbor implied, to China. Thus the audience (the Non-Aligned Movement) and the purpose served by these concepts were clear: Vietnam strove to identify itself as a non-aligned country pursuing its own social ideal (socialism) and it claimed now to be under the pressure of imperialism in the same way as most of the Third World countries.[38]

As the Vietnamese line of argument continued, the method of the imperialists was to manipulate the nationalistic countries to divert the movement and separate them from the socialist countries. Under this external pressure, the only way for a nation to maintain its independence and sovereignty is to unite with the socialist countries and progressive forces.[39]

However, the vocabulary to describe relations with China and, in fact, the new appraisal of the world situation were not made consistent before the Vietnamese Communist Party's Central Committee Plenum in July. At this plenum, the fundamental changes in the Vietnamese vocabulary were made by the resolution that named China as Vietnam's most dangerous and immediate enemy.[40] In strictly theoretical terms, there was no departure from the old definition. Vietnam's chief enemy was still U.S. imperialism; but now China had undertaken to carry out the U.S. imperialistic aims in the region, especially against Vietnam. To oppose China's ambitions in Southeast Asia involved both the question of national survival and the fulfillment of Vietnam's internationalist mission.[41] This combination of formal and pragmatic arguments was complemented by historical analogies, which persisted until the mid-1980s to describe Sino–Vietnamese relations in Southeast Asia. In line with this, the reality underlying Vietnam's foreign policy was explained by old Vietnamese metaphors: For Indochina, there exists the relation between the son of Heaven *(dang thien tu)* and his vassal *(ke bay toi)* illustrating Sino–Kampuchean relations; and behind it was an impure "alliance of ghost and devils" *(lien minh ma quy)* between socialist China and U.S. imperialism, the influence of which extended over all Southeast Asia.[42] This new identification of the enemy, as a Party document later pointed out, gave Hanoi "a more accurate and more practical appraisal of both our possibilities and strong points as well as of our difficulties and weaknesses."[43]

This resolution was remarkable for both its foreign-policy orientation and domestic ideological lineation. First, it confirmed the deterioration of the relations between China and Vietnam, which after the fall of Saigon had gradually intensified. It confirmed Vietnam's alliance with the Soviet Union, but also reoriented Vietnam's policy toward the Southeast Asian countries.[44] In the second place, it restructured Vietnam's world appraisal and ideological motivation system with respect to the *ai thang ai* struggle, taking advantage of both argumentation patterns. The resolution directed society as a whole to look to the needs of the new security situation, the economy to the war economy, and the media, culture, interpretation of history and social sciences to support the political orientation.

In the Vietnamese political parlance at "the stage of transition to socialism," before this new determination of friends and enemies, *"a single strategic task of carrying out the socialist revolution"* had been *"advancing rapidly, vigorously and firmly to socialism"* (italics by Le Duan).[45] After the new definition of friends and foes, "at the new stage of revolution ... the Party leadership must unite closely and strive to carry out two strategic tasks: *First, to build socialism successfully; second, to stand ready to defend the homeland"* (italics from the document).[46] These two tasks were coupled to a motto to "combine simultaneously the construction of the fatherland to the defense of the fatherland and to combine the productivity of labor to the struggle,"[47] thus furnishing the ideological project with a new content.[48]

The resolution pinpointing China as a concrete enemy of Vietnam meant also that the history of the Vietnamese revolution and Sino-Vietnamese relations received a new interpretation. In fact, after that resolution a situation developed where the history of Sino–Vietnamese relations had to be totally rewritten. First, the difference between the Vietnamese and Chinese revolutions was pointed out. Whereas the Vietnamese Marxists adhered to the Marxist-Leninist rule of relying on the leadership of the working class in the revolution, the Maoist theory based on the decisive role of the peasantry has been anti-Marxist and led China to a nationalist path instead of internationalism.[49] Thus one of the major themes of Vietnam's new interpretation of the Chinese revolution has been an emphasis on its nationalist character rather than on the class standpoint. This interpretation traced Chinese nationalism to the ancient Chinese idea of the world as a universe. Thus the modern Maoist idea of world (universal) revolution is derived from the old Chinese thinking in which China is the world. According to this Vietnamese argumentation, Chinese foreign policy does not conform to the class doctrine, but to the expansionism of old Chinese dynasties.[50]

The Central Committee's resolution proved that the friend/enemy concept was not neglected in the Vietnamese Communists' vocabulary.

Although it was not the central concept aired in public for the mobilization of the masses, it was the crucial element of argumentation in the political planning and decision making, as well as in the common parlance of the Party cadres. It has a vague connection to Marxist-Leninist theory, as it belongs to the vocabulary of revolutionary practice. Consequently, the Stalinist *ai thang ai* concept, which was derived from the doctrine of class conflict, replaced it in public. Accordingly, China was now pointed out as being on the capitalist road, where China's aim was "to stop and split the active and offensive role of the three revolutionary currents, to divide the socialist countries and the Communist parties."[51] However, the unsuitability of the new situation to Marxist theory and the theory of two camps, together with the new interpretation of traditional enmity in Sino-Vietnamese relations, reduced the credibility of the Vietnamese argumentation externally and created a gap between diplomatic parlance and theoretical argumentation.

Nevertheless, as of July 1978, the Vietnamese media started an all-out attack against China, which did not calm down until the end of the 1980s. Simultaneously, Vietnam joined its foreign policy more and more closely to that of the Soviet Union. From the spring of 1975 this course was not a linear one. Vietnamese foreign-policy concepts represented Vietnam's commitment as well as the distance from the Soviet bloc's policy. As noted earlier, the concept of three revolutionary currents showed the adherence of Vietnam's outlook on the world to the Soviet line. However, there existed a Vietnamese variant of this concept. Whereas the order in the Soviet concept was the socialist camp, the working-class movement and the progressive forces in the capitalist countries and, in the last place, the national liberation movement in the Third World countries, in the Vietnamese vocabulary the national liberation movement was ranked second. The Vietnamese placed the working-class movement in the capitalist countries last, emphasizing its residual role in the world revolution. Similarly, their rejection of peaceful coexistence further stressed a contrariness vis-à-vis Soviet policy. Vietnam would not accept peaceful coexistence as a method of dealing with any capitalist country, but regarded it as an approach within the sphere of Third World cooperation, which was also one principle underlying the Non-Aligned Movement. In addition, the concept of proletarian internationalism included China up to the end of 1977, contrary to the more limited Soviet concept of socialist internationalism, which was operating only inside the Soviet bloc.

Vietnam's cautious political parlance between 1975 and 1977 promoted its independence of the socialist powers. However, Vietnam's dependence on the Soviet Union increased rapidly after the year 1975. First of all, this took place in the economic sphere. Vietnam's need of economic support after the fall of Saigon was naturally acute on account of the war ravages; but a further burden was social transformation, which brought into play interesting political and ideological connections. This situation later had very much to do with the doctrinal choices made by the Communist Party leadership in recent decades. Both Vietnam and the Soviet Union kept stressing their mutual understanding of Vietnam's course of development and its Soviet model.[52] Here the *ai thang ai* concept and its doctrinal structure refer to a certain material basis. According to Stalinist doctrine, to choose the socialist, instead of the capitalist course, calls for the rapid development of heavy industry as well as for collectivization and the industrialization of agriculture. In particular, this was considered to be a very important task in South Vietnam, starting from nationalization and leading to a more advanced system of production, aimed to ward off the danger to Marxist rule of the "spontaneous capitalism" of the compradore bourgeoisie and the land-owning peasants.[53]

In this respect, the developmental model offered by the Chinese to the Vietnamese was quite different. Their first priority was the development of agriculture, after which emphasis was laid on light industry, while in third but rather distant place came heavy industry. Therefore the developmental projects in which the Soviets and the Chinese took part in Vietnam were by no means similar. Since the Vietnamese adhered closer to the Soviet developmental model, the eagerness of China to give them economic aid diminished.[54] China's unwillingness to support the Vietnamese developmental model and its ideological Soviet ties was confirmed when the Vietnamese went in the months of September and December 1975 to China, the Soviet Union and the other European socialist countries to ask for economic support. The Vietnamese were successful with the Soviet Union and its allies, but not with China. The aid promised by China did not meet Vietnam's needs; reductions were made in the amounts of non-refundable and military aid requested. By contrast, in 1975 the Soviets cancelled the debts owed to them by Vietnam, provided low-interest long-term loans and general material aid and started several large industrial projects.[55]

The Soviet aid and economic cooperation included certain preconditions. The fact that the Soviets actively encouraged the Vietnamese to adopt their model did not meet actual resistance in Vietnam, as the Vietnamese leadership deemed it to be a domestic politico-ideological matter. However, large-scale industrialization was leading to closer economic integration with the Soviet bloc along the lines laid down by Moscow. Thus the Vietnamese had to solve a difficult equation: modern, socialist large-scale production was understood to serve as the means of securing the country's independence and sovereignty, based on self-reliance; but such large-scale production called for cooperation with other socialist countries, which threatened Vietnam's own sovereign and independent line. After the Second Indochina War, there prevailed a strong belief that Vietnam was able to combine self-reliance with cooperation.[56]

The Soviet Union and Vietnam obviously differed on the way to arrange this cooperation. To the Soviet Union, it meant closer economic integration under the aegis of the CMEA (Council of Mutual Economic Assistance). In fact, Mikhail Suslov, CPSU Central Committee Secretary and the USSR's chief ideologue, suggested this more or less directly in his speech at Vietnam's 4th Party Congress in December 1976.[57] On the other hand, Le Duan in his comprehensive political report at the 4th Party Congress failed even to mention the CMEA,[58] although several developmental projects sponsored by the CMEA had already been undertaken in Vietnam. Interestingly enough, one month before the 4th Party Congress, Vietnam's Party leadership sent a message to the Albanian Communist Party in which it emphasized Albania's qualities of "self-reliance and self support" in its construction of socialism.[59] It seemed that the Vietnamese expected through this cooperation support for the construction of the material base of socialism to help generate self-reliance; and it is unclear whether they were ready for integration or for the required division of labor in a real sense inside the socialist world system.[60]

Besides this demand for the Vietnamese to abandon their strenuous pursuit of self-reliance, Moscow was also insisting on political obligations. These differences can be seen in Soviet and Vietnamese statements, with the Soviet Union stressing the importance of détente, but the Vietnamese never mentioning it. The question dealt, however, more with different levels of emphasis, owing to the international position of the two governments globally, and not on any opposing views of the world situation. On the contrary, conformity of views was expressed by both sides. The Soviet Union was recognized as a model of development for Vietnam in the light of the formal Marxist-Leninist arguments concerning social development.[61] Similarly, in a general context, the Soviet Union also recognized Vietnamese policy as following it internationally.[62]

Through the force of events, Vietnam's policy of non-commitment to the Soviet bloc officially came to an end when the Sino–Vietnamese conflict reached a new stage in the spring and summer of 1978. After the spring of 1975, the Vietnamese stance toward the Sino–Soviet power struggle was no longer symmetrical, and as early as 1976 the Vietnamese acknowledged their need to resist Chinese pressure by leaning on Soviet power.[63] Their new relation to the Soviet bloc was affirmed first by their joining by the CMEA at the end of June 1978, after China had cancelled most of its aid projects in Vietnam, and then in November, with the Soviet–Vietnamese Treaty of Friendship and Cooperation. Coincidentally with the country's joining the CMEA, the Vietnamese Communist Party identified China as the most dangerous and immediate enemy of Vietnam. This meant, of course, as it also meant to China, the confirmation of a new Vietnamese orientation toward the Soviet Union.

However, CMEA membership did not immediately change the Vietnamese view on Socialist cooperation and integration. In their first comments, the Vietnamese emphasized the role of the CMEA in saving Vietnam's construction of socialism, which was now threatened by China. Thus the CMEA was considered mainly as an aid mechanism, although the distribution of work between socialist countries was seen as an "obligation."[64] Nevertheless, as a full member of the CMEA, Vietnam limited its concept of proletarian internationalism to cover the cooperation between Vietnam and the Soviet bloc countries, accepting now Suslov's characterization of the CMEA as "the materialization of the proletarian internationalist attitude"[65] of the Vietnamese and Soviet Communist Parties.

The confirmation of this development and the harmonization of Vietnam's foreign policy to that of the Soviet Union were secured by a Treaty of Friendship and Cooperation, which Le Duan, together with Pham Van Dong, and Leonid Brezhnev, with Alexander Kosygin, signed on the 3rd of November 1978 in Moscow. Outside Vietnam, attention focussed mainly on Article VI of the Treaty, which provided for military cooperation between the two parties. China proclaimed that the treaty established a military alliance between the Soviet Union and Vietnam, and this expression became rooted in the vocabulary of many foreign observers. Indeed, this article provided for a security relationship between the Soviet Union and Vietnam. Its main clause stated that in case either country was attacked or threatened with attack, the Soviet Union and Vietnam would "immediately consult each other with a view to eliminating that threat and taking appropriate and effective measures to ensure the peace and security of the two countries."[66]

Naturally, in the very tense situation prevailing at the end of 1978 between Vietnam and China, as in Indochina as a whole, the significance of this article was emphasized. However, taken literally, the treaty was not a military pact, but signified a very close political alliance. Therefore, of considerable political importance was Article V, whereby the Soviet Union and Vietnam agreed on a common approach to the world situation. Here the Vietnamese confirmed their unreserved support of the policy of peaceful coexistence and of the Soviet approach to détente.[67] The Communist Party's daily *Nhan Dan* immediately affirmed Vietnam's new approach to peaceful coexistence without reservations.[68]

Along with the new emphases, the treaty thus reinforced the old themes of proletarian internationalism and the struggle of national liberation movements. However, the content of these concepts and their real referent were now more clearly identified. The definition of imperialism and "reactionary forces" as the main adversaries delineates proletarian internationalism as involving only the Soviet bloc and pro-Soviet Communist Parties. Therefore the ambiguous nature of this concept in the Vietnamese vocabulary disappeared when China was branded as an enemy. On the other hand, the relation of the treaty to the second main Vietnamese theme, the anti-imperialist struggle, with its close connection to Soviet foreign policy, raised the question of Vietnam's credibility as a non-aligned actor in the Third World countries' movement. Mention of the Non-Aligned Movement[69] and the treaty's orientation to the Third World soon prompted the charge that Vietnam was realizing Soviet goals in the Third World. It is hardly believable that Vietnam intended to bind the Soviet Union to its activities in the Third World countries, but rather to show Vietnam's own orientation toward the socialist countries. Nevertheless, this indicated that the problem of the split among these countries, which was the critical issue in Vietnamese foreign-policy argumentation, shifted to the other question of the credibility of Vietnam's policy toward the Third World countries.

There were other provisions in the Treaty that indicated that the Vietnamese were forced to compromise on their independence. Although the Vietnamese were inclined to use the term proletarian internationalism to express the principles of the Treaty, as *Nhan Dan* did in its editorial November 4,[70] the Treaty used the expression socialist internationalism *(chu nghia quoc te xa hoi chu nghia)* unambiguously. As this concept is known as the "Brezhnev Doctrine" in the West and it refers to the cooperation between the Communist Parties under the leadership of the Soviet Communist Party, the first and the fourth articles were important concessions to Soviet foreign policy in Asia. The parties were obligated to consolidate their relationship "in keeping with the principles of socialist internationalism" (Article I), and the Treaty similarly expected the parties to build and maintain their relations with the other socialist countries in the Socialist World System "on the basis of Marxism-Leninism and socialist internationalism," as the fourth article required.

Consequently, the Treaty forced the Vietnamese Communists to redefine the concepts of independence, sovereignty and self-reliance and the relations between them. In fact, there are interesting connotations with the Vietnamese term *doc lap*, which is used as equivalent to the English word independence. In English, independence strongly connotes freedom; but in Vietnamese, *doc lap* connotes an ambivalent situation, where in the hostile world the independent agent needs to find a protecting social network with reciprocal responsibilities to resist an external threat.[71] Whether this idea of the socio-linguistic origin of *doc lap* is correct or not, it is linked, together with the concept of patriotism, *chu nghia yeu nuoc*, to proletarian internationalism in Vietnamese political texts. The Vietnamese tended to emphasize the importance of patriotism among territorial, national, linguistic and cultural elements, which have moulded their thinking.[72] Its importance stood out in bold relief when the patriotic movement was combined with Marxism-Leninism and the international Communist movement.[73] As regards international dependency, one Communist Party cadre argued that "nowadays, in building the economy, the boundaries between countries are very important. No country can live isolated, apart from the other countries, like Robinson Crusoe on his island. To build the economy, unity *(doan ket)* and cooperation are the important conditions for establishing socialism in any country, and first of all in colonies that have gained independence."[74] Therefore the concepts of *doc lap*, *chu nghia yeu nuoc*, and proletarian internationalism, together with the principle of *phan biet ban thu* and the concept of *ai thang ai* are interrelated, while independence is maintained in a turbulent world by the correct identification of allies and enemies.

Thus there is a certain difference between the words *tu do* (freedom) and *doc lap*. The term *tu do* connotes a situation where one can act unrestrained by controls and with freedom of action. Vietnamese Marxism-Leninism combines these two words to form the syntagm *doc lap tu do*, independence and freedom. These concepts distinguish and combine the class level and the national level in Vietnamese analysis. *Doc lap* refers to the national level in terms of "independence is the basic force of the nation" and *tu do* refers to the class level, in terms of "freedom is the basic force of the working people."[75]

The point of departure in Vietnamese argumentation in new situations is the struggle of national independence movements, together with socialist forces, against imperialism and reactionary forces (China). The concept of two camps was still maintained, with "imperialism in collusion with international reactionaries opposing the development of the three revolutionary currents."[76] Under these circumstances, where the common enemy threatens the revolutionary power of the proletariat (Communist Party) in each country, independence and sovereignty are maintained with the "correct political line and keen revolutionary methods," i.e., with the Party maintaining its ability to mobilize the masses. Together with this self-reliant capability, international solidarity among the socialist countries and liberation movements guarantees the independence of each country. However, without this self-reliance, "foreign aid, no matter how important it may be, cannot replace the efforts of the people of that country."[77]

Although Vietnam's posture in the Sino–Soviet dispute changed radically during the three-and-a-half years' period after the fall of Saigon, the Marxist-Leninist doctrinal code remained unchanged. As it is closely bound to the functional tasks of ideology, the changes in this code should naturally follow the changes in the system of rule, which in the totalitarian Marxist movement was based on the ability or imagined ability of the Communist Party to mobilize the masses. However, Vietnam's new status as a unified, independent, and sovereign country, which no longer needed to wage war on its own soil against the international class enemy, emphasized the emergence of new foreign-policy concepts. They all dealt with Vietnam as a sovereign agent counterbalancing Marxist-Leninist parlance. These new concepts were connected with the double-edged argumentation in a particular way: In general, the Vietnamese held on to the theoretical premises based on a class analysis of international relations, but used both quasi-logical and pragmatic argumentation, in which Vietnam's national sovereignty was played up as a concrete objective in its opposition to China. Therefore, when dealing with its relations with China, Hanoi tended to use pragmatic arguments, including *phan biet ban thu* and historical analogies, to bolster this concept. Contrarywise, Hanoi took a formalist tack when dealing with its relations with the Soviet Union.

Two notions about the terms of independence, sovereignty and territorial integrity should be considered. First, as I noted earlier, they are closely bound to the vocabulary of the Non-Aligned Movement and its program. Second, the terms of independence, sovereignty, territorial integrity and, sometimes, self-reliance were combined to produce a theme that defined Vietnam's posture vis-à-vis China and the Soviet Union. The first three have no special connection with Marxist-Leninist theory and they were used to describe Vietnam's relations with China, especially in the fields where their interests conflicted. The concept of self-reliance has, of course, a direct connection with the domestic line of Vietnam's Communist Party, and its significance lay in showing the distance of Vietnam from the Soviet Union.

On the other hand, the Vietnamese concepts of *doc lap* and *chu nghia yeu nuoc* seemed, if their socio-cultural basis and its connection to the friend/foe concept are correct, to have the idea of proletarian internationalism as a natural counterpart. As there are historical records to show that Communism in Vietnam had been entangled since its early period with nationalism,[78] there are also reasons to believe that aforementioned aspects of the *doc lap* and *chu nghia yeu nuoc* concepts supported the inclusion and use of proletarian internationalism in Vietnamese jargon. In this respect, the Vietnamese cultural code may explain the introduction of certain terms into the Marxist-Leninist vocabulary. This did not, of course, prevent their use tactically in Vietnamese politics during the Sino–Soviet dispute. The adaptation of the concept of socialist internationalism raises, however, a difficult question in this respect. The way the Vietnamese soft-pedaled socialist internationalism in their parlance indicated that they never really accepted this concept.

VIETNAM, INDOCHINA AND THE SPECIAL RELATIONSHIP

The secret border war between Kampuchea and Vietnam, the strengthening alliance between Laos and Vietnam and, finally, Vietnam's invasion of Kampuchea have raised many questions about Vietnam's intentions regarding Indochina. In particular, the content of the key Vietnamese concept of Indochinese relations, of the "special relationship" *(quan he dac biet)* and its bearing on Vietnam's action against Democratic Kampuchea have been examined in many studies. However, because in this study motives and intentions are not any special concern, the focus being on political parlance and argumentation, the formulation of the questions is rather clear. Emphasis is therefore put on the questions: How is this concept of a special relationship related to formalism and pragmatism? How is it related to Vietnam's foreign-policy themes, to more conventional Marxist-Leninist concepts, and to the doctrinal code? And how did it develop during the changes that took place in Vietnam's foreign relations?

Initially, the use of the concept "special relationship" originates from the Vietnam–Laos relationship after the establishment of the Lao People's

Democratic Republic; but somehow a similar expression had been used many years before regarding the cooperation between the revolutionary forces in Indochina. The crucial point here was the fact that Vietnam's partners in Indochina accepted the concept of a special relationship only partly. The new Marxist regime, which took control in Laos in December 1975, wholeheartedly supported this vocabulary, but Democratic Kampuchea did not acknowledge the concept used by Vietnam and Laos, although Kampuchea itself used comparable expressions.

During the late colonial perioid and during the First and the Second Indochina Wars, there prevailed a much closer relationship between the Vietnamese and Laotian revolutionaries than between the Vietnamese and Cambodian revolutionaries. When the Laotian revolutionary movement developed and survived in close contact with the Vietnamese Communist movement, the Kampuchean Communist movement developed independently and its position was not dependent on the Vietnamese Communists. This development of a distinct path for these movements began after the Second World War, when the French colonial system was breaking down. Although these countries formed the common area of Indochina under French rule, their positions in this system differed. Therefore the nationalist and revolutionary movements (including those of the Marxists) did not develop in these countries synchroniously.

Opposite to Vietnam, where the anticolonial resistance had continued through the whole colonial period and the Communist Party as well as its organization emerged in the early 1930s, in both Laos and Cambodia, the emergence of the Marxist influence and well organized resistance against the colonial authorities took place much later. In brief, the anticolonial nationalist movement in Laos, which developed in opposition to pan-Thaiism in World War II and then turned against the French colonial power, collaborated closely with the Viet Minh, led by the Communist Party of Indochina. Similarly, the Vietnamese Communists were the grandfathers of the Laotian Communist Party, which was not established until 1955. Together with the revolutionary wing of the Laotian royal court, the Laotian Communists cooperated closely with the DRV during the Second Indochina War, until it seized absolute power in December 1975.[79]

In the big picture, after World War II, the difference between Cambodia and its Indochinese neighbors was the relatively strong position of its royal court, which was further emphasized by the postwar ruler Prince Norodom Sihanouk's ability to manipulate different political and social groups. Besides, Sihanouk could use to advantage France's pressure in Vietnam so that the French accepted Cambodia's independence in

November 1953. Sihanouk's authority was confirmed at the Geneva Conference, which obligated the armed resistance groups to integrate into Cambodian society. This meant also the elimination of rightist nationalist tendencies, which gave Sihanouk an opportunity to practice anti-American and neutralist foreign policy in Southeast Asia.

Although Marxist groups already existed at the end of the 1940s, the organized Marxist resistance did not begin before the 1960s – then as a consequence of the Sihanouk administration's policy in the rural areas. The Communist Party, known as the Khmer People's Party, was founded in 1951, after the Vietnamese decision to suppress the ICP. However, its cadres suffered heavily under Sihanouk's policy; and those in the KPP leadership who were not arrested or killed went to Hanoi or underground. The Communist Party of Kampuchea was founded in 1960 by the survivors of old revolutionary organzations and by new radical leftist elements, who had come back from France, where they had gone after World War II. To these latter elements belonged the nucleus of the power group of the future Democratic Kampuchea, including Saloth Sar (Pol Pot), Ieng Sary, Son Sen and Khieu Samphan. These two groups formed two factions inside the Party, and their struggle did not end until the massive purges of the Pol Pot administration in the late 1970s. Relations with the Vietnamese Communists became distant by the beginning of the 1960s, when the party leader Touch Samouth, an old ICP cadre, was murdered, and the Pol Pot faction forced itself into the party leadership. Although there existed cooperation between the Vietnamese NLF and the Cambodian Khmer Rouge, particularly after General Lon Nol removed Sihanouk from power at the beginning of the 1970s, relations remained indeterminate between Hanoi and the Cambodian Communists.[80]

In brief, there was a certain real historical referent to the concept of a special relationship between the Vietnamese and Laotian Communists. The concept applied only to Vietnamese–Laotian relations until the 4th National Congress of Vietnam's Communist Party, at which it was established to cover the whole of Indochina. An interesting development of the concept took place even before the 4th Party Congress, varying between formalist and pragmatic argumentation. The first authoritative Vietnamese definition of the state-to-state relations between Vietnam and Laos took place immediately after the founding of the Lao People's Democratic Republic. Interestingly, they all reflected strengthening formalism, but the concept of a special relationship does not appear yet.

The seven-page editorial in the December 1975 issue of *Hoc Tap* contained the most important expressions of the relations between Vietnam and Laos. With the repetitive definitions and phrases, the editorial represented the most typical Marxist-Leninist parlance. From the standpoint of international relations and the emerging concept of a special relationship, the expressions, which emphasized the role of the Lao revolution as a part of reinforcing socialism in Indochina and Southeast Asian, were essential.[81] Factually, these expression, with only more or less minor changes, occurred half a dozen times in the editorial.

The editorial linked the victory of the Lao revolutionary forces to three revolutionary currents in the world.[82] Besides this, there occurred several expressions which referred both to Marxist-Leninist orthodoxy and to the important orientation of the international relations of Vietnam and Laos. *Hoc Tap* emphasized that the Lao revolution had been conducted under "the leadership of the Marxist-Leninist party, which pursues a correct strategic and tactical line" and which "had been supported by the World revolutionary movement, primarily the socialist system."[83] In the Vietnamese political vocabulary, this refers to the policy of the pro-Moscow Communist Parties and to the support of the Soviet bloc. In fact, the correct line also refers to the similarities to Vietnam when the editorial describes this line with militant solidarity and the combination of patriotism and proletarian internationalism.[84] From this Soviet-based language, the editorial goes on to a definition approaching that which was later established to describe Vietnam's policy toward its Indochinese neighbors: "For the sake of the destiny of the very closely bound relationship between two nations, Vietnam and Laos, we esteem more and more this special, friendly and cooperative solidarity in the cause of defending and building a prosperous homeland by advancing along its own course of development in each country."[85]

The Vietnamese defined their relations with the new Lao system according to this interpretation, including several elements they used to deal with the socialist countries. There were, however, particular definitions with respect to Vietnamese–Laotian relations in Indochina. First, the theme of proletarian internationalism was one qualifier in these relations.[86] The second epithet was *the particularly great militant solidarity,* which refers to the common origins of the Laotian and Vietnamese Communist Parties from the ICP and the more or less joint struggle of the Viet Minh and Pathet Lao against the French and the Americans.[87] The third qualifier was the theme of struggle for national independence, the significance of which was emphasized when the Vietnamese and the Laotians coordinated their international relations, especially toward the other Southeast-Asian countries.[88] The first and the third qualifiers were the central elements in the Vietnamese foreign-policy vocabulary and the Marxist-Leninist doctrinal code. Hence they serve a strong autocommunicative purpose. The second epithet, which contains a strong reference to the common tradition of revolutionary action in both countries, points to the other countries, including the rest of Indochina, and refers to the arguments regarding the structure of reality. It likewise refers to the fact that Vietnam has its own sphere of foreign and security policies, which is not included in the main currents of the international relations of the socialist countries.

The fact that the concept of a special relationship did not emerge until the formation of the Lao People's Democratic Republic emphasizes the state-to-state relations between the Indochinese countries. Moreover, the concept did not seem to be a purely Vietnamese creation intended to define the relations between the Indochinese countries. Whether its origin is Vietnamese or Laotian, both countries started to use the concept to give a particular content to their relationship.[89] Interestingly, the particular emphasis given the unique nature of Vietnam–Lao relations was promptly utilized in Vietnam's political parlance to suppress the other elements defining these relations, marked especially by the temporary omission of the concept of proletarian internationalism in Vietnam–Lao relations shortly after the formation of the Lao People's Democratic Republic. The omission of this concept was important in the respect that proletarian internationalism was used in reference to the countries with which Vietnam maintained relations at the party level. This reinforced the view that the Vietnamese stressed the distinct nature of its relations with the Marxist governments in Indochina as contrasted to its relations with socialist countries in general. This did not mean that the Vietnamese disregarded the significance of the political and ideological line of its neighbors. On the contrary, the common political and ideological line played the central role in the concept of a special relationship. In this respect, the Vietnamese emphasized the similarities between them and the Laotian Communists both internally and externally, including national united front tactics and policy toward socialist countries. Therefore the expression that the Laotian Marxist-Leninist party had "a correct strategic line" constitutes the significant part of the special relationship. However, this common politico-ideological line in Vietnam's Indochina policy did not refer to proletarian internationalism, indicating that this concept was reserved to determine Vietnam's relations with the Soviet Union and China.

When the Lao Party and Government Delegation visited Vietnam in February 1976, this formal premise was dropped from Vietnamese statements. Proletarian internationalism was not used in Vietnamese jargon with respect to Vietnamese–Laotian relations. Le Duan did not

mention the concept in his speech in honor of the Lao delegation, nor was
it cited in the context of Vietnamese–Laotian relations in the joint
statement signed by Le Duan and Kaysone Phomvihan. However, the
concept appeared, together with other established Vietnamese concepts,
in the part of the joint statement in which the countries defined their
relations with the socialist countries, stressing the mutual view of
Vietnam and Laos with respect to the Soviet Union and China.[90]

The use of the concepts, despite the harmony in the joint statement,
was not identical. There is an interesting parallel between Vietnam's
policy toward the Soviet Union and China and the policy of Laos toward
Vietnam and the Soviet Union. In both cases, the deliberate use of the
Marxist-Leninist concepts indicated foreign-policy orientation. Naturally,
the geographical position of Laos and the overall dependence of the
Laotian Communists on their Vietnamese comrades did not allow very
much space for their foreign policy to move. Similarly, as the Vietnamese
counterbalanced the pressure coming from either the Soviet Union or
China by, on the one hand, emphasizing the role of the world socialist
system and three revolutionary currents and, on the other hand, by
ignoring the Soviet concept of détente, the Laotian Communists used the
socialist community to counterbalance Vietnamese influence. By
emphasizing the role of the socialist world system, the Lao leadership
tried to play down the Vietnamese interpretation of Indochinese relations
as a separate part of the relations inside the socialist system. In contrast
to Le Duan's speech on the same occasion, Kaysone Phomvihan mentioned
the concept of proletarian internationalism three times in the context of
Vietnam–Lao relations, linking a concept of special relationship to the
overall relations among the socialist countries.[91] The Laotians boosted
this approach by stressing the leading role of the Soviet Union in the
Socialist World system; and the "correct" Laotian line was reciprocally
acknowledged by the Soviets.[92]

Notwithstanding this different use of words and phrases, which had
certain different political meanings for Vietnam and Laos, a special
relationship was accepted as a general approach by both sides. Despite
the fact that the joint statement issued during this visit included formal
premises for Vietnam–Lao relations, with regard to the special relationship,
the emphasis is laid on a pragmatic note. The concept was bound, first of
all, to the common policy program of the two countries and not to the
theoretical premises of Marxism-Leninism. The difference in the views
held on the nature of the special relationship between Vietnam and Laos,
which came out in February 1976, were harmonized when the delegation
representing Vietnam's party and government went to Vientiane to sign

the Treaty of Friendship and Cooperation with Laos. The pragmatic tones that still prevailed in the Political Report of the 4th Congress of Vietnam's Communist Party in December 1976 were mollified by the formalist vocabulary. In the treaty and in the joint statement signed during this visit, all the epithets of a special relationship were now balanced. The joint statement of July 18, 1977, by Le Duan and Kaysone Phomvihan stated unambiguously: "The two sides agree that the Vietnam–Laos solidarity bloc *(khoi doan ket)*, which has been built on the basis of Marxism-Leninism and proletarian internationalism ... has helped increase considerably the strength of each nation and is a guarantee of the successful development of each country's revolution. The advance steps of each country's revolution are closely related to the fine steps of development of the special relationship between the two countries."[93]

The Treaty of Friendship and Cooperation signed during the visit combined the theme of anti-imperialist struggle and the theory of two camps. In Article I of the Treaty of Friendship and Cooperation, the connection of the special relationship to proletarian internationalism was confirmed.[94] Similarly, as in both joint statements, the first issued in February 1976 and the second in July 1977, the treaty raised two other themes, the particular common experience of these nations and the national liberation struggle as the epithets of the special relationship in the context of the two camps theory. Thus both sides agreed that "the independent and sovereign line *(duong loi doc lap, tu chu)* and correct leadership of Vietnam's Communist Party and the Lao People's Revolutionary Party, the tradition of very warm solidarity *(truyen thong doan ket tham thiet)* between the two nations," in their struggle against imperialism and their dedication to constructing socialism "constitute the fundamentals for the development of the Vietnam–Laos special relationship."[95]

The theme of the national independence struggle as the epithet characterizing relations between Vietnam and Laos was emphasized in the fifth article, which was formulated according to the concept of three revolutionary currents. In this respect, and as earlier practice of uniting Vietnam–Lao foreign policy, for example at the Non-Aligned Summit, held in Colombo in 1976, had proved, the common policy of Vietnam and Laos should be directed to the region of Southeast Asia.[96] The common, coordinated policy pursued in the Non-Aligned Movement was not particularly mentioned in the Treaty; but it was pointed out in the joint communiqué, which went over the regional and global questions in detail, with regard to which the Vietnamese and the Laotians took a common stand.[97]

There are similarities between the fifth article of this treaty and the fifth article of the Treaty between Vietnam and the Soviet Union signed in November 1978. The difference between these articles lay in their spirit; whereas the Lao–Vietnam treaty emphasized the national independence struggle, the USSR–Vietnam treaty promoted détente. Like the treaty with the Soviet Union, this treaty also included a military article, in which the obligation of mutual defense was even more binding than with the Soviet Union.

With respect to the common orientation in foreign policy, some attention deserves to be paid to the connection of the special relationship in the dealings between the new Marxist government of Democratic Kampuchea and the two other Indochinese countries revealed in this treaty as well as other documents. It was essential that the Vietnamese did not link Cambodia to a concept of special relationship either in the Treaty and the joint statement or the speeches made during the visit of the Vietnamese delegation to Laos. Both sides pledged their support of Kampuchea, explicitly "the revolutionary organization" *(to chuc cach mang)*, i.e., the Pol Pot administration,[98] but without the same reciprocity that marked the relations between Vietnam and Laos.

However, this was not the whole picture involving the use of this concept in Vietnam's Indochina policy. On the part of the common approach of Laos and Vietnam there existed also Vietnam's own orientation, where the concept of the special relationship appeared. First, the report of the 4th Party Congress construed the concept to deal with Indochina as a whole. Later, this interpretation recurred in a Vietnamese definition of relations among the Indochinese countries.[99] Second, the Vietnamese emphasized that the relations between Vietnam and Laos were a model of how the future relations between the Indochinese countries in a general context ought to be arranged. According to Le Duan, the special relationship between Vietnam and Laos "is a rare model of the relations *(moi quan he mau muc hiem co)*," which "is the pride forever of our two nations."[100] This model was realized in the border treaty, which was signed during the Vietnamese leaders' visit to Laos.[101] Although the details of the border treaty were never published, their import became clear during the serious border conflicts between Vietnam and Kampuchea since May 1975. Third, a couple of months after the Vietnam–Laos Treaty was signed, the Vietnamese connected the concept of the special relationship to their bilateral relationship with Kampuchea, something they had avoided earlier. Therefore, when the concept was separated from the goal-oriented reasoning occurring in Vietnamese–Laotian documents, it acquired prerequisities, which connected it to the Marxist-Leninist orthodoxy.

The vocabulary and rhetoric that were entering the Vietnamese policy to deal with Vietnam's relations with other Indochinese countries adhered to the general formalist lines. In its relations with Kampuchea, Hanoi could already draw on some tradition to describe its relations in formal terms. The main qualifier of the relationship, according to the Marxist-Leninist doctrine, was the fierce struggle between two camps. This was introduced into the common struggle against the imperialist enemy.[102] When Phnom Penh fell into the hands of the Khmer Rouge, Hanoi stated that the Khmer Rouge's triumph belonged to the victories of the Indochinese peoples that had turned the balance "in favor of the revolutionary forces and to the disadvantage of the colonialists, imperialists and international reactionaries."[103]

It should be noted that this language was not only the Vietnamese way of describing the relations between two countries. In fact, Democratic Kampuchea's vocabulary describing the relationships in Indochina did not deviate essentially from this. The Kampuchean documents, actually rather few in number, that dealt with relations with Vietnam explained them in terms of "militant solidarity" or "long-standing bonds of militant solidarity and friendship" in which the Vietnamese and Kampucheans were "comrades-in-arms."[104] This orientation, which also marked Vietnam's foreign policy toward the Third World and especially toward the Non-Aligned Movement, was the decisive principle of Democratic Kampuchea's policy in a new situation.[105]

Although this neutralist approach was fully acknowledged by the Vietnamese, it delineated clearly the limits of the cooperation between these two countries in Indochina. Kampuchea's main foreign partner was China and the Vietnamese, Lao, and Korean peoples were "three other close comrades-in-arms."[106] Furthermore, according to the Kampucheans, the basis of this solidarity came from the Indochinese people's summit conference, where the Vietnamese, the Kampucheans and the Laotians at the beginning of the 1970s coordinated their policy against the U.S. The Khmer Rouge leadership clearly disregarded the heritage of the Indochinese Communist Party in this respect.[107] Nevertheless, the new leaders of Democratic Kampuchea seemed to accept the Vietnamese view of a struggle between two camps as the general point of departure in their relations with Vietnam.[108] They did not recognize the Chinese appraisal of the world situation explicitly before 1977, when the Kampuchean affirmation of the Chinese international orientation was acknowledged during Pol Pot's visit to Beijing in September.[109]

In the early period following the spring of 1975, Vietnamese and Kampuchean documents indicated that there had developed some kind of consensus regarding the vocabulary dealing with the relations between the two countries. However, the documents of the 4th Congress of Vietnam's Communist Party proved that Vietnam had taken a unilateral approach vis-à-vis Democratic Kampuchea. The use of the concept of a special relationship before the 4th Party Congress had restricted the definition of Vietnam–Lao relations, and it had been only one qualifier in this definition. But in the Political Report of the Congress, this concept was emphasized as a basis of Vietnamese policy in Indochina, and it dealt unambiguously also with relations with Kampuchea. The Vietnamese did not specify what this really meant in the case of Kampuchea, but its definition was formulated in documents concerning Lao–Vietnamese relations.

In the Vietnamese leadership's message on the occasion of the first anniversary of the Kampuchean Communist Party on September 28, 1977, the concept of a special relationship was emphasized. However, the secret border war between Kampuchea and Vietnam had already escalated to large-scale battles, and at that moment Pol Pot's troops had just made serious military raids on Vietnamese territory, notably Tay Ninh Province. The Vietnamese counterattacked in October, penetrating deep inside Kampuchea. In this situation, however, the fact that the term "special relationship" appeared in a short message three times, proved that use of it was not an accident. This indicated that the Vietnamese were formulating their premises according to the orthodox Marxist-Leninist model. The message noted the importance of the special ralationship between Vietnam and Cambodia in the past and present and stated further that the Vietnamese Communist Party was committed in the future "to preserve and develop the special relationship between the parties and the peoples of Vietnam and Cambodia."[110] During his visit in November to Beijing, which took place simultaneously with the massive Vietnamese military operation in Kampuchean territory, Le Duan reiterated a similar expression of the special relationship.[111]

Owing to the Khmer Rouge's ignorance of the special relationship, Vietnam's unilateral use of the concept in this context seemed to express Vietnam's objectives relating to Kampuchea. Nevertheless, it should be pointed out that this did not happen until as late as September 1977. However, to study Vietnamese–Kampuchean relations in 1975–1977 by examining only the texts published during this period by the Vietnamese or the Pol Pot administration leads one to an utterly artificial world. Naturally this tells something about Marxism-Leninism as political parlance, and reveals how the doctrine creates its own reality. Actually, the only symptom of the real referent of Vietnamese relations with Democratic Kampuchea was the amount of Vietnamese documents concerning the matter – actually quite small. An illustrative example is the party review *Hoc Tap*, in which there appeared in 1975–1976 only one article on Democratic Kampuchea and where Vietnam–Kampuchean relations were examined in the mood of anti-imperialist struggle.[112]

As Vietnamese and Kampuchean documents later revealed, clashes on the border of these two countries began as early as the spring of 1975. There occurred several border clashes in 1975–1977. Hanoi and Phnom Penh differed in their interpretations of border lineations, which dated back to the colonial period; but the disputed areas were not large enough to explain the intensity of the border conflict. Negotations on the border disputes were held on a high level twice, first in June 1975 in Hanoi and then in May 1976 in Phnom Penh. The clashes intensified during the course of 1977, when negotiations deadlocked. Simultaneously, China, which had tried to keep a balance in relations with these countries, started in 1977 to support Phnom Penh diplomatically.[113] In September 1977, the Khmer Rouge made swift coordinated raids along the border, penetrating several kilometers inside Vietnam and killing hundreds of civilians. A few days after these raids, during Pol Pot's visit to Beijing, China gave remarkable support to Democratic Kampuchea's policy "in the struggle against imperialism and hegemonism."[114] The Vietnamese responded with a large-scale military operation against Kampuchea, which was still going on when Phnom Penh suspended its diplomatic relations with Vietnam at the end of December 1977.[115]

Certainly, the origins of the conflict can be found by studying a complex combination of different factors, including the colonial heritage, the Sino-Soviet rivalry and the policies of two totalitarian states, whose societies were not organized according to constitutional rules but by waging war. The Vietnamese tried to keep the façade of a common enemy, imperialism, until Democratic Kampuchea broke this façade by suspending diplomatic relations and by starting to make a public issue of the conflict. Actually, Pol Pot's ultratotalitarian regime had supported anti-Vietnamese sentiments earlier; this was partly connected with the purges inside the Kampuchean Communist Party, partly with the isolationist policy of the Khmer Rouge, based on absolutist self-reliance, and partly with the extreme conditions of Kampuchean society, to which Khmer Rouge rule had led.

Evidently, the publicity about the conflict between two Marxist states broke the picture of the unity among the socialist states that Vietnam had carefully tried to maintain. However, this did not mean that the Vietnamese had abandoned its Marxist-Leninist doctrinal code. This code does not call for the coherence of Marxist theories on social and international relations, but the ability of the political parlance to keep mobilizing the masses. The Vietnamese turned, however, more to formal Marxist-Leninist argumentation so as to emphasize the correct line of the respected Communist Parties in the common struggle. From these premises, the Vietnamese used an argumentation resembling that used by the Soviets when the Warsaw Pact troops marched into Czechoslovakia. Although the harmony between foreign-policy concepts and Marxist-Leninist language in general was preserved, the commitment to the established vocabulary in a new situation brought along with it diplomatic troubles, for which Vietnam had to suffer for many years.

One reason for the use of the concept of a special relationship was obviously tactical. Vietnam wanted to give the impression that this kind of relationship had really existed in the past; and by seeking to restore this condition, Vietnam tried to put the blame on Pol Pot's regime for spoiling the relationship. Second, by promoting the special relationship, Hanoi emphasized that good relations with Kampuchea represented a priority in its foreign policy on which many other political choices depended. Although this point of departure was closely connected with the structure of Marxist-Leninist parlance, it also raised questions about Vietnam's intentions to dominate Indochina.

It was the Pol Pot administration that made an issue of Vietnam's "special relationship."[116] This was taken up quickly by Western analysts, who tied the concept to the Brezhnev Doctrine, or the doctrine of "limited sovereignty,"[117] which was used to claim the right of the socialist community, led by the Soviet Union, to control and preserve the community's unity.

Notwithstanding the sometimes highly provocative nature of this claim, it deserves closer attention. What was labelled in the West as the Brezhnev Doctrine was developed by the Soviets to justify their intervention in Czechoslovakia in 1968. It was a concrete case of socialist internationalism, and it embraced the following principles, many of which had already been accepted by the Vietnamese: 1) the class basis of social development, 2) the two camps theory, 3) the unity of the world's socialist system, and 4) socialist self-determination and the responsibility of the socialist community to act as the guardian of the sovereignty of the Communist Party in each country.[118] Owing to the Vietnamese emphasis on self-reliance and independence, the last point of the doctrine was clearly in contradiction to established Vietnamese thinking. Despite the fact that Hanoi never questioned the legitimacy of the Warsaw Pact troops' intervention in Czechoslovakia, the Vietnamese resisted the idea of the dominance of the socialist community in the internal affairs of each member state by avoiding use of the term "socialist internationalism" and eluding strong institutional ties with the Soviet bloc. Moreover, the Vietnamese concept of proletarian internationalism was connected much more with a wider approach to joint revolutionary action by the Third World and the socialist community.

However, Vietnam's commitment to the concept of a special relationship with that country after its rejection by Kampuchea called for the persuasive application of it. The Communist Party declared that the Vietnamese would keep the bonds between the Communist Party of Vietnam and the Communist Party of Kampuchea. Accordingly, "no reactionary force whatsoever can possibly break these special relations of solidarity and friendship."[119] Moreover, excepting the right of intervention in the domestic affairs of the members of the socialist community, Vietnam had accepted all the other general principles of the Brezhnev Doctrine, including the class basis of international relations, the two camps theory, and the unity of the world socialist system. In this connection, "building a special relationship between Vietnam and Cambodia" had been based on the common struggle against imperialism demanded by the class division.[120]

Just as the "special relationship" conforms to the doctrinal code of Marxism-Leninism in the same way as the Brezhnev Doctrine does, the Vietnamese also pursued their own approach to Vietnamese–Kampuchean relations in a similar way, as Moscow considered it its right to control the members of the socialist community. The Vietnamese leadership tried to affirm that the special relationship did not include that control function. They tried "to preserve and develop the special relationship" in view of "the struggle for the common ideal," the countries having been "associated with one another in the struggle for national liberation."[121] Thus the special relationship resulted from the mobilization of forces to achieve a common goal, just as national unity was formed in early Vietnamese revolutionary texts.

The question arises: who was leading this mobilization? The Vietnamese do not give a clear answer to this question. In fact, in the Vietnamese documents, the question of leadership was not brought up; and it seemed to suffice for Hanoi that the parties recognize in common who are their enemies and who their allies. However, the concept of a special relationship was used to legitimate Vietnam's right to intervene in Kampuchean politics. Interestingly enough, the argumentation for that was basically the same as for the Brezhnev Doctrine. Accordingly, "Cambodian reactionaries" had destroyed the traditional unity between the countries. As in the Soviet argumentation in the case of Czechoslovakia, which charged "imperialists" with attempting to detach the country from the socialist community, the Vietnamese claimed that Vietnamese-Kampuchean unity was being undermined by "imperialists and reactionaries who have great ambitions in Southeast Asia."[122] Thus this argumentation included two elements: There was a deviation in the Communist Party leadership, which went against the interests of their own country and the other socialist countries (here the other Indochinese countries). And this leadership was supported and controlled by an external power that sought to divide the socialist (Indochinese) countries. Moreover, this deviation ran counter to history and led to bankruptcy.[123] The Vietnamese did not say that they would witness that bankruptcy, but affirmed that they were "determined to preserve and enhance the militant solidarity and fraternal friendship among the three Indochinese countries."[124] This argumentation followed the formal pattern of logic in which the premise is the correct or incorrect line of the Communist Party and, as governed by the objective laws of social development, leads to inevitable consequences.

Outside this argumentation pattern, there also occurred later an element that supported the interpretation of the "special relationship" as the Vietnamese version of the Brezhnev Doctrine. This was the admission of socialist internationalism into the Vietnamese vocabulary as it appeared in the Soviet–Vietnamese Treaty on the eve of the intervention in Kampuchea. Although the acceptance of this concept was perhaps mainly a concession to the Soviet Union, it also directed Vietnam to keep Indochina as a uniform entity in the socialist camp.

Thus the original idea of the special relationship, as it appeared to represent the relationship between Vietnam and Laos adhered to two main Vietnamese themes of proletarian internationalism and the national liberation struggle in the context of the *ai thang ai* struggle and the formal argumentation pattern. However, the third theme determining the special relationship, the peculiar historical and geographical conditions obtaining in the Indochinese countries, followed the pattern of pragmatic argumentation. The conflict with Cambodia and Vietnam's orientation toward the Soviet Union changed a degree of this. The rhetorical structure of the Brezhnev Doctrine changed the concept to make it more specific and pushed aside the other epithets contained in the concept. Together with the concept of socialist internationalism, it was also used to explain the relations between Indochina and the socialist community and this reduced its value for Vietnam to emphasize the independence of Indochina from Soviet influence.

VIETNAM, ASEAN AND THE TWO CAMPS THEORY

The political vocabulary, including that of foreign relations, had developed during Hanoi's struggle to unify Vietnam and carry out the socialist revolution in the North. The starting points were the *ai thang ai* struggle and the two camps theory, which supported both of these two tasks as well as forming the basis of the doctrinal code. Although Marxist-Leninist parlance possessed the vocabulary to deal with the new situation following the unification in the spring of 1975, the Vietnamese data published after the fall of Saigon proved that Hanoi had difficulties creating an unambiguous policy toward its capitalists neighbors in Southeast Asia. Obviously, there were external reasons for this, such as the competition between the Soviet Union and China to increase their influence in the area while the United States was withdrawing its military presence from Southeast Asia; but this explained things only in part. The problem brought by the Sino–Soviet dispute to Vietnam's Southeast Asian policy was followed by new problems arising from the conflict between Vietnam and Democratic Kampuchea and involving Southeast Asia as a whole.

This chapter seeks answers to the questions about how Vietnam fit its foreign policy concerning the rest of Southeast Asia into this context so as to conform to the Marxist-Leninist doctrine.

The reasons for Vietnam's ambiguous orientation may lie in the Southeast Asian countries themselves. They were Third World countries with a colonial heritage; but, at the same time, they had a strong capitalistic orientation, some of them having very close political and military ties with Vietnam's main enemy, the United States. Similarly, most of them had supported South Vietnam's government during the war and the involvement of the U.S. in it; and two of them, Thailand and the Philippines, had even participated in the hostilities by sending troops and offering air bases to the Americans.

In fact, the Southeast Asian capitalist countries seemed to be better prepared for the new political situation than Hanoi. When the power of the United States in the area appeared to be on the wane, the Southeast Asian countries, including Thailand, Malaysia, Singapore, Indonesia and the Philippines, took a purely Southeast Asian alignment under consideration. However, it is simplistic to claim that ASEAN (Association of Southeast Asian Nations) was founded solely to oppose the influence of Socialist Vietnam or the Cultural Revolution of China; but there also existed interstate factors behind the Southeast Asian countries' need to create a regional organization. Despite this, when the charter of ASEAN was signed in Bangkok in 1967, the defeat of the U.S. in Vietnam was not yet to be seen and there were in effect both bilateral and multilateral military commitments between the Southeast Asian countries and the Western powers. But contrary to these older agreements, which served the strategic needs of external powers more, the central idea behind ASEAN aimed at regional resilience and independence – first from their old colonial masters and then from the influence of the superpowers.[125]

Naturally, the ASEAN members had their particular interests and different kinds of security options, which did not allow any homogeneous alliance. In fact, one basic idea underlying ASEAN was to build an organization to reconcile the conflicting interests behind these countries.[126] The idea of regional resilience through regional cooperation for economic growth toward stabilizing the several societies was taken as a principal method to prevent the spread of Marxist movements in those countries.[127]

The Association rested on a loose institutional base, which was reinforced by separate agreements. Its political orientation was guided mainly by three declarations and one treaty: the Bangkok Declaration, the Kuala Lumpur Declaration of 1971, the Declaration of ASEAN Concord formulated in Bali in 1976, and the Treaty of Amity and Cooperation in Southeast Asia, signed in Bali in 1976. The Kuala Lumpur Declaration, known also as the ZOPFAN (Zone of Peace, Freedom and Neutrality) Declaration, continued the tendency, which could be observed already in the Bangkok Declaration, namely, to work toward preventing any superpower from gaining control in Southeast Asia. The Bangkok Declaration proclaimed that all the foreign bases were temporary,[128] and the ZOPFAN Declaration stressed this view further. The idea of neutralism was firmly rooted in the foreign policy of one ASEAN member, Malaysia, and it lay somewhere between the neutralism pursued by the Non-Aligned Movement and the neutralism recognized traditionally by international law.

The ZOPFAN proposal reiterated reconciliation as a principal means of maintaining stability and security in the area. Its general principles fit well into the ideology of the Non-Aligned Movement. In fact, there was only one clause that referred to neutrality. The Declaration did not offer any means of putting it into practice. It did, however, call upon the ASEAN members to seek international recognition from the major powers. In this respect, it resembled the traditional neutrality, thus departing from Non-aligned practice.[129] Nevertheless, the central issue here was to prevent outside powers from interfering in regional affairs.[130]

China was the only major power to recognize the ZOPFAN proposal without reservations. With respect to Vietnam, the attitude of China and the Soviet Union toward ZOPFAN was most interesting. In fact, owing to the Soviet idea of collective security and after the influence of the cultural revolution had diminished in China's foreign policy, the Sino–Soviet rivalry for diplomatic success in Southeast Asia really gained momentum. Interestingly enough, both countries had at first reacted coldly or at least unresponsively to the ZOPFAN proposal. The Soviet attitude turned within a relatively short time to qualified support, when common ground began to be found for ZOPFAN and the Soviet idea of an Asian collective security system. However, when the Malaysian prime minister visited Moscow, the differences were accentuated owing to the support given by the Soviets to a broader system, including all the major powers in Asia, contrary to the ZOPFAN proposal, which was made on a regional basis.[131] After the Sino–American rapprochement, China renewed its policy toward Southeast Asia and entered into diplomatic relations with the ASEAN countries (except Indonesia and Singapore). China took advantage of the cool reception given by the ASEAN member states to the Soviet idea of collective security and expressed its full support of the ZOPFAN proposal to keep the Great Powers out of the Southeast Asia region.[132]

When the Declaration of ASEAN Concord and the Treaty of Amity and Cooperation in Southeast Asia were signed in February 1976, socialist Indochina already existed. The Treaty and the Declaration aimed at closer political collaboration between the ASEAN countries. They did not include military cooperation, but the Declaration suggested security cooperation on a non-ASEAN basis between the member states.[133] The aim of a common united political line among the ASEAN countries had evidently much to do with the emergence of socialist Indochina. However, the ASEAN leaders denied that these documents were directed against Indochina, although the Malaysian foreign minister admitted that the whole development of ASEAN was closely connected with the situation in Indochina. On the other hand, he believed that the Declaration, together with the Treaty, would lead to a closer dialogue with the different parts of Southeast Asia.[134] Indeed, the Treaty gave an option to the other countries of Southeast Asia to sign it and thus join ASEAN.[135] Therefore the Treaty offered the possibility of demolishing the Cold War structure in Southeast Asia; but owing to the course of events and the possibilities allowed by the Treaty of strengthening political cooperation, it helped to bolster the Cold War constellation.

The omission of the concept of peaceful coexistence and détente from Vietnam's political vocabulary gave it an interesting aspect vis-à-vis the ASEAN countries. The absence of peaceful coexistence, together with the emphasis given the *ai thang ai* struggle as a dominant characteristic of international relations, notably when connected to the theme of national liberation, constituted one approach toward the ASEAN countries in Vietnam's foreign-policy argumentation. However, on the side, another approach was developed, one that used familiar expressions dealing with peaceful coexistence, although the relevant concept was rarely cited.

The first coherent representation of Vietnam's political line involving the ASEAN countries as a collective bloc appeared in the May 1976 issue of *Hoc Tap*. All the other broader articles on Southeast Asia had ignored the whole organization or described it briefly as a more or less dependent instrument of U.S. foreign policy.[136] The May 1976 article consisting of anonymous *Binh luan* (comment) followed the general Vietnamese trend and pointed out the theme of the struggle for national liberation as a qualifier of Vietnam's policy aimed against the ASEAN bloc. There were two important events to which the article can be connected. First, there was the Bali summit of ASEAN held in February, at which the cooperation of Southeast Asia as a whole was on the agenda; and, second, the Non-Aligned summit was scheduled to take place three months later in Colombo, Sri Lanka. In this respect, it was a response, on the one hand, to the ASEAN countries' offer of cooperation to Indochina; and, on the other hand, it was a part of the joint policy of Vietnam and Laos, first proclaimed during the Lao leadership's visit to Vietnam at the beginning of that year and then at the Colombo summit the following August.

The argumentation of *Binh luan* was based on a class analysis of international relations. It rejected the independence of ASEAN as a regional agency, but portrayed it as representing the neocolonialist Nixon doctrine in Southeast Asia. ASEAN was depicted as a collusion of U.S. strategic interests and the interest of the "ringleaders" *(nhung nguoi cam dau)* of the two dominating classes in the Southeast Asian countries: namely, those of the land-owning class and comprador bourgeoisie *(tu san mai ban)*.[137] According to this argument in the ZOPFAN Declaration of 1971, "the neutralization *(trung lap hoa)*" was aimed to "draw the puppets of Saigon, Vientiane and Phnom Penh to their [the ASEAN ringleaders'] system by making them observer members of the Association;" and it intended to eliminate the victories of Indochinese countries "by strongly promoting the status quo *(nguyen trang)* between Indochina and Southeast Asia, and defending the wavering positions of neocolonialism in the area."[138]

Interestingly enough, this Vietnamese analysis of ZOPFAN deviated from both the Soviet and Chinese approaches to neutralism in Southeast Asia. When the Soviet Union combined it with a larger arrangement in

Asia that depended on peaceful coexistence, and China accepted ZOPFAN's aim to reject all foreign powers in the area, the *Binh luan's* analysis connected it directly to the U.S. policy of suppressing the national liberation movements in the region. It concluded that the relationship of the forces between the revolutionary national independence movements and imperialism had changed, causing profound contradictions inside and between the ASEAN countries and between the peoples in power in those countries, which prevented the application of this doctrine directly in Southeast Asia. Therefore the ZOPFAN proposal was launched as an effort to lessen these contradictions in Southeast Asia.[139] Thus by emphasizing the class nature of ASEAN and its connection to the U.S., the Vietnamese pressed their different approach toward both the Soviet Union and China.

Vietnam's effort to create an independent line vis-à-vis the Soviet Union and China in its Southeast Asian politics ran very closely parallel to its relations with Laos. It is obvious that Vietnam tried to counterbalance its stance toward Sino-Soviet relations with a policy of its own, which included cooperation with Laos, in Southeast Asia. Similarly, the theme of anti-imperialist struggle, when dealing with Southeast Asia as an entity, emphasized the role of Indochinese revolutions in the area and the need to have foreign-policy objectives in harmony with current social and political developments. The coordination of Laotian and Vietnamese policies in line with this theme of national liberation movements was undertaken as early as the Laotian leaders' visit to Hanoi in February 1976. Like the *Binh luan* later, the joint statement accused the U.S. of using ASEAN as its tool to sabotage the revolutionary forces in order to maintain its positions in the Southeast Asian countries.[140] Evidently, this vocabulary tried to create the constellation of a two-bloc structure in Southeast Asia, where Indochina was one entity and a rear base of revolutionary forces in Southeast Asia and ASEAN appeared as a reactionary political phenomenon and a tool of American imperialism. Vietnam and Laos continued the similar language in their joint statement of July 18, 1977, in which they asserted that there existed aspirations to turn ASEAN into a "de facto military alliance" *(mot lien minh quan su tren thuc te)*, which opposed the main currents in Southeast Asia.[141]

However, the diplomatic turning point of the joint Lao–Vietnamese approach to Southeast Asia occurred as early as August 1976 at the Non-Aligned Summit in Colombo. The two countries coordinated their policy for Colombo earlier in February and stated as their aim promoting cooperation with the Non-Aligned and socialist countries.[142] Interestingly enough, the attack against ASEAN, or rather against the ZOPFAN proposal, was made by the Laotian president. The question involved the position of ZOPFAN in the political declaration of the Summit. The Kuala Lumpur Declaration was adopted for the Political Declaration of the Algiers Conference of 1973, where the Heads of State or Government of the Movement's member countries considered "it to be a positive contribution to the establishment of international peace and security," and appealed "to all States to respect its principles and objectives."[143] In Colombo, Laotian President Souphanouvong, supported by Vietnam's Pham Van Dong with somehow similar expressions, suggested the creation in Southeast Asia of "a zone of genuine peace" to guarantee that the countries in that zone live in "peaceful coexistence and friendship."[144] Pham Van Dong did not deal with the ASEAN proposal for the formation of the zone in detail, but he did mention Vietnam's new approach, the four-point program for a solution to the problems of Southeast Asia.[145] However, Souphanouvong went deeper with his extraordinarily strong attack against ASEAN and ZOPFAN. Thus he was following the lines that the *Binh luan* represented in *Hoc Tap*. According to this, he proclaimed that the ZOPFAN declaration was "made in 1971 at a moment when the U.S. imperialists had intensified their aggressive war in Indochina and sought to require the ASEAN member countries to suppress the national liberation movement in Laos, Vietnam and Kampuchea. The content of this declaration thus hides this implication of the ASEAN member states in the action against the national liberation movements."[146]

The interesting point is that the diplomatic jargon of Vietnam here was far more modest than that of Laos, although nearly identical expressions had been used before the Colombo Summit.[147] In fact, Souphanouvong also repeated expressions Vietnam had managed to include in the political declaration of the preparatory conference of the Colombo Summit, namely, the Non-Aligned foreign ministers' conference held in Lima the preceding year.[148] Following this, the Vietnamese did not reject the Laotian view and when Laos's representative opposed the inclusion of ZOPFAN in the final Declaration of the Colombo Conference "in view of the significant change that has occurred in Southeast Asia," they supported the Laotian proposal.[149] Thus it is more than believable that the Vietnamese and Laotian policies in Colombo were coordinated in advance. Although the Non-Aligned Countries of ASEAN (Indonesia, Malaysia and Singapore), primarily Malaysia, supported by Indonesia, tried to defend ZOPFAN as part of the political program of the Movement,[150] the ZOPFAN proposal was dropped from the Political Declaration of the Colombo Conference.[151]

Before the Colombo Conference, the way Vietnam raised the theme of the revolutionary struggle for liberation, when dealing with the Southeast Asian capitalist countries and especially ASEAN, indicated that its targets were not these countries, for the themes were part of the autocommunication between Vietnam and Laos, on the one hand, and, on the other hand, inside Vietnam's political structures. In fact, the *Binh luan* proved that the Vietnamese had difficulties criticizing the contents of ASEAN's declarations as such. Therefore the *Binh luan* did not try to decide what the realization of ZOPFAN might mean, but claimed that it was a "scheme and trick" *(am muu thu doan)* by which the dominating class was trying to conceal its dependence on U.S. imperialism. It emphasized that there was a striking contradiction between the Kuala Lumpur declaration and the presence of U.S. troops in Southeast Asia. The *Binh luan* also pointed out that at the same time as the ASEAN leaders at the Bali Summit emphasized respect for the independence and freedom of other countries, Indonesia sent its troops into East Timor to suppress the freedom of its people.[152] In the same tone, it concluded that at the Bali Summit, the five ASEAN member countries discussed in public mutual economic and cultural cooperation also with Indochinese countries, but its real aim was "mutual collusion *(viec cau ket voi nhau)* together with American imperialism" in order to oppose national independence movements in the member countries and to prevent the influences of the Indochinese revolutions.[153] The only answer in this situation in Southeast Asia was, according to the *Binh luan*, to resolve the contradiction between the great majority of the people and the ruling class, which was in collusion with neocolonialism. Only after the demolition of the neocolonialist system would there be a possibility to progress toward "the future of independence, peace and genuine neutrality." Thanks to three victorious revolutions in Indochina, the *Binh luan* affirmed that Southeast Asia has a bright future.[154]

There is a need, however, to examine more closely what the *Binh luan's* argumentation meant for the revolutionary national liberation struggle and the demolition of the neocolonialist system, particularly in the ASEAN countries. First, in Hanoi's vocabulary the national liberation struggle did not necessarily mean a socialist revolution, although it supposed that at a later stage these two main trends would join together. In the case of the Southeast Asian capitalist countries, it did not necessarily indicate support for the armed insurgency movements, which existed in, for example, Thailand, Malaysia and the Philippines. It rather emphasized the change in foreign policy in a national and "anti-imperialist" direction by rejecting all commitments made during the Vietnam War, notably with the Western Powers, including the ASEAN declarations and treaties. This did not call immediately for social revolutions in depth, but Hanoi insisted that the interests of the majority of the population had to direct politics. In this respect, "the main part of the upper strata *(ca nhung tang lop tren)*, which seek to develop the national economy," can lead these countries to the anti-imperialist line of foreign policy.[155]

Despite the rejection of ASEAN as a dialogue partner, Vietnam expressed its readiness to develop bilateral relations with individual Southeast Asian countries, including Thailand and the Philippines, which had political and military commitments with the U.S. However, after the Communists' complete victory in the South, the theme of national liberation and anti-imperialist struggle was brought out in Vietnam's bilateral relations with the other Southeast Asian countries. Soon after the fall of Saigon, a delegation representing South Vietnam's provisional government went to Bangkok to claim all the military matériel captured from South Vietnam. Similarly, the Vietnamese insisted that Thai authorities remove the U.S. military bases and troops from Thai territory. Thailand announced its willingness to establish diplomatic relations with Hanoi, but rejected the Vietnamese claims on grounds of international law. Hanoi let it be known that there could hardly be progress in relations with Thailand insofar as "the Thai government has provided Thai territory to the U.S.A. as important strategic areas for its neo-colonialism."[156] Similarly, these themes were raised when Hanoi gave its support to Laos and Kampuchea in their border clashes with Thailand and when diplomatic support was given to the FRETILIN (Frente Revolucionária de Timor Leste Independente) in East Timor against Indonesia to bolster the national independence struggle in Southeast Asia.[157] Even after diplomatic relations were established with Thailand, the theme of anti-imperialist struggle was not totally discarded. An expression used frequently by Vietnam and Laos, one following the definition adopted by the 4th Party Congress, affirmed that these countries "support without reservations the Thai peoples' struggle for national independence, democracy, peace and genuine neutrality, without the military bases and forces of imperialism in their territory."[158]

The Vietnamese were ready to apply the concept of peaceful coexistence in dealings with the capitalist countries of Southeast Asia, but not with ASEAN. This critical approach toward ASEAN serves Vietnam's policy in several ways: It showed both to the Soviet Union and China that Vietnam had an independent line in its foreign policy toward the rest of Southeast Asia. Similarly, it connected the foreign policy of

Laos and Vietnam and strengthened the identification of Indochina as a bloc in the *ai thang ai* struggle in Southeast Asia. Along with the theme of the national liberation struggle, Vietnam's foreign policy toward Southeast Asia was linked to the previous struggle against the U.S. and the Saigon government, thus joining the foreign policy in this way to the ideological basis of the Vietnamese Marxist-Leninist movement. Therefore the viewpoints expressed by the *Binh luan* as well as the foregoing diplomatic parlance draw the conclusion from the premises of class struggle that adhere consistently to the pattern of formal argumentation.

However, this was only a part of Vietnam's foreign policy in relations with the rest of Southeast Asia. When Vietnam's approach to ASEAN is connected to its policy to individual Southeast Asian countries, the general picture becomes more complicated. The double-edged approach to the other Southeast Asian countries appears in documents of the 4th Party Congress, which state that Vietnamese foreign policy "fully supports the just struggle of the peoples in Southeast Asia for national independence, democracy, peace and genuine neutrality, that is to say, without military bases and troops of the imperialists in their territories," but was, however, ready to develop the relations with the ASEAN countries "on the basis of respect for each other's independence, sovereignty and territorial integrity, non-aggression and non-interference in each other's internal affairs, equality, mutual benefit and peaceful coexistence."[159]

This definition of Vietnam's foreign policy in Southeast Asia thus divides into two. First, there was the theme of anti-imperialist struggle in rather unambiguous form, which was concentrated on the efforts to have the American bases and troops removed from Southeast Asia. This theme was described in the foregoing. The other part of the definition dealt with the necessity to recognize certain realities in the area. This emphasizes the pragmatic tones in the foreign-policy arguments.

The Vietnamese expression of "independence, peace and genuine neutrality" has been considered as a counterpart, or even counterproposal, to ASEAN's ZOPFAN. It is more or less uncertain when the expression occurred for the first time. Nguyen Duy Trinh used it when he defined Vietnam's policy toward Southeast Asia in 1974. He connected the expression to the U.S.'s total withdrawal from Southeast Asia.[160] In the Political Declaration of the Non-Aligned foreign ministers' conference held in Lima in August 1975, there was a passage that referred clearly to the Vietnamese expression, which became established only later.[161] In its most restricted form, a language problem crops up where *doc lap, hoa binh va trung lap that su* can be translated in two ways. First, as it occurs mainly in the official translations of Vietnamese documents, *that su* (genuine) qualifies only the term *trung lap* (neutrality). However, there also exists the translation used most often in the ASEAN countries, where the word "genuine" qualifies every term of the expression. This did not cause any confusion so far as the expression "without the military bases and forces of imperialism" was connected to the sentence; but the problem arose when this was omitted. Thus the syntagm "genuine independence, peace and neutrality" connoted differently from "independence, peace and genuine neutrality." In the former case, the form of neutrality does not appear in special focus as it does in the latter. The former expression can also be used to question Hanoi's starting points in Vietnam's policy toward the ASEAN countries, if it does not recognize that these countries are genuinely independent.[162] The latter refers clearly to the meaning of neutrality, which differs according to whether foreign troops and bases are involved or not. There was also the expression *moi that su doc lap, tu do* (genuinely independent and free), which was used with reference to the future of Southeast Asia.[163] So far as the Vietnamese did not consider that fundamental improvements in their relations with the ASEAN countries were necessary, they did not regard this as an essential question. However, when Vietnam's deputy foreign minister was visiting Singapore after his government had started their new approach to ASEAN, he denied that Vietnam had put forward any clause of "genuine independence" when it had dealt with the zone question.[164]

The Vietnamese expression of "peace, independence and genuine neutrality" can be called a "proposal" only with strong reservations. It is true that it was a counterpart of ZOPFAN, emphasizing the demand for the withdrawal of all U.S. troops from Southeast Asia. Contrary to what is believed,[165] no official proposal like the Kuala Lumpur declaration was ever formulated. The most authoritative documents to come to light were the political report of the 4th Party Congress and the Vietnam-Laos Treaty. The expression was rather part of Vietnam's anti-imperialist vocabulary in Hanoi's struggle to boost the prestige of the Non-Aligned Movement, and the language reflected Vietnam's position in Southeast Asia. When the Vietnamese named China as their immediate enemy in the summer of 1978, Hanoi abandoned this expression.

Actually, Vietnam did submit a comprehensive proposal on how to arrange the relations between Southeast Asian countries. Instead of working on a collective basis, the proposal called for a system of bilateral relations. Vietnam managed to include it in its joint communiqué with Thailand on the establishment of their diplomatic relations, and Bangkok welcomed Hanoi's "four-point policy" as a correct approach toward the other Southeast Asian countries.[166] The four-point policy, which Nguyen Duy Trinh presented a day before the Vietnamese–Thai communiqués were issued, did include an expression about the development of relations "for the sake of independence, peace and genuine neutrality in Southeast Asia,"[167] but this was only part of a broader entity. In fact, it was formulated after a model used by the Non-Aligned Movement, including respect for the independence, sovereignty and territorial integrity of nations, non-aggression, non-interference and peaceful coexistence, together with cultural exchange and economic cooperation (first and third points). The second point, which forbade "any foreign country to use one's territory as a base for direct or indirect aggression and intervention against any other country or countries in the region;" and the fourth point, which reiterated the theme of independence, peace and genuine neutrality in Southeast Asia, reflected more clearly the common Vietnamese parlance about Southeast Asia.[168]

Evidently, the four-point program included elements quite different from pure anti-imperialist struggle. It deviated from formalist vocabulary. However, the attention given peaceful coexistence here is most interesting. It drew on the mature Marxist-Leninist jargon as well as the established vocabulary of the Non-Aligned Movement, which was surely familiar to the non-aligned members of ASEAN. Thus the concept included two code systems. It therefore has a double meaning to Hanoi. By means of the concept, Hanoi communicated its intention to approach the ASEAN member states. Simultaneously, by expressing the concept, Hanoi kept the vocabulary within the limits of the Marxist-Leninist doctrine. Nevertheless, the ASEAN members refrained from resorting to it when dealing with Vietnam. More important to them was the fact that the first point convinced the ASEAN governments that Vietnam dissociated itself from the Marxist insurgency movements in these countries. The second point was acceptable also to Thailand in the situation where it had just decided to close the U.S. military bases in the country. In the four-point program, there was an obvious lack of a common anti-imperialist and Marxist-Leninist vocabulary, indicating strongly that this program was really directed to the other Southeast Asian countries and not for the purpose of enforcing the doctrinal code.

Although Vietnam's negative attitude toward ZOPFAN was confirmed at the Colombo Summit, it did not dramatically change Vietnam's bilateral relations with the ASEAN countries. There were at least two reasons for this. First, the ASEAN countries were not unanimous about the real content of the concept. The concept reflected mostly Malaysian and, with respect to a minor part, Indonesian foreign-policy objectives, whereas Thailand and the Philippines were not ready to realize it; and, as it seemed, the idea of Southeast Asia without the counterbalancing factor of the superpower rivalry ran counter to Singapore's intention.[169] In the second place, no strong hopes were held that Vietnam might join ZOPFAN in the post-Indochina war situation. Rather did there exist worries that Vietnam was going to join hands with either the Soviet Union or China in its Southeast Asian politics. Against this possibility, it was well enough that Vietnam followed an independent line in relations with the ASEAN countries, one that did not include support to the Marxist movements in these countries.[170]

In this respect, Vietnam's four-point policy satisfied the ASEAN countries. Their attitudes toward Vietnam varied, with Malaysia and Indonesia maintaining the most moderate stance toward Indochina, although recognition of ZOPFAN in the Non-Aligned Movement was an important part of Malaysian foreign policy. However, according to the official optimism of the Malaysian government, the growing dialogue between Indochina and the ASEAN countries would reveal to Vietnam the real intentions behind ASEAN and ZOPFAN.[171] Thailand's approach was divided when the civilian administration tried to develop relations, but the military maintained a rather hard line against Communist Indochina. The Singaporean leaders' statements about Indochina and Vietnam remained rather cautious. Singapore paid attention to Hanoi's vocabulary of anti-imperialist struggle and suggested that the other ASEAN countries take Hanoi's rhetoric seriously. Despite the fact that it did not reject closer relation with Indochina, Singapore emphasized the fundamental differences between the social systems of Indochina and the ASEAN countries so that the cooperation between these two blocs could never rise above a certain degree and never reach the same level as that between the ASEAN countries.[172]

Hanoi's rhetoric relating to the other Southeast Asian countries tended to depend on the realities in the area instead of maintaining its former quasi-logical character. Vietnam began to reconsider its approach toward the ASEAN countries in the latter part of 1977, when its conflict with Kampuchea worsened and the tension with China had started to increase. The turning point occurred in the summer of 1978, when Hanoi identified China as its immediate enemy. Hanoi's new approach culminated in two high-level Vietnamese tours of Southeast Asia, first Foreign Minister Nguyen Duy Trinh's visit to the ASEAN countries at the end of 1977 and the beginning of 1978 and that of Prime Minister Pham Van Dong in September 1978.

In line with its new approach, Hanoi made known its intention to develop closer interaction with these countries; but it also gave signals that the Vietnamese were ready to open up relations with ASEAN on an institutional basis. The first sign of this was seen when the Vietnamese dropped the word "genuine" out of its policy objective aiming at peace, independence and neutrality in Southeast Asia. In the joint communiqué issued at the end of Nguyen Duy Trinh's visit to Indonesia, the formulation was that the relations between the countries in the region should be "based on peace, neutrality, independence and cooperation."[173] Although this formulation had strongly approached ASEAN's ZOPFAN and ignored the theme of anti-imperialist struggle, Hanoi hesitated to discuss ZOPFAN publicly.

However, there took place in Vietnam's Communist Party circles discussions on how to deal with ZOPFAN and ASEAN in general. This discussion emphasized terms like "peace" and "stability" *(on dinh)* as a policy objective in the field of Southeast Asian cooperation in a situation where China tried to separate Vietnam from the rest of Southeast Asia. Interestingly enough, these terms were now connected to the principles of peaceful coexistence, a theme that Vietnam had avoided using since the fall of Saigon. Moreover, there were expressions of Vietnamese interest in ZOPFAN. In regard to ZOPFAN, the Vietnamese, as one Party cadre argued, were ready to change their "views to discuss, together with the other countries in the region, the matters connected with the creation of a Southeast Asian zone of peace and neutrality *(mot khu vuc Dong Nam A hoa binh trung lap)*."[174]

Vietnam's representative at the UN's tenth special session on disarmament in June 1978 used the somehow obscure expression "zone of peace," which had been common in the Soviet vocabulary when dealing with neutralism. However, the Malaysian foreign minister had also used the expression "zone of peace" when speaking of ZOPFAN.[175] Evidently, the context in which Vietnam's representative commented on this question referred to regional disarmament and neutralism, issues relating to which Vietnam was ready to take part as an answer to the Malaysian offer to put ZOPFAN into practice. He did not reject the ZOPFAN concept, but emphasized that "all aspects of such a zone should be clearly defined by agreement among the countries of the region, without interference from countries outside it,"[176] while the Malaysian proposal at the same session was "not intended to curtail the rights of outside Powers to pursue their legitimate political and economic relations with the zonal States."[177]

During Pham Van Dong's visit to the ASEAN states in September, Vietnam continued its rapprochement with ASEAN and obviously tried to find a compromise in the zone question. However, both Democratic Kampuchea and China had also intensified their diplomatic activities in the ASEAN countries, and the reaction of the ASEAN countries to Pham Van Dong's visit, although it was welcomed, was also cautious. The ASEAN leaders turned down the idea of a non-aggression treaty proposed by Vietnam's prime minister to each ASEAN member country. The formulation of the joint statements of the visit, however, referred to Dong's proposal.[178] Nevertheless, the ASEAN countries wanted to stay neutral in the conflict between Vietnam, Kampuchea and China, and though some of them (Indonesia and Malaysia) had earlier showed a tendency to compromise with Vietnam, they wanted to maintain a common ASEAN stand in the zone question. Thus the bilateral joint statements of Vietnam and the respective ASEAN countries contained nearly the identical expression concerning this question. Vietnam had even accepted the term "freedom," which it had avoided using in dealing with the zone question but the ASEAN countries refused to compromise with the ZOPFAN concept, as in their joint statements with Vietnam, they expressed their commitments to the ZOPFAN.[179]

Despite the fact that Vietnam's new ASEAN policy got stuck on the Kampuchean question, there had already taken place major changes in Vietnam's foreign-policy orientation. When, after the fall of Saigon, Vietnam's Southeast Asian policy stressed the theme of anti-imperialist struggle and connected it to Vietnam's previous struggles against U.S. imperialism, the relation to the Marxist-Leninist doctrinal code was very close. Nonetheless, this theme regarding ASEAN emphasized Vietnam's independent policy relating to Southeast Asia vis-à-vis the Soviet Union and China.

However, the changes from the anti-imperialist struggle to a more conventional foreign policy impeded the linking of foreign policy to internal mobilization, and forced other themes to rise to formulate and promote a new approach. This took place simultaneously with the change from formal to pragmatic argumentation in Hanoi's relations with the governments of ASEAN. Interestingly enough, Hanoi's tendency to turn from the formalist to the pragmatic approach was opposite to its dealings with Sino–Soviet realations as well as with Democratic Kampuchea. This showed how the Vietnamese rhetoric was closely related to the audience, and, in this case, did not indicate that the general "formalist" trend was developing in Hanoi.

VIETNAM, THE NON-ALIGNED MOVEMENT AND THE UNITED NATIONS

In contrast to many other newly independent countries, unified Vietnam kept a high profile in its international relations immediately after it had joined international organizations. Although it was not admitted to membership in the United Nations until the 32th general session in the fall of 1977, it took part in the activities of the Non-Aligned Movement as early as the summer of 1975. In fact, the Provisional Revolutionary Government of South Vietnam had been a full member of the movement since the Algiers Summit of 1973 and as an observer at the Lusaka Summit of 1970.[180] On account of anti-imperialism's and anti-colonialism's being held as the main elements of the Non-Aligned ideology, Hanoi had enjoyed a high status in the movement even before Vietnam became a member. This was further advanced by Vietnam's policy of staying neutral in the Sino–Soviet conflict, which was in conformity with the principles of non-alignment.[181]

From the point of view of rhetorical analysis, this chapter differs from earlier chapters in one important respect: the crucial question is not the specific substance of argumentation, but the themes by which Vietnam selected its audience. The special interest here focuses on how the Vietnamese dealt with the question of addressing a particular audience, in addition to the "global audience," on how the use of themes are formulated in the course of political developments and on how these are related to the different argumentation patterns. The "global audience" means here the whole gamut of people committed to the basic principles of the organizations involved. In this respect, this "global audience" differs from the membership of the Non-Aligned Movement and the United Nations. Although Vietnam appeared in these organizations as a champion mainly of the themes not including concrete issues of Vietnam's foreign policy, the political and theoretical commitments underlying these themes connected them closely to such issues as the Sino-Soviet dispute and Vietnam's position in Southeast Asia.

After the fall of Saigon, the Non-Aligned Movement was the arena in which Vietnam's foreign-policy profile took shape. It was the place where the action, foreign-policy themes, and the Marxist-Leninist doctrinal code seemed to be in the greatest harmony. There may be several reasons for this, but three of them were quite obvious. The first was the ideology of the Movement, into which it was easy for Vietnam to fit its foreign-policy themes. The second was the international situation in the Third

World at the time that Vietnam's activities began in the Movement. Finally, there were certain elements in the organizational structure of the Non-Aligned Movement that strengthened Vietnam's positions there.

The theme of anti-imperialist struggle as a part of Vietnam's revolutionary national struggle, in particular, and that of the national liberation struggle in the colonial countries, in general, were emphasized as early as 1960 in the 3rd Party Congress documents. Similarly, they gained an important part in the concept of three revolutionary currents at the beginning of the 1970s. Consequently, the anti-colonialist Third World movement was a natural forum for Vietnam in which to proclaim its foreign policy. In contrast to the other Third World group, Group 77, which includes all the Third World countries, the Non-Aligned Movement had more specific common denominators than economic underdevelopment alone. Moreover, the membership has consisted not only of independent states but also national liberation movements and other organizations. Originally, non-alignment was an expression of the sovereignty of newly independent countries in Africa and Asia in the context of the Cold War. Thus it included two characteristics. The expression of its anti-colonialist nature, which took on more anti-imperialistic features, toward the 1970s, was a fundamental element, which brought the founding countries together. Along with this anti-colonialist stance of the member countries, the intent of keeping out of the Cold War conflict was similarly a basic component of the Movement. In brief, the Movement tried to promote the struggle to raise the status of these countries vis-à-vis the developed countries by the policy of avoiding involvement in the Cold War. In connection with these two denominators, the member countries adopted certain basic principles on how to work out mutual relations as well as relations with the Third World and with industrialized countries.

These two determinators also determined the various member countries' positions in the Movement. Therefore the emphasis laid by members on either neutrality in the conflicts between the superpowers or the anti-imperialistic stance had pointed out their place in the axis between the moderates and the radicals in the Movement. However, the form given the concept of peaceful coexistence, which the Movement had adopted, emphasized the degree of tolerance toward different social systems in the international community. In the Non-Aligned Movement's vocabulary, the concept of peaceful coexistence did not deal, though not excluding it, with the relations between the superpowers but rather with the relations between a Non-Aligned country and other countries, including both Third World and industrialized countries, whether they belonged to two major blocs or not. The concept amounted to a basic principle in international relations and not a particular application of diplomacy in the special circumstance of the international class struggle.[182] The original documents did not suggest preferences for political, social and economic systems, which members should adopt, but stressed the fact that there existed, and was going to exist, distinct kinds of systems. Consequently, despite its anti-colonialist and anti-imperialistic stance, the Movement represented the interests of its members only on the international level and had not brought them together on account of common social and political ideals.[183]

In the 1970s, there began to occur a remarkable shift from the neutralist position of the Non-Aligned Movement in the Great Power competition to a more radical stance. There were several factors behind this. First, both China and the Soviet Union had started to show interest in the Movement. In the second place, there emerged between 1973 and 1976 several new Marxist-oriented states that joined the Movement, and finally certain radical members, especially Cuba, intensified their activity in the Third World and raised their profile inside the Movement. These factors surfaced for the first time at the Algiers Conference. The political declaration of the Algiers Summit still reflected strong neutralist tendencies and an intention to avoid the Great Power struggle inside the Movement.[184] However, behind the scenes there existed clear differences about how to deal with the Chinese and Soviet approaches toward the Third World in general and toward the Movement in particular. In fact, the draft resolution, which was authorized by the host country, Algeria, criticized both East and West, in tones similar to those of China. Together with the Soviet response, in which L.I. Brezhnev proclaimed that the socialist countries were the natural allies of the Non-Aligned countries, Cuba attacked the Algerian view of the superpowers and managed to prevent Algeria's draft resolution. There occurred in the political resolution a single word, "hegemonism," which referred to Chinese terminology and obviously also to Algeria's draft resolution; but, contrary to this, the economic declaration contained vehement anti-imperialist vocabulary, reflecting a clearly antiwestern attitude and putting special blame for the Third World's economic straits on the developed capitalist countries.[185]

The tension between these different tendencies increased at the Colombo Summit. The appearance of Vietnam, together with other new Marxist-oriented member states, turned the Movement in a more anti-imperialist and antiwestern direction. There are some organizational factors in the Movement that facilitated the formal approval of Vietnam's policy and also strengthened the radical tendency in the Movement, especially after the Colombo Summit. The Movement has been based on a loose organization without any permanent institution or secretary. The highest authoritative organ is the Conference of the Heads of States or Governments of the Non-Aligned members. Since the Lusaka Conference of 1970, it has met at three-year intervals. The host country in each case becomes the leader of the Movement until the next meeting; and, similarly, this country coordinates the activities of the Movement and takes care of the secretarial responsibilities of the Non-Aligned group. Besides this influential status bestowed on the presidential country, the Coordinating Bureau, which includes approximately one-fourth of the members, is given the important task of directing the Movement. Its function is to form the preliminary consensus, which is further reinforced at the foreign ministers' conference of the Non-Aligned Countries, for the Summit Conference of the heads of state. The consensus of the Summit Conference has been represented by declarations, action programs and resolutions, which require formal unity. No formal votes are cast, and if any member disagrees, this is registered as a dissenting opinion. Thus the decisions of the Movement bind its members only morally; and there have been only a few that have presupposed concrete action on the part of the member country.[186] However, this kind of decision making, directed to declarations and to decisions that do not call for concrete measures opposed to member countries' interests, fits well into Vietnam's interests to expres its anti-imperialist stance with like-minded governments. Vietnam's possibilities to direct the Movement from its side strengthened substantially when it was elected to the Coordinating Bureau at the Colombo Conference.

When Vietnam joined the Non-Aligned Movement on the eve of the Colombo Conference, some signs appeared that Vietnam might adopt a radical approach like Cuba's inside the Movement. The first Vietnamese comments on non-alignment and Hanoi's policy, as brought out at the preparatory meetings before Colombo, added to this impression. The analysis of *Hoc Tap* immediately after the Non-Aligned's Foreign Ministers' Conference in Lima clearly supported the anti-imperialist tendency in the Movement. In fact, this analysis concluded that it was also the dominating tendency of the Movement. Accordingly, "the essence of non-alignment of the Movement – as the Summit Conferences of the Non-Aligned Countries have decided – is a constructive principle, which is definitely different from passive neutralism." This analysis, which was also partly broadcast by Hanoi Radio,[187] placed the Movement into the framework of Marxist-Leninist theory. Thus "the Movement of the Non-Aligned Countries is a side of the national liberation movement and is leading the offense of the world revolution against imperialism."[188] Therefore it argued that Vietnam "has joined the Organization of the Non-Aligned Countries mainly for the sake of the revolution of the world peoples of which the Vietnamese revolution is a part." It did not hesitate to connect its policy in the Non-Aligned Movement to Vietnam's revolutionary project, which was extending now to a global scale: "Being a socialist member country of the organization of Non-Aligned Countries, the Democratic Republic of Vietnam, together with other socialist countries, will not only struggle for peace, independence, democracy and socialism, but also unite with revolutionary world forces in the struggle against imperialism, colonialism and neo-colonialism." However, the assurance that Vietnam "undertakes never to participate in a military alliance on its own territory" proves that also the element of non-committal to any great-power alliance was useful to Vietnam at that moment.[189]

This sophisticated anti-imperialist delineation occurred as early as August 1975 at the Conference of Non-Aligned foreign ministers in Lima. The Vietnamese, who actually had two delegations, one representing the DRV and the other the Provisional Government of South Vietnam, did not totally reject the rather moderate appraisal of the international situation in the Political Declaration, but wanted to revise it somewhat. Vietnam made a proposal in which the Non-Aligned Countries were urged to intensify "their struggle against colonialism, neo-colonialism and racism," and to "oppose the aggression by imperialism against developing countries."[190] Although this revision was not accepted for inclusion in the Political Declaration of the Lima Conference, it contained obvious expressions of the influence of Indochinese countries. The most apparent were the paragraphs dealing with Southeast Asia, to which I already referred to in an earlier chapter. The foreign ministers stated their "profound concern that imperialism persists in maintaining its military presence in Southeast Asia, thus constituting a threat to the peace and security of the region." Therefore "the Non-Aligned Countries reaffirm their unconditional support of the struggle of the Southeast Asian countries for genuine independence, peace, freedom and neutrality, for the liquidation of the military bases and of the military presence of imperialism in this region, for the dissolution of SEATO, thus permitting the peoples of Southeast Asia to live in peace, good neighborliness and cooperation, in conformity with the ten Bandung Principles."[191]

These paragraphs contain several interesting points. First, the affirmation was nearly identical to the one adopted later by the Vietnamese and the Laotians. The word "freedom" refers to the fact that there had been some kind of compromise with the ZOPFAN concept and consensus arrived at by Vietnam and Laos with the non-aligned ASEAN members. However, in the light of ASEAN's later policy line of defending the ZOPFAN concept, the ASEAN countries gave up the concept surprisingly easily. Together with the total omission of the concept from the Political Declaration, which also served as the preparatory draft for the Colombo Declaration, the ASEAN countries passed the item without any reservations. In fact, this was a continuation of practices from the preceding Coordinating Bureau's meetings, where the ZOPFAN concept had failed to be mentioned in the Bureau's documents, although Malaysia was one of the members of the Coordinating Bureau. This all indicated that not even the ASEAN members of the Non-Aligned Movement shared any similar interest in the ZOPFAN proposal and that their views differed from each other on its importance in the Non-Aligned Movement at that moment.[192]

There were also other statements in the Non-Aligned's documents that reflect the growing influence of the Marxist governments and especially that of Vietnam in the Movement. In the Lima Declaration, the theme of anti-imperialist struggle was strengthened further. Indochinese revolutions were mentioned as "a favorable feature of present international developments," and the expressions "American imperialism" and "United States imperialism" occurred several times, referring directly to the one superpower without any balancing statement about the other. However, the Declaration did not directly support the Soviet Union's policy either. There occurred a paragraph directed critically at the progress of détente, which was, according to this, "limited in its scope by the hardening of hegemonic and imperialistic pretensions in all their manifestations," referring to Beijing's language.[193] Characteristic of Vietnam's policy at that moment, Hanoi let this language be passed over without any reservations. This indicated that it was Vietnam's purpose to avoid carrying out Soviet or Chinese objectives in the Movement.

Although Hanoi continued to give qualified support to connecting the policies of the socialist countries and the Non-Aligned Countries, it did not want to back Soviet policy the way Cuba did. In this respect, Vietnam's situation was difficult, as both Moscow and Beijing tried to influence the results of the Colombo Summit. They accused each other of attempting to use the Movement for their own purposes both at the global level in general and in the Sino–Soviet struggle in particular.[194] In this context, the Soviet Union joined the Indochinese countries' policy in the Non-Aligned Movement as part of the "progressive" member countries' move to unite the socialist and Non-Aligned countries in a common front.

Moscow tried to persuade Vietnam to accept the Soviet détente at Colombo by claiming that détente was the precondition to Indochinese victories.[195] On its part, China claimed that Moscow was trying to divide the Non-Aligned Countries into progressives and conservatives, and thus eliminate the danger the Movement represented to Soviet imperialism.[196]

In this context, Vietnam's performance at the Colombo Summit was most interesting. Pham Van Dong's speech at the Conference reflected Hanoi's disapproval of China's and the Soviet Union's meddling tactics toward the Movement. He avoided using Marxist-Leninist vocabulary, and his intention to emphasize Vietnam's non-aligned profile was obvious. Thus, in this respect, there emerged a striking difference from Hanoi's earlier attitudes. Dong acknowledged the importance of the economic cooperation between the Third World and the socialist countries. Speaking of the shared interests of Vietnam and the socialist countries, he emphasized that their relations should be developed on "the basis of the principles of respect for each other's independence and sovereignty, equality between partners, mutual aid, and mutual benefit." But what followed then was one of the strongest manifestations of self-reliance that Vietnam had made at the international forums. Dong did not hesitate to bring the capitalist and socialist countries together: "So, by the growth of our own economic potential, by the strengthening of cooperation among the Non-Aligned countries, by the expansion of our relations with the socialist countries and the developed capitalist countries, we create the necessary forces for ourselves to develop an independent economy, to impose the suppression of the old economic order, and to advance toward establishing a new international economic order. This struggle is an arduous and protracted one, but we will win."[197]

In the light of this broader framework, it was quite understandable that the Vietnamese did not want to emphasize the ZOPFAN question at Colombo. Thus the four-point policy cited by Pham Van Dong referred both to the principles of the Non-Aligned Movement and Vietnam's independent policy toward Southeast Asia. Equally, just as there was no mention of the ZOPFAN concept in the Political Declaration of Colombo, neither was there any hard-line characterization of the Southeast Asian situation as in the Lima Declaration of foreign ministers. Moreover, he used rather moderate phraseology when dealing with the theme of anti-imperialist struggle, avoiding any deviation from the general trend of the Non-Aligned countries. The argumentation was based purely on pragmatic patterns, ignoring typical Marxist-Leninist formalism. In this respect, the Lao president, for example, represented a far more radical approach. In fact, there occurred in the Political Declaration, in the paragraphs dealing with the Indochinese countries, condemnations of imperialism and comments about U.S.–Vietnam relations nearly identical to those in Pham Van Dong's speech. These included Vietnam's demand that the U.S. contribute to the restoration of Vietnam's economy from the damages of the war, according to the Paris agreement of 1973, and that the United Nations Security Council accept Vietnam's application for membership in the UN. In every case, Dong's language proved that Vietnam was trying to adhere to the general lines followed by the Movement.[198]

Pham Van Dong's speech at the plenary meeting in Colombo did not support the Soviet Union or China in their policy toward the Non-Aligned Movement, but tried to emphasize Vietnam's participation in this movement. Therefore the Sino–Soviet conflict moderated Vietnam's anti-imperialist stance and placed emphasis on Vietnam's non-aligned politics. Thus there developed a rather different kind of parlance when Vietnam was dealing with the Movement as compared with Vietnam's general foreign-policy language. Although the theme of anti-imperialism supported strongly Vietnam's Marxist-Leninist doctrinal code, there was also the danger that it might connect Vietnam with the Sino–Soviet rift in the Movement, as opposed to Vietnam's obvious intention to emphasize its independent policy. However, despite the fact that Vietnam considered itself to be a socialist country, it avoided being counted, in the context of the Non-Aligned Movement, as a representative of the socialist bloc. Even after Vietnam's relations with China were disrupted, it characterized its foreign relations as socialist and non-aligned.[199]

In spite of the fact that the same themes recurred in both Vietnam's non-aligned policy and its policy presented at the UN, the difference between the audience at Colombo and at the UN caused clear changes in Vietnam's foreign-policy themes. Just as at Colombo Vietnam had tried to avoid themes that might divide the audience, at the UN it used themes that selected their auditors quite discriminatingly. Following the line of Vietnam's foreign-policy orientation, this was quite natural. Broadly speaking, all the Non-Aligned Countries, so far as they were committed to anti-imperialism, were considered in Vietnamese vocabulary as revolutionary forces and the allies of Vietnam's revolution. By contrast, the United Nations consisted of all kinds of states, including the imperialist powers, especially Vietnam's arch-enemy, the United States. Although there were some contacts between Hanoi and Washington regarding the normalization of relations after the Carter administration took power, Vietnam behaved toughly in public toward the U.S., in conformity with Vietnam's anti-imperialist theme.[200] While in Colombo the Sino–Soviet rift restrained Vietnam from emphasizing the theme of the anti-imperialist struggle, this situation did not prevail in the United Nations. In the United Nations, Vietnam did not need to watch its words in order to avoid falling into the middle of the Sino–Soviet struggle, because the Soviet Union and China did not have the same interests in this forum as in the Non-Aligned Movement. Thus Hanoi was better able to wage its anti-imperialist struggle through UN diplomatic channels.

Foreign Minister Nguyen Duy Trinh's first speech at the United Nations' General Assembly in September 1977 departed thus in many ways from Pham Van Dong's address in Colombo. It followed in major respects the formalist Marxist-Leninist foreign-policy line drawn at the 4th Party Congress. Accordingly, Trinh's speech argued for the central significance of three revolutionary currents. By using this concept, he analyzed the main international trends taking place at that moment. As noted earlier, the concept justified the view linking the national liberation movements and socialist countries together. In conformity with this, Trinh contended at the General Assembly that the developing socialist system had provided a universal way for national liberation and social emancipation.[201] He described Vietnam's victory over the United States as a common victory of mankind against imperialism, and drew the following conclusion: "The victory of Viet Nam demonstrates this shining truth of our times: that a nation, however small, provided it is closely united and determined to fight according to a correct line and provided that it enjoys the sympathy and the support of progressive mankind, is wholly capable of defeating all aggressors... Such is the raison d'être of all peoples and the goal of our international community."[202] He thus made of this domestic project of Vietnam's, which was extended also to its foreign relations, a universal principle. This foreign minister's revolutionary vocabulary indicated that Vietnam did not undertake to communicate with all the UN members, but to show its place in this organization at the forefront of the world's revolutionary forces.

However, the foreign minister's speech was not purely self-motivation between like-minders, but it also marked out a political delineation. When dealing with Vietnam's partners on the level of foreign relations, Nguyen Duy Trinh offered some clarifications, meant to emphasize Vietnam's own approach to the United Nations. To the socialist countries, he stated that Vietnam was carrying out an independent foreign policy, intended to strengthen solidarity and cooperation with both the Soviet Union and China.[203] He was thus trying to affirm that the adoption of the Soviet vocabulary did not mean Vietnam's shifting to the Soviet side in the Sino–Soviet rift. With respect to Southeast Asia, the emphasis on peaceful coexistence as the base for dealing with different social systems, together with the four-point policy, was intended to reduce the suspicions of the Southeast Asian region about Vietnam's anti-imperialist and revolutionary language.[204]

At the United Nations, there were few concrete issues in connecetion with which Vietnam could argue for its anti-imperialist aims. The Vietnamese claim of U.S. responsibility in part for payments to Vietnam in the reconstruction of its war-damaged economy, according to the Paris Agreement, was not on the UN's agenda; but the organization did provide Vietnam a suitable forum to manifest its stance. In fact, negotiations had taken place between the U.S. and Vietnam for the normalization of relations, and American aid was also discussed; but Washington's point of departure was that the Paris Agreement was dead and that aid could be discussed only as a humanitarian question – and after normalization. This did not satisfy the Vietnamese, who were reluctant to receive humanitarian aid from the Americans and who wanted to show who had won the war.[205] Vietnam's claims received support from the Non-Aligned Colombo Conference. Pleading for such support, the Vietnamese demanded in the United Nations that the U.S. take real measures, "in terms of honor and responsibility."[206] Obviously, by referring to this point of departure, Trinh was arguing that the problems between Vietnam and the United States were "still outstanding with a view to normalizing the relations between the two countries."[207]

Apart from the questions concerning Vietnam itself, no major questions were on the UN's agenda at that moment to give Vietnam an opportunity to state its foreign-policy themes. Therefore the main areas in which Vietnam could show its activity now tended to involve minor global issues. These issues appeared during the last national liberation wave in the mid-1970s, and they dealt with the self-determination of certain ex-colonial territories and the question of political power there. These questions were discussed at the General Assembly under the heading of "the implementation of the declaration on granting of independence to colonial countries and peoples," which was based on the United Nations' Resolution 1514. Vietnam's interests had a twofold focus: first, the United States military bases in the Third World, namely in the Caribbean, Indian Ocean and Pacific; and, second, the East Timor question in the region of Southeast Asia.

The Vietnamese focused their policy mostly on the small islands of the so-called U.S. Outlying Territories, where the U.S. maintains important air and naval bases and other military facilities. Among these, Puerto Rico, in the Caribbean, represented a special case which Vietnam considered to be under direct colonial rule – rejecting the legacy of periodic local elections, which had given legitimacy to the U.S. sovereignty.[208] However, the Pacific region claimed Hanoi's particular attention. In Hanoi's argumentation, there were two questions that can also be connected to Vietnam's experience. The first question dealt exclusively with national self-determination, i.e., whether the military bases established in the respective areas were against the will of the local populations.[209] In their arguments the Vietnamese considered American military bases and sovereignty over "unincorporated areas" as a direct heritage of colonial rule and connected it to the United States' past policy in Indochina. Accordingly, all these refer to Washington's attempt at "the subjugation of the peoples of those territories and the destruction of their national liberation movements."[210]

Hanoi's argumentation that the bases were directed against the local people's struggle for self-determination was rather vague, as no real separatist movements had existed, excluding some legal opposition parties in these territories, notably in Puerto Rico. This was enough for Hanoi to claim that the local people were waging "a valiant struggle" against the U.S.[211] However, the economic significance of these bases to the tiny Pacific islands was so crucial that it is questionable whether the opposition elements had real support from the local inhabitants in general.

Consequently, Hanoi focused its argumentation more on the second question, namely, the threat these bases posed to other nations. Vietnam paid particular attention to one of these "unincorporated" American territories, namely, the Pacific island of Guam, from which B 52 planes made bombing raids against North Vietnam during the Vietnam war. The argumentation of Vietnam's representative in the General Assembly on its main theme of anti-imperialist struggle was revealing. He stated that Vietnam supported "unreservedly the struggle of peoples against imperialist military bases in other countries... because those bases are not only designed for the subjugation of the colonial peoples in question but also constituted a threat to the peace and security of other peoples and countries." Accordingly, the question of Guam should be considered in the context of the anticolonial struggle. The Vietnamese diplomat pointed to the use of the Guam airbase during the Vietnam war; and in the light of the General Assembly's resolution endorsing the view that the Guam base should not be directed against the right of local peoples to exercise self-determination, he urged its total and immediate dismantling. Hanoi emphasized the connection of these questions with its theme of support for national liberation struggles. The rating of the anti-imperialist struggle above other Vietnamese diplomatic activities was further demonstrated when a U.S. spokesman connected Vietnam's stance on the American bases and presence in the Pacific as well as other Third World areas to the attempt to normalize relations between the two countries. Hence the Vietnamese representative responded that the recalling of past facts illustrates "the commitment of the Vietnamese people to the common struggle of peoples" against the existence of imperialist military bases in colonial territories.[212]

The question of East Timor and the theme of anti-imperialist struggle were far more complex from the standpoint of Vietnam's foreign policy than the issue of the American military bases. In fact, the East Timor question divided in certain respects the traditional East–West and South–North axis of the United Nations. The question cropped up when the Portuguese colonial administration was demolished in the mid-1970s in the Third World, including the eastern part of the island of Timor in the Indonesian archipelago. During the colonial period, Indonesia was under Dutch rule, excepting the island of Timor, which was divided between the Dutch and Portuguese colonial administrations. When Indonesia became independent in 1949, the former colony of the western part of the island became part of the new state. During the late period of Portuguese colonialism, there developed in East Timor a Marxist-oriented national liberation movement, FRETILIN, which declared the independence of East Timor when the Portuguese gave up control. However, in July 1976, after occupying East Timor, Indonesia formally annexed it. FRETILIN's claim to independence gained diplomatic support from other old Portuguese colonies, from the socialist countries, including the Soviet Union and China, and from the Movement of Non-Aligned Countries.

The discussion on East Timor started as early as the 30th session of the General Assembly. There were aspects of the two-bloc power constellation in the discussion, but they were broken repeatedly. In fact, the Western Powers, which had never taken action to condemn Indonesia's policy regarding East Timor, were absent from most of the voting on the question. Similarly, Singapore's absence from many votings dealing with East Timor indicated its disagreement with the ASEAN front, which wanted to suppress discussion of the issue in the United Nations.[213] Singapore did not relinquish its reservation on Indonesia's policy until the 34th session, in October 1979. Interestingly enough, it happened simultaneously with the emergence of the Kampuchean question, when Singapore became one of the most active ASEAN countries to condemn Vietnam's aggression.[214] It was also rather difficult for the socialist countries and the Third World countries to take a dogmatic stance toward the issue, because Indonesia was a Third World country. However, the only reliable supporters of Indonesia were the ASEAN countries, excepting Singapore and certain conservative Arabic countries, which were standing on Indonesia's side, chiefly for religious reasons.

Already at quite an early stage, Vietnam had taken a stand in support of the FRETILIN in the common front with the socialist and Non-Aligned countries. The Vietnamese had made this known before the UN membership at the Non-Aligned's meetings and through their direct contacts with the FRETILIN leadership. Similarly, right after the fall of Saigon, they used the East Timor issue to prove the political nature of ASEAN, as discussed in an earlier chapter. An article appearing in January 1976 in the *Hoc Tap* examined the question characteristically in the light of anti-imperialist struggle and national liberation. Published several months before the annexation of East Timor by Indonesia, this article examined Indonesia's policy in the framework of "Indonesian colonialism."[215] It branded Indonesian policy as imperialistic by stating that "the plan of Indonesia to annex East Timor is laid down by the U.S. strategy in Southeast Asia," which is part of the American policy in this region in the post-Vietnam period.[216] This defines Indonesia's position in the *ai thang ai* struggle: "Resorting to this kind of aggressive action, the reactionary Indonesian clique has itself revealed that it is the enemy of the national independence movements in Southeast Asia."[217]

However, this kind of parlance disappeared nearly completely when Vietnam dealt with the question at the United Nations. At the time Vietnam entered the United Nations, it was obvious that Hanoi had already started to re-evaluate its foreign policy toward Southeast Asia. Relations with Democratic Kampuchea had been badly damaged and the prospects with China did not seem to be much better either. Obviously, this was a central element in the political context of Hanoi's approach to the East Timor question at the United Nations.

The question of East Timor and the questions relating to non-self-governing territories held by the U.S. were dealt with simultaneously by the Fourth Committee. If comparisons are made, the questions involving U.S. bases and military presence commanded Vietnam's interest in the first place and the question of East Timor was clearly secondary. In their statements, in contrast to their stands taken earlier, the Vietnamese hesitated to condemn Indonesia's East Timor policy directly. Vietnam's spokesman said at the Fourth Committee's meeting in November 1977 that "with regard to East Timor, the Socialist Republic of Viet Nam felt bound to state its disapproval of Indonesia's policy toward East Timor, which was not conducive to stabilizing the situation in Southeast Asia."[218] This was rather far from the anti-imperialist language of the foregoing article attacking Indonesia on this question. The phrasing and the concept of "stabilizing" reflected the new approach of Vietnam toward Southeast Asia, which the Vietnamese were just introducing and which they reaffirmed during Nguyen Duy Trinh's visits to the Southeast Asian countries two months later.

Hanoi tended to transfer the issue to a more general level in order to keep it in harmony with its theme of anti-imperialist struggle but simultaneously to avoid too sharp an attack against Indonesia. Although Hanoi reiterated its support of the "just struggle of the people of East Timor, under the leadership of the FRETILIN," a Vietnamese diplomat argued that "Vietnam remained convinced that the real problem lay in the treacherous maneuverings of imperialism, which were intended to divide peoples struggling against colonialism and countries recently liberated from the colonial yoke and to set them against each other, divert them from their shared objective and make them forget that their common enemy was aggressive imperialism."[219] Obviously, Vietnam intended to make it known that, although it opposed Indonesia's occupation of East Timor, it did not want to challenge Indonesia's regional role in Southeast Asia.

Vietnam's anti-imperialist struggle did not last long with this intensity at the United Nations. At the very next UN session, Vietnam's conflict with Democratic Kampuchea and China confused its possibilities of addressing the theme of anti-imperialist struggle. Nguyen Duy Trinh's speech on October 4, 1978, dealt largely with the same themes as in the previous year. However, the speech contained new elements, which reflected the changes that had already occurred in Vietnam's foreign policy. Trinh refrained from mentioning Democratic Kampuchea and China, but used the expressions of "expansionism," "big nation hegemonism" and "international reactionaries in collusion with imperialism," to describe Vietnam's problems with "some of its neighbours."[220] Nevertheless Vietnam had to justify its policy toward Kampuchea after Phnom Penh had unfolded its relations with Vietnam in detail at the General Assembly. Vietnam's representative did not blame imperialism for the troubles between Vietnam and Kampuchea, but argued that "the only obstacle to a peaceful settlement between the two countries is the policy of a great Asian power that has long had ambitions of expansion and hegemony in Southeast Asia, setting the three Indo-Chinese countries as well as the Southeast Asian peoples against one another so that it may carry out its policy of 'divide and rule'."[221]

Trinh did not ignore the theme of anti-imperialist struggle and mentioned routinely Vietnam's previous stand in support of the peoples of "those islands 'under trusteeship,' the Non-Self-Governing Territories and other countries which are now struggling for their fundamental national rights." He failed, however, to mention East Timor and gave an optimistic appraisal of the prospects with Vietnam and other Southeast Asian countries, using the expression used by Pham Van Dong on his visit to the ASEAN countries just one month earlier. Moreover, Trinh expressed his confidence that the normalization of relations with the U.S. would took place soon.[222] When, during the previous session, he estimated that "the balance of forces has radically changed in favor of peace and revolution ... bringing about extremely favorable conditions for the nations to forge ahead and to achieve the lofty objectives of our times, namely, peace, national independence, democracy and socialism,"[223] he now ventured to speak rather moderately, emphasizing that "the struggle of the people of the world for peace, national independence, democracy and social progress has consistently gained new successes."[224]

Thus there was an interesting parallel between the enunciation of Vietnam's policy in the Non-Aligned Movement and in the United Nations. Vietnam's policy as brought to the fore in these organizations started with a very strong commitment both to the theme of anti-imperialist struggle and to formal argumentation. In the Non-Aligned Movement, the emergence of the Sino–Soviet conflict effectively suppressed Vietnam's commitment to the anti-imperialist theme. Similarly, during their first session at the UN, the Vietnamese emphasized this theme. However, Vietnam's troubles with its neighbors, primarily China, caused the Vietnamese to soft-pedal their anti-imperialism in this organization. Interestingly enough, simultaneously with the squelching of the theme of anti-imperialist struggle, Trinh's speech at the 33th Session emphasized Vietnam's role as representing the socialist community. To show his own country's place in this system, Trinh acclaimed the role of Cuba as a socialist and Third World country.[225] This did not mean the radicalization of Vietnam's approach to international relations, but rather reveaed its urge to be identified, like Cuba, as a Third World country strongly supported by the Soviet bloc. Thus Trinh's promotion of Vietnam's aim to develop its relations with the other systems in the spirit of détente and peaceful coexistence indicated both commitment to Soviet foreign policy and also a desire to reach as wide as possible audience within the limits of the doctrine.

5 Isolation and Formalism 1979–85

VIETNAM AFTER THE OCCUPATION OF KAMPUCHEA

Vietnam's military invasion of Kampuchea started on December 25, 1978, with strong military forces, amounting to 12 divisions. Phnom Penh was captured on January 7, 1979; and, three weeks after the beginning of this military operation, all the major cities and main roads were under the control of Vietnamese troops. The Vietnamese did not originally recognize their major role in the occupation, but explained the fall of the Pol Pot administration as a consequence of "the Kampuchean people's stormy revolution." However, Hanoi's own role was not totally denied, as the Vietnamese exercised "their legitimate right of self-defense."[1] In order to cover Vietnam's major military role, or at least to give a justification for the new prospective regime of Phnom Penh, the invasion was preceded by the establishment of the Kampuchean National United Front for National Salvation (KNUFNS) at the beginning of December 1978. This organization, created for practical purposes by Hanoi, did not deny the harmonization of its policy to that of Vietnam's. At its inaugural meeting, the "Central Committee" of the Front proclaimed its close contacts with Vietnam and Laos in Indochina, and it shared the Vietnamese view that emphasized China's role behind the Indochina conflict.[2] After the fall of Phnom Penh, the People's Revolutionary Council of Kampuchea, headed by Heng Samrin, was formed on January 8; the new regime adopted the name People's Republic of Kampuchea (PRK); and finally, on February 18, it signed the Treaty of Peace, Friendship and Cooperation with Vietnam.

Vietnam's invasion of Kampuchea was followed by the Chinese "lesson" to Northern Vietnam in February, after Deng Xiaoping had guaranteed the formal neutrality of the United States but its practical support to China's military attack against Vietnam. After a two weeks' military campaign, during which the Northern border areas and provinces of Vietnam were badly damaged and systematically destroyed in part, the Chinese troops started to withdraw, the withdrawal being completed on March 17, 1979.[3]

Despite this relatively short period of hostilities in Indochina, when the Kampuchean question became a matter of international diplomacy, it developed into a crucial issue for Vietnam's foreign policy over the next decade. Vietnam was effectively prevented from raising other issues in international organizations when the ASEAN countries questioned the legitimacy of Vietnam's military action and the introduction of the PRK to the UN agenda and similarly its emergence at meetings of the Non-Aligned Movement. The parties and alliances concentrated on the cold war issues in Southeast Asia, and this situation was not eradicated before the end of the 1980s and the early 1990s. The Western and Western-oriented countries in Asia, including the ASEAN countries, joined the economic blockade that the U.S. had already started after its withdrawal from Indochina in 1975, and the diplomatic and economic blockade on a broader basis continued up to the withdrawal of the Vietnamese troops from Kampuchea in September 1989. This meant the growing dependence of the Indochinese countries on the Soviet bloc economically, militarily, and politically. There were certain Third World countries, such as Cuba and India, with which Vietnam had active dealings, especially with regard to Third World questions; and there were some Western countries, such as Sweden, that continued to give development aid to a relatively large extent, but they could not change the ever-growing dependence of Vietnam on the Soviet Union.

All these things supported the development and establishment of the orthodox Marxist-Leninist political parlance in Vietnam. There were also some internal factors that equally supported this development, as has previously been noted. In the new situation in Southeast Asia, these tendencies reinforced each other and crystallized Vietnam's political language. Crucial to the need for orthodox vocabulary was the second five-year plan (1976–1980), which was based largely on the Soviet model of building a socialist economy, bypassing the capitalist phase of development. This model emphasized the role of heavy industry at the expense of agriculture and light industry. On account of the primitive stage of Vietnam's economy and the dogmatic application of this model, including the collectivization of agriculture and the suspension of private trade, especially in the South, this policy failed, for the national product and the living standard remained constant at a very low level during this five-year plan. The disappointment was rather severe as the general optimism about socialist construction had been very high after the victorious war.[4] This economic failure coincided with political rivalry in the Communist Party leadership, which led to the ousting of the China-oriented cadres and to the demotion of certain other old-guard leaders to minor posts in the Party. These changes in the leadership meant the concentration of power in the faction led by Le Duan.[5]

The encounter of these Vietnamese domestic tendencies with external pressures led to a more orthodox Marxist-Leninist language, as the texts of Vietnamese cadres at the end of the 1970s and the beginning of the 1980s proved. This happened although the Party made remarkable revisions in the third five-year plan (1981–1985) aimed at the construction of a socialist economy, including partial abandonment of collectivization, and gave more weight to the development of agriculture.[6] Similarly, the country's international relations, which had undergone dramatic changes since the mid-1970s and turned old friends into enemies, had brought about no changes in the political doctrine. The Vietnamese doctrine now connected the *ai thang ai* struggle, the nation's economic difficulties, its social transformation, the Hoa-problem, the Chinese threat, the Kampuchean question and the blockade of Vietnam to the international class struggle as an entity, where the solution of one part of the problem was supposed to lead to the gradual solution of this struggle. In Vietnam, the Marxist-Leninist doctrine turned now to the manner of speaking, regardless of whether the doctrine had any reference to reality or not. In this respect, political argumentation was turning more to the theoretical premises of Marxism-Leninism and was losing its ability to mobilize the Vietnamese.

The examination of the development of the doctrine on foreign relations is divided here in two. The first question is: how did the discussion between the Party cadres try to fit into the new international situation within the limits of the doctrinal code and Marxist-Leninist theory? How were these evaluations reflected to the top level when the leadership formulated and defended its policy? Then, the question arises as to what arguments Vietnam's diplomacy has tried to bring up to justify the country's position in Indochina, Southeast Asia and the world after it had turned from the avant-garde of national liberation to become "an aggressor"?

THE TAKEOVER OF FORMALISM

Vietnam's doctrinal structure of foreign-policy argumentation, which was described in the fourth chapter, was responding to the situation where China posed an immediate threat to its foreign policy. In this respect, there was no need to change its elements. After "the two wars to defend the homeland," as the Vietnamese called the invasion of Kampuchea and the war against China, some of the elements were more crucial to Vietnam's foreign policy than ever before. Although these elements were hard to fit into the Marxist theory of class relations on the international level in a situation where the immediate enemy was a socialist country and an old comrade-in-arms in the anti-imperialist struggle, the concepts of *ai thang ai* and three revolutionary currents were widely called up to justify Vietnam's foreign policy. The emphasis was not on theoretical consistency but on political expediency to join Vietnam's domestic line to the orientation of its foreign policy.

As for linking domestic politics and foreign policy, the crucial theme was "raising the two banners of national independence and socialism" *(giuong cao hai ngon co doc lap dan toc va chu nghia xa hoi)*.[7] This theme combined the construction of socialism with the defense of the country, and connected Vietnam's foreign-policy line to that of the socialist bloc. The adaptation of the motto about "building socialism and defending the homeland," which was affirmed at the 5th Party Congress, gave a broad framework also to the theoretically oriented discussion on Vietnam's international relations. "Building socialism" refers both to Vietnam's domestic rule and to its international orientation toward the Soviet bloc. "Defending the homeland" refers both to the threat of China and to the relationship between the Indochinese countries. The concept of proletarian internationalism was emphasized, the re-established relations between Vietnam and Kampuchea were illustrated as "militant solidarity" and, after the subjugation of Pol Pot's administration, the concept of special relationship was not abandoned but used to describe the relations between the countries of Indochina rather than Vietnamese–Kampuchean relations in particular.

However, there is certain evidence that the political line and the vocabulary adopted by the 5th Party Congress to appraise Vietnam's new international position were not unambiguous. Although the orthodox Marxist-Leninist doctrine about two courses of development was dominant and much time was devoted to bind this and foreign policy together, the revolutionary pragmatism did not disappear. In fact, part of its terminology was re-established in the 5th Party Congress documents. To illustrate this line of argumentation in Vietnam's foreign policy, I will examine first Vo Nguyen Giap's five essays issued between October 1978 and April 1979 and published as a book titled *Ca Nuoc mot long bao ve vung chac to quoc Viet Nam xa hoi chu nghia*.[8] These writings were obviously a symptom of the foreign-policy delineation defeated in the Party leadership at the beginning of the 1980s, when General Giap had to leave his post of minister of defense, finally losing his seat in the Politburo at the 5th Party Congress. He was accompanied also by Foreign Minister Nguyen Duy Trinh, together with two other old guard members, who were dropped from the Politburo.[9] Therefore Giap's writings do not represent a mainstream political doctrine, but it is analyzed here as an alternative style of arguing replaced by formalist thinking.

To what extent formalism and pragmatism can be connected to two different kinds of political orientations is still an open question. There exist interpretations on both fractionalism and the unity of the Party leadeship. Here the issue is whether the changes in the Party leadership before the 5th Party Congress reflected the longer political struggle in the Party leadership. It is arguable that Giap's pragmatic approach reflected a different kind of delineation from that adopted by the official Party line. However, I am inclined to believe that the changes in the Party leadership reflected, first of all, the question of "what kind of attitude should be adopted to the growing dependence on the Soviet Union?" and perhaps on the distinct attitude toward the policy in Kampuchea. Although there exist some testimonies of the longer power struggle in the Party leadership, the evidence is still unambiguous.[10]

In Giap's essays, there were similarities to the political delineations adopted by the 5th Party Congress. First of all, the phrase about defending the homeland and building socialism as a general theme for mobilizing the masses was crucially significant already in Giap's writings. This indicated that the Party leadership had to choose this theme at least during the summer of 1978. However, despite the fact that Giap articulated many concepts commonly used by the Party's mainstream, the differences between his vocabulary and the vocabulary established after the 5th Party Congress were evident. Naturally, these variances suggest broader differences in political orientation. There were certain concepts used by both Giap and mainstream representatives, but the meanings and positions of which differ in the broader context. Such a concept was that of the three revolutionary currents, which Giap used sparingly (five times in the space of over two hundred pages) and apparently in a limited context, where he listed the forces that supported Vietnam's international position.[11] The concept of proletarian internationalism *(chu nghia quoc te vo san)* appeared only once[12] and he ignored completely the concepts of socialist internationalism, special relationship and *ai thang ai,* thus emphasizing his disagreements with the Soviet-oriented Marxist-Leninists. These differences were obvious, as Giap's essays dealt with both the Indochina question and Vietnam's foreign policy in general.

In the big picture, Giap was presenting his own version of Vietnam's strategy for survival in the new international situation. Accordingly, the building up of socialism merely represented the course chosen by Vietnam in the global revolutionary struggle, and this did not as such justify

Vietnam's orientation toward the Soviet bloc. He derived his analysis from the distinction between friend and foe in the global struggle between imperialist and anti-imperialist forces, and placed it on such a concrete level that the Marxist class division can hardly be detected in it. Giap saw this distinction first on a general level, where the fundamental enemy *(ke thu co ban)* among the anti-imperialist forces was the United States, and then on a concrete level, where Vietnam's immediate enemy *(ke thu truc tiep)* was "the reactionary clique of Beijing" *(bon phan dong Bac Kinh)*.[13] According to this latter concrete distinction, the strategy and tactics are determined and the allies are chosen. Hence he linked the initiative *(chu dong)* and the principle of separating friend from foe in order to gain the upper hand on the battlefield.[14] Securing the initiative was crucial for the defense of the country, being a part of "the ideology of offensive strategy" *(tu tuong chien luoc tien cong)*;[15] and it was therefore both a justification of Vietnam's occupation of Kampuchea and part of the ideological project. This project resembles that of Vietnam's national liberation war: It involves all the sectors, and has "to combine military, political, ideological and cultural factors and to integrate the military, political and diplomatic struggle."[16] In fact, this ongoing war was retrospectively viewed by Giap as a continuation of the national liberation struggle: It is "the ideology to arm all the people and fight against the aggressor" and it originates from Vietnam's remote past and has grown to a military-political synthesis.[17]

From this formulation of the friend/foe distinction and the project of "defending and building the socialist homeland," Giap developed his program for Vietnam's survival in the new situation. In his report to the National Assembly, Giap pointed out five "tasks for all our people and the army in the new situation." These tasks were 1) to integrate the economy and national defense, 2) to organize national defense and (internal) security, 3) to develop the economy and the culture, 4) to improve the leadership and consolidate the Party organization, 5) connecting these tasks to Vietnam's foreign policy.[18] These issues emphasized Vietnam's own line of development and although the concept of self-reliance had disappeared from the Vietnamese political vocabulary, Giap tried to avoid acknowledging Vietnam's dependence on the Soviet bloc. He defined the role of the socialist countries according to the line of the 4th Party Congress without the commitments to the Soviet bloc's economic and political line at variance with the course laid out in the documents of the 5th Party Congress. Giap even gave his support to the Chinese revolution, and limited the definition of the direct enemy to the political élite in Beijing.[19] Evidently, his theses were aimed at maintaining the greatest possible independent line vis-à-vis the Soviet bloc as regards both domestic issues and international alignments in a situation where the isolation of Vietnam was growing.

Obviously, the Marxist-Leninist class analysis and the vocabulary closely associated with it for the justification of the course followed by Vietnam in both foreign relations and domestic affairs were alien to Giap. Contrary to Giap's starting points, the trend worked out at the 5th Party Congress based its estimation of international relations and Vietnam's foreign policy mainly in terms of the conventional Marxist-Leninist vocabulary. However, a part of the vocabulary used by Giap was adapted also to the dominant trend. In this respect, the friend/foe concept was re-established in the common vocabulary, and thus the pragmatic pattern appeared in the 5th Party Congress documents.[20] This was the specification of the general line "to build and defend the socialist homeland," on which the 5th Party Congress based its ideological work.

Despite these similarities, the vocabulary adopted by the Party Congress differed from Giap's essays in many respects. The expressions used in the Political Report of the Congress were then repeated in the cadres' texts. In this respect, the justification of Vietnam's international position by Hoang Van Thai, who was also a general and a member of the Central Committee, is illustrative. Thai concentrated in his writings mainly on the situation of Indochina, but he dealt also with Vietnam's foreign relations in a broader perspective. His theoretical foundations linked the justification of Vietnam's policy in Indochina clearly to the Marxist-Leninist point of view.

According to Hoang Van Thai's rhetoric, the alliances between the countries all over the world are a natural phenomenon based on the objective laws of development in the relations between different countries. Hence he connected the geopolitical reasoning with the class analysis by emphasizing that the geographical facts had been a crucial precondition for political alliance.[21] Equally, the social classes had sought alliances to secure or win the power in the class struggle. This appeared in Marx and Engels' *Communist Manifesto*, but from the point of view of Vietnam and Indochina, Thái emphasized Lenin's modification of it: "The proletariat in all the countries and oppressed nations, unite." He argued that this was the theoretical basis of the general alliance, formed by the three revolutionary currents of the world, the alliance of the socialist countries, the national liberation movements and the workers' movements in the developed countries. Specifying the Indochinese level, his analysis concluded that the alliance of Vietnam, Laos and Kampuchea was based on Marxism-Leninism and proletarian internationalism and "it is an organic part of the international alliance of the socialist countries and the world's revolutionary forces, supported by the Soviet Union," just as "it is a creative application of proletarian internationalism in the concrete situation of the three countries in the peninsula of Indochina."[22]

This definition reveals the striking differences in the premises laid down by Vo Nguyen Giap for Vietnam's foreign policy. Giap emphasized Vietnam's own national strategy, which presented a strong independent character; and the alliances, a word which Giap in fact ignored, were based purely on Vietnam's own interests. He concentrated his analysis on distinguishing the enemy on a concrete level, which helped him to avoid any problematic class analysis in Vietnam's foreign relations. On the other hand, Hoang Van Thai represented Vietnam's foreign relations as an organic part of the Soviet bloc's foreign policy. At the theoretical level, if his analysis is compared with Giap's, it does not operate with the clear distinction between the concrete, direct enemy and the fundamental enemy. Following the line of the 5th Party Congress, Thai mentioned this distinction;[23] but as a general approach, he tended to treat Vietnam's foreign policy more with the respect of the fundamental enemy of the revolutionary forces. His point of departure was in Marxist-Leninist premises, which he tried to fit into the conditions prevailing in Indochina. This led him to a class analysis, which had strong political consequences. His premises were therefore more radical than the pro-Soviet line that the 5th Party Congress adopted.

In fact, the vocabulary used by Thai was equally revealing. The concept of three revolutionary currents, proletarian internationalism and a special relationship formed a hierarchy of the concepts that bound Vietnam's policy in Indochina to that of the Soviet Union. The starting point of this logic was the three revolutionary currents, which alone can turn, and have already turned, the relation of forces in favor of the revolutionary forces of the world. The strongest pillar of these forces was the Soviet Union, together with the other socialist countries, and the relationship between them was based on proletarian internationalism. As the revolutions of the three Indochinese countries were part of the proletarian revolution of the world, "the alliance of the three countries was part of the international alliance of the socialist countries and other revolutionary forces of the world."[24] The prerequisite for the victory of the socialist revolution in each Indochinese country was the alliance of these countries based on a special relationship between these countries.[25] Thai used also the expression of a "special relationship of cooperation" *(quan he hop tac dac biet),*[26] perhaps to assuage the negative connotation the concept had received when it was attached to Vietnam's invasion of

Kampuchea. Nevertheless, the concept was used to illustrate the entity constituted by Indochina's mutual relations and not Vietnam's bilateral relations with Kampuchea.

Despite this, there were obvious characteristics in Hoang Van Thai's approach that revealed that he had appropriated elements similar to those existing already in the Brezhnev Doctrine. The emphasis on the common threat to the Indochinese countries' revolutions was very much like the justification of the Soviet invasion of Czechoslovakia. In fact, the Vietnamese declared their support of the Soviet Union in preventing Czechoslovakia and Hungary from turning to the enemy's camp, presenting thus arguments nearly identical to those justifying the Indochinese alliance and the occupation of Kampuchea.[27] Actually, Thai's statements about a common ideology and culture referred more to the control aspect that existed in the relationship between the Indochinese countries than to the possibility of guaranteeing the sovereignty of these countries. Thus, according to Thai, the common ideological ground together with the Communist Party rule in each country were the most important qualifiers of the Indochinese alliance.[28] In this respect, his reasoning bore a distinct affinity to the definitions used to characterize Vietnamese–Laotian relations. In Vietnamese and Laotian vocabulary, the "special relationship" referred sooner to historical and geographical factors than representing a serious attempt to become bound to the Marxist-Leninist doctrine, like Thai's.

Hoang Van Thai seemed to accept all these pro-Soviet emphasizings, which Giap tried to avoid. This grafting of Soviet Marxism-Leninism to Vietnam's political language and to the parlance of foreign relations in particular characterize the cadres' texts during the period immediately following the 5th Party Congress. At the general level, the Soviet Union was accepted as the leader of the socialist camp and of the world's revolutionary forces,[29] and the 5th Party Congress adopted a pro-Moscow definition of socialist internationalism as a basis for the relationships between the socialist countries.[30] However, this concept did not become established in the general vocabulary of the Party cadres' texts. Ignorance of the concept was so prevalent as to reflect the conscious policy line of the Party. Among the few references to the concept, socialist internationalism was associated with the aid given by the Soviet government to build socialism in Vietnam; but the concept was not used systematically to illustrate Soviet-Vietnamese relations.[31] In fact, the 5th Party Congress limited reference to socialist internationalism to the economic cooperation with the Soviet bloc, in particular, and employed proletarian internationalism to illustrate its relationship with the Indochinese countries.

In the general political parlance of the Party cadres, "socialist internationalism" was practically abandoned and replaced by "proletarian internationalism," also when referring to the Soviet bloc.

With respect to the nearly complete discarding of the term "socialist
internationalism," there existed still more striking peculiarities in
Vietnamese use of Marxist-Leninist language, as the re-establishment of
the friend/foe dichotomy in their political parlance proved. The re-
emergence of the friend/foe concept involves Vietnam's relations with
China to a large extent. The orthodox Marxist-Leninist vocabulary had
considerable difficulty fitting China's international position into the
Marxist theory, as the Soviet example had already shown. Attempts were
made to accomodate Vietnam's complex international situation in the
Stalinist theory of two roads and to adapt this theory to fit Sino–
Vietnamese relations in particular.[32] Despite the poor utility in a concrete
analysis, *ai thang ai* between the two roads was not abandoned and
remained as an official dogma at the 5th Party Congress.[33] However,
Hoang Van Thai gave up this concept and accepted the friend/foe
dichotomy to deal with Vietnam's, or, better, Indochina's, relations with
China.[34] The emphasis on China as the common enemy of all the
Indochinese countries underlies the interpretation of Vietnam's
Communist Party that these countries had common security needs.[35] On
the other hand, connecting this Indochinese security question to the
commonly held view of China's foreign policy, which had turned against
the world's three revolutionary currents, and against the principle of
proletarian internationalism, was the most common, though rather vague,
attempt to examine Chinese policy from the Marxist-Leninist point of
view.[36] On account of the difficulties of Marxist-Leninist formalism to
explain the hostilities between two Communist governments – those of
Vietnam and China –, pragmatic explanations with historical analogies
were often used. Thus the Vietnamese cadres, like the official propaganda,
concentrated on the historical threat to Vietnam posed by China during
different dynasties as well as the present, represented by "the great power
hegemonism of Beijing's ruling circle."

As Marxist-Leninist concepts did not offer any real support to the
concrete friend/foe analysis, the Vietnamese had to resort to more
theoretically and politically neutral concepts of territorial integrity and
sovereignty in their policy toward China. There were also reasons for this
when, after the Sino–Vietnamese war, the territorial dispute, involving
first of all the question of the sovereignty of Hoang Sa (Paracels) and
Truong Sa (Spratlys) islands, became one of the most concrete issues
complicating the relations between Hanoi and Beijing. The question of
sovereignty was raised in the pragmatic argumentation regarding foreign

policy. Thus the Vietnamese described the Chinese threat as double-edged: the politico-ideological threat to Indochina as a whole, where Beijing had been in collusion with U.S. imperialism, and the concrete territorial threat to Vietnam based on old Chinese ambitions involving the whole of Southeast Asia.[37]

The Vietnamese view of a united Indochina, or Indochina as a bloc, was crucial to the Vietnamese approach to the ASEAN countries. This included both the theoretical presuppositions regarding the role of Indochina and the ASEAN countries in the two camps struggle in Southeast Asia and also the complexity of Vietnam's foreign policy toward the ASEAN countries in practical diplomacy. Despite the fact that the ASEAN countries were leading the international front against Vietnam's occupation of Kampuchea, these countries were clearly the audience for Vietnam's foreign-policy declarations. The Kampuchean question dominated Vietnam's foreign relations in every field of multilateral policy, preventing the Vietnamese from raising their own foreign-policy themes. This was the case especially at the United Nations. In the Non-Aligned Movement, there was more room for Vietnam to present its views on international issues in general; but also here, as in the UN, the Kampuchean question tended to rise to the fore for Vietnam as a result of the diplomatic activities of the ASEAN countries. It also remained one of the main themes of Vietnam's foreign policy despite Hanoi's every attempt to evade it and despite the difficulties in dealing with it according to the theoretical premises of Marxism-Leninism. Thus there seemed to open up a gap between the theoretical analysis of international relations, which emphasized the theme of Vietnam as an outpost of socialism and independence in Southeast Asia, and the actual diplomatic rhetoric, which was forced to explain Vietnam's occupation of Kampuchea to the heterogeneous international audience. Consequently, the "theoretical" discussion, which had previously formed a rather unified entity with practical diplomacy, took a dualistic turn. Interestingly, the approach toward the Southeast Asian countries culminated in the two concepts of *ai thang ai* and friend/foe. Theoretically solid, though quite abstract, *ai thang ai* supported a confrontative attitude toward ASEAN, but the friend/foe distinction, which was based on the realities of foreign policy, was used in an effort to find some kind of common ground with ASEAN for preventing China and ASEAN from entering into a closer alliance.

In 5th Party Congress documents, Vietnam's definition of its relations with the ASEAN countries followed clearly the outlines of the friend/foe distinction, despite the fact that the general trend at this Congress went in the direction of conventional Soviet Marxism. The complexity of the power constellation in Southeast Asia was acknowledged, and the Congress avoided utilizing the class analysis to illustrate the policy of the ASEAN countries. Similarly, instead of the phrase "peace, independence and genuine neutrality," which was used at the 4th Party Congress, a more neutral expression of Vietnam's willingness to build with the ASEAN countries "a zone of peace and stability" was used.[38] This expression was retained in Vietnam's attempt to compromise with the ZOPFAN proposal of ASEAN during its diplomatic activities in 1978.

Nevertheless, the moderate and optimistic mood marking Vietnamese relations with ASEAN in 1977–1978 turned back a degree to criticism of this organization's policy, when Vietnam's diplomacy toward ASEAN failed as a consequence of the occupation of Kampuchea. This also reflected the texts and the vocabulary of the Party cadres. Vietnamese diplomatic spokesmen had tried, especially during the year 1978, to search for a common language with the ASEAN countries, and theoretically oriented texts had been used in an attempt to find the premises for this policy. One central point in both Vietnam's ASEAN diplomacy and Vietnamese discussion, in particular, was that Vietnam appeared as an independent political actor when dealing with the ASEAN countries and not as a member of any bloc or group of countries, such as Indochina or the Socialist bloc. This point of view was emphasized during Pham Van Dong's visit to the ASEAN countries and in subsequent Vietnamese comments, where the independence of Vietnam's line from the Soviet or any other bloc was pointed out.[39]

However, these premises of Vietnam's policy toward the ASEAN countries changed radically. In the new situation developing during late 1978 and early 1979, the main premise was evidently Vietnam's relationship with the Soviet Union. The political report of the 5th Party Congress confirmed this by stating that the relationship with the Soviet Union is "the keystone of the foreign policy."[40] This postulate determined also the Vietnamese discussion on the international situation in Southeast Asia and Vietnam's policy toward ASEAN. Although in Vietnamese diplomacy there occurred attempts to separate Vietnam's relationship with the Soviet Union from its relations with the Southeast Asian countries, the theoretical discussion of the Party cadres emphasized the Soviet–Vietnamese relations in the sphere of foreign policy. The Soviet–Vietnamese relations were represented as a crucial factor in establishing peace and stability in the area, as these relations were "joined in an important manner to the independence of three Indochinese countries and to the peace and stability in the area."[41]

This argumentation was based on the two-bloc structure existing in Southeast Asia. The critical prerequisite for this structure was the formation of a unified Indochinese bloc. It was equally important to acknowledge ASEAN as a bloc, which practically happened already during Vietnam's Southeast Asian diplomatic maneuvering in 1978 and officially at least at the 5th Party Congress. Vietnam's rather late recognition of ASEAN was attributed by the Vietnamese to its loose organizational structure, which prevented them from realizing its importance.[42] Interestingly enough, this situation involving two different groups allowed the Vietnamese to adopt wholeheartedly the concept of peaceful coexistence: Accordingly, the emerged socialist system of Indochina has provided peaceful coexistence between two state systems in Southeast Asia, which coincides, as this reasoning concludes, "with the need to develop peace and stability" in this area."[43]

This point of departure reveals two interesting and mutually supporting elements in Vietnam's foreign-policy rhetoric. First, the emphasis on peaceful coexistence indicated that Vietnam had abandoned anti-imperialist struggle as a theme for Southeast Asia, after it had managed to create a unified Indochina. Thus the Vietnamese were not stressing the need for fundamental social and political changes in Southeast Asia, but the stability of the structure of the regional state system. In the second place, the emergence of peaceful coexistence, together with the orthodox Marxist-Leninist vocabulary, reflected the Soviet influence in Vietnam's foreign policy. This indicated that, on account of their close relations with the Soviet Union, the Vietnamese Communists were adopting the general Soviet approach in international affairs, including détente *(giam cang thang)*, as a positive method to promote the aims of the socialist countries – instead of looking to a confrontation between the two blocs.[44] These changes in Vietnamese vocabulary implied also, especially owing to the concepts of peaceful coexistence and détente, that the orthodox Marxist-Leninist argumentation evolved along the lines of the new developments of Marxism-Leninism. This meant that the political language of revolutionary pragmatism, on the one hand, and the orthodox Stalinist theory of the two roads, on the other hand, were complemented with more modern Soviet vocabulary, in a way similar to what happened at the beginning of the 1970s, when the concept of three revolutionary currents was introduced. This vocabulary belongs to the argumentation pattern that stands, like the Stalinist orthodox vocabulary, on quasi-logical argumentation. Similarly, although the concepts now represented better the reality of Southeast Asia at the beginning of the 1980s, the point of departure was also here the two camps theory.

Despite the criticism the Vietnamese leveled at ASEAN's policy on the Kampuchean question, there were clear differences in the cadres' attitudes toward this association, when compared with the situation that prevailed after Vietnam's victory in the spring of 1975. The main difference was, of course, recognition of the organization and the legitimacy of the Southeast Asian state system. This point of departure drove the Vietnamese to re-examine the basic documents of ASEAN, primarily the Kuala Lumpur and Bali declarations. The differences between these new interpretations and the Vietnamese attitudes after the fall of Saigon were striking in this respect. While these declarations had previously been considered to be part of the imperialist scheme to bind the Southeast Asian countries to American foreign policy in Asia, the new approaches emphasized the positive impact of these declarations on the stability of the whole region.[45] The origin of ASEAN was attributed to an attempt to reduce the influence of Communist China and the socialist camp in Southeast Asia.[46] The same analysis went on to say that the low political profile of this association could be seen as an effort to thwart aims of turning ASEAN into a stronghold of the "free world." The development of ASEAN into a Cold War alliance in the region was prevented by limiting the membership to the founding members and inactivating military cooperation inside the organization.[47]

Against this positive general approach, the problem arose as how to explain ASEAN's stance toward the Kampuchean question. There existed two kinds of explanations. The first concentrated on the external factors of ASEAN and the other focused more on the factors at work inside the ASEAN countries. Naturally, these approaches overlapped. One analyst pointed out that the greatest threat to the stability of the Southeast Asian state systems had always come from outside the region. He referred to the historical threat of imperial China, followed by Western colonialism, and to the present situation, where China's hegemonism, together with American imperialism, was manipulating the relationships between the Southeast Asian countries.[48] He emphasized that "compared with the threat of Chinese expansionist hegemonism, which lasted thousands of years, Western colonialist rule has been much shorter in Southeast Asia."[49] However, the argumentation based on external elements requires an internal factor, which makes it possible for a nonregional power to become involved in Southeast Asian politics. This retrospective approach was therefore supported most often by a more or less coherent class approach. Accordingly, the reason why the ASEAN countries turned against Indochina was "the class character of the ruling circles *(ban chat giai cap cua gioi cam quyen)*" in these countries.[50] Although there are, as this analysis continues, progressive tendencies that support the peaceful development of the region, owing to their class nature, part of the ruling class has always tried to take advantage of every situation in which they can use ASEAN against socialist Indochina. Therefore the Kampuchean question was one of the issues that was used to prevent the progress of the Indochinese countries' revolution.[51]

Thus there existed, as the example of the Vietnamese discussion on ASEAN proved, three kinds of elements in the Marxist-Leninist argumentation about Vietnam's international relations. First, there was the friend/foe concept, which turned China into an adversary in Southeast Asia and supported the moves aimed at developing the relations with ASEAN. Second, the emergence of the modern Soviet vocabulary indicated that the new elements had been admitted into Vietnamese foreign-policy argumentation in the early 1980s. Finally, the orthodox class analysis also continued to hold its place in this argumentation structure. Concerning Vietnam's foreign relations as a whole, it is arguable that these trends prevailed among the Party cadres in general.

VIETNAM'S DOCTRINE ON INDOCHINA

The next two chapters will deal with the question of how this formalist pattern, which had become dominant in the Party cadres' discussions, was then applied in Vietnam's foreign-policy practice, particularly at sessions of international organizations and in Indochina's relations with the ASEAN countries. However, in the present chapter, the crucial question is how the Vietnamese leadership determined its policy in Indochina along formal and pragmatic lines. For the purpose of shedding more light on Vietnam's regional policy, I am examining the elements of argumentation about Vietnam's policy toward Kampuchea, which I shall try to summarize as "Vietnam's doctrine on Indochina." This "doctrine" includes the theoretically orientated arguments of the Party cadres together with the statements of the top leadership. However, it does not include the Vietnamese argumentation at sessions of international organizations or the arguments belonging to regional diplomacy. These arguments are examined as an application of this "doctrine." The particular characteristics of these arguments depended on the special nature of the audience. That is to say, Vietnam was forced to respond to one particular question, i.e., how to resolve the Kampuchean question internationally.

In fact, the formalist approach was complemented and even challenged by pragmatism immediately after the invasion. Besides several patterns of argumentation intended to address different kinds of audiences which Hanoi had to face, it obviously had something to do with distinct political approaches entertained by the Communist Party leadership. Beyond the theoretically oriented discussions between the Party cadres, there existed some major documents in which the development of formalism for a wider audience can be followed. Two aspects of these documents should be observed: They were addressed, if not for a "global audience," for a rather broad audience pointing up the importance of these documents. Secondly, by following the formal line, they approached the arguments of the Brezhnev Doctrine. However, only after the pragmatic arguments of the invasion of Kampuchea are connected to it, a balanced version of Vietnam's doctrine concerning its Indochina policy can be formulated.

The first document examined here is Le Duan's broadcast speech held at the celebration of the 50th anniversary of the Party in February 1980. The general importance of this speech was heightened by the Politburo's removal of Nguyen Duy Trinh, the foreign minister, from the top leadership. Probably Vo Nguyen Giap's dismissal took place at this time.[52] The second document is the political report of the 5th Party Congress, while the rest of the material consists of the group of documents published during the Soviet delegation's visit to Vietnam during October and November 1983. Characteristic of these documents, the first two were addressed primarily to the native public and secondarily to a general foreign audience, and the third group of documents first and foremost to the Soviet guests and secondarily to the general foreign public.

Notwithstanding that all setbacks to the unity of the world Marxist movements, Le Duan's belief in the "scientific" predictions of Marxism-Leninism seemed to be watertight. At the Communist Party anniversary, he argued that the victories of the Marxist national movements and "the complete victory of socialist construction in a series of countries are "speeding up the victory of scientific socialism throughout the world." Therefore "the strength of socialism is definitely surpassing that of imperialism and international reaction."[53] Within the three revolutionary currents in which the Soviet bloc was the prime mover, as Le Duan argued, Vietnam was performing its historical task of carrying out the revolution in Southeast Asia. The special alliance between the Indochinese countries is its particular manifestation.[54]

There were other expressions by which Le Duan connected Vietnam's policy to that of the Soviet Union's economically, ideologically and politically. In his speech, he mentioned socialist internationalism, a concept that had very seldom appeared in Vietnamese texts except those that were published in collaboration with the Soviet Union. The other exception to this was the Political Report of the 5th Party Congress. However, the concept brought out in Le Duan's speech in February 1980 did not directly signify the political preeminence of the Soviet Party over other Communist Parties, but the acceptance of the Soviet model of economic integration and its suitability to Vietnam's domestic development in meeting the needs of the socialist world system.[55] This called for strengthening the industrialization process, and it likewise served to justify the Party line and the development of the political system under Communist Party rule. In the Political Report of the 5th Party Congress, the content of the concept of socialist internationalism was more political and referred to the political relations between the socialist countries.[56] At the 6th Party Congress of December 1986, the concept was again limited to the economic relations within the socialist community.[57]

Despite this limitation, the concept of socialist internationalism appeared also in purely political contexts in the joint statement issued after the Summit Conference of the Indochinese countries in February 1983.[58] This Vientiane statement used several particularly strong expressions to connect Indochina to the Socialist World system. It included the Indochinese countries' overall commitment to Soviet foreign policy and the role of these countries in promoting it in Southeast Asia.[59] All these arguments, including socialist internationalism, together with the concept of three revolutionary currents, when they were connected to emphasis of the correct political line, close relations between the Indochinese countries and the presence of Vietnamese troops in Kampuchea, sounded very much like the Brezhnev Doctrine.

This kind of vocabulary took on an even stronger tone during the visit to Vietnam of the Soviet delegation led by G.A. Aliyev, a Politburo member of the CPSU and first vice-chairman of the Council of Ministers. The Soviet-Vietnamese joint statement published during the visit stressed that the struggle between different social systems was more acute than ever. The Soviets were confident that the Vietnamese were following the correct line in this struggle, particularly in "consolidating the socialist unity" in Southeast Asia. Both sides expressed their determination to develop their relations "on the basis of Marxism-Leninism and socialist internationalism" and continue their ideological cooperation "against hostile ideology," which was, in the current situation, "of particularly important significance" and they were "determined to coordinate their actions in the area."[60] Thus this formalism was linking both mutual understanding of socialist construction in each of the countries and the common ideological line connected to the foreign policy of the socialist community. Also the role of Vietnamese foreign policy as a part of the socialist countries' international role was understood to belong to the sphere of mutual understanding between Vietnam and the Soviet Union. It was thus aspired to build the broad frames for Vietnam's foreign policy on the basis of Marxist-Leninist doctrine.

Nevertheless, in Vietnam's policy toward Kampuchea and its relations with China, the pragmatic arguments were rather strong, particularly immediately after the invasion of Kampuchea and the border war with China. Hence the scope of Vietnam's foreign policy was more limited and the foreign-policy goals much more modest than in Marxist-Leninist formalism. The description of the socialist countries as the strategic allies of Vietnam illustrates well the role of the Soviet bloc in this approach. In this context, the independent lines of the Communist Parties were emphasized; but also the convergent general goals of Vietnam and the socialist countries were acknowledged. Allies were needed while Vietnam was defending its independence and the epithets connected with it, sovereignty, territorial integrity and the right to determine its own internal line. Accordingly, the invasion of Kampuchea was explained by Vietnam's right and duty to defend its sovereignty against China's ambitions to govern Indochina. This argument was often combined with a tendency to create a new reality with the historical analogy of the present situation in Indochina to the relations between feudal China and Vietnam.[61] The characteristic of revolutionary pragmatism stemmed for the negligence of both the formal Marxist-Leninist premises and the socialist blocs' role behind Vietnam's policy in Indochina.

Interestingly enough, the Treaty of Peace, Friendship and Cooperation between Vietnam and the new government in Phnom Penh, which was signed in February 1979, lacks all these Marxist-Leninist expressions and vocabulary that characterize the treaty of 1977 between Vietnam and Laos and the treaty between the Soviet Union and Vietnam of 1978. The essence of the Vietnam–Kampuchean treaty lies in the mechanism that prohibits the use of Kampuchean soil against Vietnam (Article II). The fifth article, which was designed for the benefit of an international audience, describes the foreign policy of the two countries as based on "independence, peace, friendship, cooperation and nonalignment," limiting their relations with the Soviet bloc to the expression of an intention to "strengthen their relations in all fields with the socialist countries." Therefore the treaty was clearly addressed to the Non-Aligned countries and the UN member countries rather than to the limited domestic audience and the socialist countries.[62]

In the pragmatic arguments, which also appeared in the Vietnamese statements after the invasion as well as during and after the Sino-Vietnamese border war, the role of Vietnam as an independent and sovereign agent was emphasized as contrary to the formal Marxist-Leninist tendency to connect Vietnam's foreign policy to the broader perspective of the socialist camps' international role. Vietnam was realizing its sovereign revolutionary line, including revolutionary violence, in order to achieve its ends. With respect to the "two wars for national defense," Hanoi did acknowledge the support given by the Soviet camp to its policy in Indochina and its war against China, but emphasized that the essence of Vietnam's actions was the defense of the nation's independence. The wars against the Khmer Rouge and China were thus means of securing the independence of Vietnam. The other consequences, such as, for example, the growing influence of the Soviet Union in Southeast Asia, were its by-products and not the end in itself.[63]

However, the Vietnamese argumentation on this issue usually combined different patterns of argumentation. Truong Chinh's article on Kampuchea, which was published in the Vietnamese media and was also broadcast in English by the VNA in November 1979, is typical. This article also reflects the broad audience to which it was addressed. In order to gain both the domestic public and the Non-Aligned countries as his audience, Truong Chinh chose the anti-imperialist struggle for the basic theme of his article. The general context of his article was the defeat of Vietnamese policy at the United Nations. Besides the fact that Hanoi failed to get international recognition for the Peoples' Republic of Kampuchea, the UN's General Assembly also passed a resolution on the Kampuchean question that demanded Vietnam's withdrawal from Kampuchea. Therefore Truong Chinh tried to prove the legitimacy of the Heng Samrin government and to defend Vietnam's policy in Indochina.

According to the article, the Kampuchean revolution, like the Indochinese revolution, was originally an anti-imperialist revolution. However, after the victory of three Indochinese countries over American imperialism, China, manipulated by the U.S. and in order to realize its power ambitions in Southeast Asia, took advantage of the deviation of Marxism in the Kampuchean Communist Party to oppose Vietnam. Here Truong Chinh turns his argumentation to the pragmatic pattern when describing the situation of Vietnam, encircled by Beijing, as the old model of Chinese feudalism. The agression against Vietnam was an old Chinese "strategic goal" which produces "a life and death problem" to Vietnam.[64] Thus the Vietnamese used violence to secure their national independence and domestic line against Beijing's ambitions. Because Kampuchea was the weakest link in Beijing's strategy, Vietnam struck there.

However, the Vietnamese invasion was followed immediately by a more conventional Marxist-Leninist argument in the article when Truong

Chinh tried to argue that Pol Pot's administration was defeated also by a domestic mass movement. Thereby Hanoi tried to deliver both the formal Marxist-Leninist argument of a mass uprising and the moralistic argument about the despotic rule of the Khmer Rouge. Referring to the relationship between the mass purges carried out by the Khmer Rouge and the demise of Pol Pot's rule, he maintained that the resistance was a consequence of oppression. He did not hesitate to state that "the revolutionary civil war of the Kampuchean people broke out and developed entirely within the country of the Angkor civilization." This war was combined with Vietnam's defense of its southeast border.[65]

In the light of the Vietnamese statements regarding Kampuchea, the following conclusion on its Indochina doctrine can be drawn: the dominant pattern in the doctrine is the formalist argumentation based on the two camps theory. In this respect, it resembles the Brezhnev Doctrine. It acknowledged the interests of the socialist world system in Indochina and emphasized Vietnam's role in maintaining the features of this system in the region. One aspect of this was the Vietnamese aid to the PRK, including the presence of Vietnamese "voluntary" troops in Kampuchea. However, the Vietnamese angle here appears as the pragmatic arguments based on Vietnam's own security interests, particularly as opposed to China. These elements in Vietnam's policy are therefore of special interest when Vietnam's multilateral policy pursued at international organizations are dealt with.

THE INDOCHINA DOCTRINE AND THE GLOBAL AUDIENCE

The discussion carried on by the Party cadres and the argumentation of the political leadership proved that Marxist-Leninist formalism had gained the dominant position in international relations. However, as we have seen, Vietnamese Marxism-Leninism did not depend solely on this quasi-logical pattern of the Marxist-Leninist doctrine. Notwithstanding the fact that the Vietnamese leadership formulated its doctrine on Indochina along the lines of a formal Marxist-Leninist pattern, the pragmatic element there allowed different kinds of arguments. Therefore examination of Vietnam's policy at international organizations opens up a significant point of view, owing to the fact that Vietnam had to meet there quite heterogeneous audiences.

On account of the bad international reputation of Pol Pot's administration, Hanoi obviously estimated erroneously the international reaction to Vietnam's occupation of Kampuchea.[66] In any case, on the side of formal argument, deviating from the genuine revolutionary line, Vietnam started, with evidently shattering but authentic material, to accuse Democratic Kampuchea's authorities of genocide.[67] This kind of approach was emphatically brought to the fore in both propaganda and international diplomacy.[68] It tried to employ humanistic and ethical tones in order to attract as broad as possible an audience. Consequently, this moralistic style deviated strikingly from pragmatism and formalism; the doctrinal code of Marxist-Leninist argumentation was rather vague and seemed, from time to time, to lose its force entirely.

At first, these arguments were tangled up with the question of who had the right to accredit a representative of Kampuchea to the international organizations, the old government of Democratic Kampuchea or the People's Republic of Kampuchea supported by Vietnam. The role of the ASEAN countries in the Non-Aligned Movement and, especially, at the United Nations became an obstacle to Vietnam's diplomacy.

Immediatelly after Vietnam's invasion of Kampuchea, the ASEAN countries met in Jakarta to coordinate ASEAN's joint policy toward the issue. Despite the fact that the tense situation in Indochina had already lasted a year, not until the invasion were the ASEAN countries pushed to agree on the common foreign policy presupposed by the Bali Concord as early as 1976. As a result of this Jakarta meeting, a document was drawn up on which, notwithstanding its rather general outlines, the ASEAN countries based their arguments against Vietnam's policy toward Kampuchea during the 1980s. Vietnam was not mentioned in the document and no concrete measures were proposed for the termination of the hostilities. It did include, however, clear principles, on the basis of which the political contents of this document can be worked out. Its vocabulary was based on the Bandung Declaration and the UN Charter, and it called upon the countries in the region to respect "each other's independence, sovereignty, territorial integrity and political system" and "to refrain from using force or threatening to use force in their bilateral relations, and carrying out subversive activities, directly or indirectly."[69] After the Jakarta meeting, by referring to these principles, ASEAN published several statements before the 34th Session of the General Assembly and the Non-Aligned's Summit in Havana, where Vietnam was more or less directly urged to withdraw from Kampuchea.[70]

Vietnam started its campaign to obtain international recognition for its protégé, the Heng Samrin government of the People's Republic of Kampuchea as early as January 1979. However, Hanoi failed to get the UN Security Council's support for the right of Heng Samrin's government to represent Kampuchea at the United Nations' organizations.

Simultaneously, ASEAN's attempt to bring the issue of Indochina before the Security Council was prevented by a Soviet veto. Therefore these issues had to wait until the beginning of the following UN Session in September 1979.

Before the 34th UN session, there was a bitter fight on the right to represent Kampuchea at the Havana Non-Aligned Summit. At this Summit, a general debate took place on the course of the Non-Aligned Movement, which focused on the two denominators of nonalignment, namely the principle of keeping outside the Great Power blocs and that of anti-imperialism. However, these denominators did not as such determine each country's position inside the Movement when both elements were accepted as its general principles. Thus the question was one of the emphasis given to these denominators. Although this debate was exaggarated in the Western media, and there occurred no essential shift in the Movement's direction,[71] the arguments on how to deal with the two superpowers did, indeed, indicate the most conspicuous dispute about the Movement's line. To it was joined the debate started by Brezhnev during the Algiers Summit of 1973 on the socialist countries as the natural allies of the Non-Aligned Movement and which was eagerly pursued at the Havana Summit by the host country, Cuba.[72] This was challenged by Yugoslavia's line of emphasizing the distance of the Movement from both Great Powers. The ASEAN member countries in the Movement, especially Malaysia and Singapore, supported this approach and linked the Kampuchean question to this debate. Together with Yugoslavia, they considered that the recognition of the claim by the People's Republic of Kampuchea to the Kampuchean seat would be a symptom of the influence of one Great Power inside the Movement.[73]

Hanoi moderately followed Cuba's approach. Consistently enough, Pham Van Dong argued in Havana against the emphasis on "standing clear of blocs" and considering this "the highest objective," which "is in essence aimed at making the Non-Aligned Movement deviate from its anti-imperialist objectives."[74] Although he did not deny the concept of nonalignment, he stressed that when becoming "a strong anti-imperialist force" the Non-Aligned Movement demonstrates that it "is going in the right direction."[75] However, Dong did not deal directly with the question of the relationship between the socialist countries and the Non-Aligned Movement. As far as the Soviet Union was concerned, he touched only on the bilateral relations between the USSR and Hanoi. He therefore painstakingly tried to avoid expressions that might be interpreted to indicate that Vietnam's foreign policy, particularly in Indochina, was being conducted from Moscow.

Nevertheless, Dong used various expressions that revealed the pro-Soviet stance of his argumentation. His speech was clearly based on the Marxist-Leninist doctrine and his analysis of the world situation on the two camps theory. Accordingly, the general trend of the global developments is determined by the three revolutionary currents of the era, which "are surging up like storms" and "which are attacking, from all directions, imperialism and expansionism, and bringing the peoples' revolutionary cause to splendid victory."[76] Thus China's role was reduced, according to the lines of the two camps theory, to the part played by the imperialist forces; and the Kampuchean problem – particularly the question as to who had the right to occupy the Kampuchean seat at international organizations – was masterminded by American imperialism and Beijing's hegemonism.[77]

However, there existed a clear difference between Pham Van Dong's argumentation for the right of Heng Samrin's government to represent Kampuchea and his arguments justifying Vietnam's invasion of Kampuchea. When dealing with the overthrow of Pol Pot's regime, Dong concentrated on the illegitimate domestic role of Pol Pot's administration. He did not admit the direct intervention by Hanoi, but emphasized that the Khmer Rouge's rule was smashed by the Kampuchean people's victory. He argued that the Kampuchean people's right to overthrow the genocidal regime was combined with Vietnam's right to self-defense and the right of the Indochinese people to defend themselves "against their common enemy – U.S. imperialism and Chinese reactionaries."[78] Thus all these contained the same elements as the Indochina doctrine formulated in the previous chapter.

Vietnam's policy at the Havana Summit succeeded partly: the Kampuchean seat was left vacant. The reason for this was, however, sooner in the institutional practices of the Non-Aligned Movement than in Hanoi's success in persuading the majority of the audience. The institutional factor in the settlement of the Kampuchean credentials in the Movement was enforced by Cuba's position in the leadership. The treatment of the Kampuchean credentials in the new situation started as early as the end of January 1979 at the meeting of the Coordinating Bureau in Maputo, Mozambique, where Vietnam and Cuba tried to prevent the participation of the delegation representing the old Phnom Penh government as an observer. Since the Heng Samrin government failed to send a delegation and the interest of this meeting lay elsewhere, the attempt by Vietnam and Cuba failed.[79] However, when the Coordinating Bureau held a meeting in Colombo in June 1979, the question of the Kampuchean seat in the Movement had become highly divisible. Excepting the members of the Coordinating bureau, 50 members of the Movement had come as observers. Both Pol Pot's party and Heng Samrin's government sent a delegation and both claimed the status of observer. The old status of Democratic Kampuchea's delegation was defended particularly by two Bureau members, Yugoslavia and Indonesia; and two of the observers, Malaysia and Singapore, who were afraid of the pro-Soviet grouping's influence in the Movement, also spoke up on its behalf. Vietnam and Cuba, both Bureau members, supported the right of the People's Republic of Kampuchea to observer's status. When it became obvious that no consensus was possible, what with the negotiations behind the scenes led by Sri Lanka's Foreign Minister A.C.S. Hameed, it was agreed that Pol Pot's government could maintain its status as an observer but without the right to speak, which normally belongs to such status. In fact, Hameed ruled that the Kampuchean question would not be allowed to be dealt with at the delegations' formal meetings. This ban was disregarded only by the Laotian and Singaporean delegations.[80]

Notwithstanding these preliminary victories of the Pol Pot administration in the Non-Aligned Movement, the advantage gained was effectively negated by the Movement's consensus principle and the power of the host country. As the host country automatically takes the chair in the Coordinating Bureau, Cuba decided to keep the Kampuchean seat vacant during the three-year period of its leadership of the Movement. Thus the decision reached two months earlier on Democratic Kampuchea's right to represent Kampuchea was nullified. The solution, which was called consensus by Cuba and Vietnam, was loudly questioned by Yugoslavia and the ASEAN countries. The Democratic Kampuchean delegation was allowed to enter Cuba during the summit, but the hosts prevented it from taking part in the meetings, including the general debates of the summit and other functions of the Movement. Simultaneously with the Havana Summit, Heng Samrin was invited to Cuba on a state visit, receiving the highest possible protocol from Fidel Castro. Khieu Samphan of the Pol Pot government had to follow the procedure of ordinary passengers, including the normal immigration formalities.[81]

However, the final Declaration of the 6th Summit did not reflect the growing influence of the pro-Soviet grouping in the Movement. The theme of anti-imperialist struggle was in no more central a role than at the Colombo Summit. The Political Declaration of the 6th Conference affirmed that the essence of the policy of non-alignment involved both the anti-imperialist struggle "and all forms of foreign aggression, occupation, domination, interference or hegemony, as well as being against great-power and bloc policies."[82] In fact, the Political Declaration included expressions that might be interpreted as rather directly critical of Vietnam's regional role. "The Situation in South-East Asia" in the Declaration followed ASEAN declarations on the Kampuchean situation. It urged that peace and stability in the region could "be realized on the basis of the nonaligned principles of respect for sovereignty, independence, territorial integrity, noninterference in internal affairs, nonuse of force and non-aggression."[83] Furthermore, the ZOPFAN concept re-emerged in the vocabulary of nonalignment and the Political Declaration ignored Hanoi's earlier formulations.[84] This obviously reflected both the changes in Hanoi's attitude that took place at the end of the 1970s and the reduced prestige of Vietnam in the Movement, owing to growing criticism of its regional policy. Vietnam's acceptance of the ZOPFAN concept was affirmed a couple of weeks later, when Vietnam's representative applied the concept at the United Nations, together with its earlier expression of "peace, independence, freedom and neutrality."[85]

Immediately after the Havana Summit of the Non-Aligned Countries, the question of Kampuchean credentials was made even more subversive at the General Assembly's 34th session than in Havana. Contrary to the political parlance used by the Vietnamese cadres in domestic discussion, the Vietnamese diplomats did not play the role of the avant-garde of anti-imperialist struggle and socialism in the Third World. Especially the speech of Vietnam's representative in the Assembly's general debate lacked almost all the expressions characteristic of the vanguard Marxist. He also avoided using the Marxist-Leninist vocabulary most often heard in Vietnamese speeches dealing with international affairs, such as the three revolutionary currents, anti-imperialist struggle and proletarian internationalism. The main target in his speech was China's international and regional role. As he depicted it, Vietnam's role in Kampuchea was a response to China's threat to Vietnam's independence and Chinese expansionism in Southeast Asia.[86]

However, in the debate over the Kampuchean question, which was accepted as an agenda item at the General Assembly, Vietnam had to use several different arguments to defend its regional policy. Two central elements made up the context of Vietnam's rhetoric. First, the Vietnamese were addressing a "global audience," i.e., they had to confront a highly heterogeneous international audience with quite generally accepted premises. This emphasized the function of moralistic argument. Without considering the theoretical purity of its arguments, Hanoi condemned the crimes of the Khmer Rouge against the Catholic, Buddhist and Moslem religions, the national minorities and the educated strata of Kampuchean society.[87] At the UN, Hanoi now had a real political issue, which it tried to turn in its favor by pursuing supporters for its cause; and its rhetoric was not aimed simply to proclaim its own political stand. Secondly, Hanoi was arguing against the ASEAN initiative for the solution of the Kampuchean question, which involved the central principles of international law and, more particularly, ASEAN's ZOPFAN proposal.

The policy pursued by the ASEAN countries at the General Assembly was double-edged. Its first part dealt with the question of Kampuchea's credentials at the UN, and the second ASEAN's initiative, agenda item 123, "the Situation in Kampuchea." These were important to the international publicity about the Kampuchean question. They turned into an annual spectacle at the beginning of the Sessions throughout the 1980s, owing to the practice of deciding the credentials of each country annually. The Kampuchean question therefore rose onto the scene automatically, and it was rather simple for the ASEAN countries to link the draft resolution on the situation in Kampuchea to the question of credentials as long as such credentials were not given to the Heng Samrin government.

The Kampuchean credentials became one of the very first questions to be taken up at the 34th Session. The General Assembly had to consider the appeal of the permanent representative of Democratic Kampuchea in the UN, who requested that the Kampuchean credentials be awarded the delegation of Democratic Kampuchea. Moreover, the Heng Samrin government announced that the Peoples' Republic of Kampuchea was sending its delegation to the Session. This forced the General Assembly to refer the issue to the Credentials Committee.[88]

In this preparatory committee, the political division, which remained more or less a permanent feature of the Kampuchean issue during the 1980s, was already evident. At the committee sessions, three proposals for its solution were presented. Based on the decision reached at the Non-Aligned Summit in Havana, Congo and Panama suggested that the Kampuchean seat also at the UN should remain vacant. China and the United States supported the appeal of Democratic Kampuchea, and the Soviet Union claimed that the Kampuchean credentials belonged to the Peoples' Republic of Kampuchea. When it became obvious that the stance of China and the U.S. would win, the Soviet Union suggested the draft of Congo and Panama as a compromise. However, the chairman of the committee, together with the delegates from the rest of the countries (on the basis of the technical role of the committee), decided to recommend awarding the credentials to Democratic Kampuchea.[89]

At the General Assembly, the ASEAN countries, together with China, formed an opposite pole to Vietnam and the socialist countries. When the majority of the developed Western countries, with the backing of some Third World countries, supported the credentials of Democratic Kampuchea, the only acceptable solution for Vietnam being India's proposal, which followed the lines of the draft suggested by Congo and Panama in the Credentials Committee. The idea of the Indian draft was that it was not presented as an independent proposal but as an amendment to the solution arrived at by the Credentials Committee. This possibility seemed to attract the greater part of the member countries, which wanted to stay neutral in the Assembly's voting. However, the ASEAN countries managed to prevent this kind of interpretation and the Indian draft was considered as an independent proposal. In a twofold vote, the Indian draft was set first against ASEAN's proposal; and when Vietnam, together with the socialist countries, supported the Indian proposal, the juxtaposition between the acceptance or the rejection of Vietnam's policy toward Kampuchea emerged as the main question. In this situation, the countries that had hesitated to take sides found it impossible to support the Indian proposal. After that, the proposal of the Credentials Committee was accepted with 71 in favor, 35 against and 34 abstaining (UN resolution 34/2).[90]

Knowing the constellation at the General Assembly, and realizing the difficulty of geting the majority of the countries to support its position in the Kampuchean question, the Indian proposal was acceptable to Vietnam in this situation. Thus Vietnam argued both for its draft proposal for the recognition of the Heng Samrin government and for the Indian proposal to leave the Kampuchean seat vacant. Hanoi therefore emphasized the illegitmacy of the Pol Pot government in representing the Kampuchean people on both moralistic and factual grounds. Hence Pol Pot's government had no administrative power in Kampuchea. Against Singapore's argument, in particular, that Heng Samrin's government functioned only with the support of Vietnamese troops, Vietnam's representative countered by appealing to the Kampuchea–Vietnam treaty. While arguing in favor of this position, Vietnam's spokeman approached the familiar Marxist-Leninist tones. He emphasized that "the militant solidarity between the peoples of Vietnam and Kampuchea ... are in no way prejudicial to the legitimate interests of anyone." As he continued, "this includes the ASEAN countries, some of which have joined in one way or another in the American war of aggression against Vietnam."[91] Therefore, the presence of Vietnamese troops was due to the need to preserve this militant solidarity of Indochina in order to defend itself against the common enemy, whose aim was to turn Indochina into a single battlefield.[92]

There is no evidence that Vietnam and India had put forward their proposals in coordination. Vietnam expressed, however, particular understanding of the Indian move. In fact, in the discussion on the Kampuchean situation at the General Assembly in the following year, Vietnam's representative stated that to leave the Kampuchean seat vacant would be "the most judicious solution."[93] Hanoi presented India's draft resolution as a proposal of the nonaligned countries, which was claimed to be in harmony with the decisions of the Non-Aligned's Havanna Conference, thus giving the impression of a broad consensus among the Non-Aligned members.[94] Although India's policy did not succeed at the General Assembly, it indicated India's positive attitude toward Vietnam's regional role, which was realized at the 7th Non-Aligned Summit in New Delhi three years later and in India's recognition of the Heng Samrin government as an exception among the socialist countries. India's proposal opened up the possibility of Vietnam's being identified as a member of the Non-Aligned Movement, fending off particularly Chinese accusations that Vietnam was realizing Soviet global policy.

The other part of the ASEAN double-edged policy on Kampuchea was even more embarrassing to Vietnam than the issue of Kampuchean credentials. The item "Situation in Kampuchea" put Vietnam near the position used by Hanoi to blame imperialism. Particularly the paragraph in the resolution adopted by the General Assembly calling for the "immediate withdrawal of all foreign forces from Kampuchea" and calling upon "all States to refrain from all acts or threats of aggresssion and all forms of interference, subversion or coercion, and to respect scrupulously the sovereignty, territorial integrity and independence of Kampuchea"[95] was totally unacceptable to Hanoi.

Hanoi's proposal was an answer to ASEAN's initiative, which was not yet a formal draft resolution. Interestingly enough, a crucial argument behind both ASEAN's and Vietnam's proposal was the establishment of the conditions of ZOPFAN. The Vietnamese used in their draft resolution the expression "a zone of peace, freedom, neutrality and stability in the region,"[96] but among other expressions they also used explicitly the ZOPFAN concept in their statements when they described the ideal relations between the Southeast Asian countries. ASEAN's draft resolution did not mention the concept, but it was used in the arguments for their proposal. ASEAN's initiative stated its members' concern about the armed intervention against Kampuchea. It pointed out the danger of an escalation of the Kampuchean situation to a conflict in which external powers were involved, referring thus to the central idea of the ZOPFAN concept.[97] The selfsame idea was repeated in the revised version of ASEAN's draft resolution.[98] In the ASEAN countries' statements, the demand for Vietnam's withdrawal was connected directly with this central ZOPFAN objective. Malaysia's representative urged a political solution "so that we do not become the pawns of outside countries in their power or ideological struggles" and stressed that "our ultimate objective is the establishment of a zone of peace, freedom and neutrality."[99] Similarly, Singapore's Tommy Koh pointed up the risk of Great Power involvement in Southeast Asia. As a precondition for regional relations in Southeast Asia, ZOPFAN was also demanded by Indonesia and Thailand.[100] The draft resolution presented by ASEAN at the UN's 35th Session the following year stated explicitly that, after a comprehensive political solution was achieved, the Southeast Asian countries should renew their efforts to establish a zone of peace, freedom and neutrality in Southeast Asia.[101]

The appearance of the ZOPFAN concept together with the expression of peace, freedom, neutrality and stability in the Vietnamese vocabulary during the debate on the Kampuchean issue proved that Vietnam was seeking some common ground with ASEAN. It indicated the political shift that had taken place in Vietnam's leadership when Hanoi abandoned the anti-imperialist struggle as a general theme in its relations with the ASEAN member countries. ZOPFAN thus became a foreign-policy theme in order to attract an audience in the ASEAN countries. It also indicated that Vietnam had accepted ASEAN as an important regional actor. However, as the Vietnamese draft resolution and following argumentation proved, there were striking differences about the contents of the concept between ASEAN and Vietnam. For ASEAN, the idea of ZOPFAN was to keep the cold war conflicts out of this region. For Vietnam, following the foreign-policy argumentation that developed in the late 1970s and early 1980s, the expressions about regional relations – with the ZOPFAN concept sometimes applied – was adapted to the general lines of the two camps theory.

Accordingly, the conditions of ZOPFAN would prevail if only both sides recognized the existence of two blocs in Southeast Asia and agreed on a status quo between them. Vietnam's draft resolution included three crucial points. First, it gave the green light to the elimination of any genocidal government that threatened peace and stability in Southeast Asia. Second, it rejected the right of foreign countries to intervene in Kampuchean affairs. Moreover, it called for continuation of the effort to build a zone of peace, freedom, neutrality and stability in Southeast Asia.[102] The draft resolution therefore justified Vietnam's right to control Kampuchean affairs, rejected ASEAN's proposal for neutral mediation in resolving the Kampuchean issue, including participation by the United Nations. And finally, it was asserted that to recognize these points would mean that the foregoing characterization of peace, freedom, neutrality and stability prevailed in Southeast Asia. According to this "ZOPFAN" of Vietnam, it could be enforced by signing treaties of peace and nonagression in Southeast Asia.[103] Vietnam's interpretation of ZOPFAN was therefore in harmony with the Soviet concept of peaceful coexistence, which was entering the Vietnamese political vocabulary.

The concept of ZOPFAN was becoming an important element in Vietnam's relations with the ASEAN countries. Its significance was that the same concept could be applied by different language codes. Thus, by this concept, the Vietnamese tried to connect two different kinds of political language systems, just as Soviet diplomacy had used the concept of peaceful coexistence in dealing with the capitalist countries. This is an important element when a Marxist government tries to adjust to the international system without giving up the theoretical premises and the task of domestic mobilization of the doctrine. In order to avoid the blending of Marxist-Leninist elements with their concept, particularly the two camps theory, the ASEAN governments were very cautious when they used it in dealing with Vietnam. Therefore Vietnam – after the ASEAN countries had rejected all the ostensibly very small attempts made by the Vietnamese (substituting the word independence for freedom, or adding the word stability to the concept) to make revisions in the concept – started to use the concept itself, though giving a special twist to it.

The draft resolution sponsored by ASEAN was adopted by the General Assembly by an even greater majority than the credentials of Democratic Kampuchea. In the voting, India again attempted to mediate with its own draft resolution, which in fact followed Vietnam's draft resolution quite closely. It aimed to reinforce the current situation, though interestingly putting even more weight on the two-blocs structure (Indochina-ASEAN) in Southeast Asia.[104] The Vietnamese failed to persuade the member countries of the United Nations to give their support and the ASEAN draft resolution received growing support during the 1980s.[105]

Analysis of Vietnamese rhetoric, particularly at the UN, but also to some extent at the Havana Summit Conference of the Non-Aligned Movement, proved that there was a growing gap between the Party cadres' discussions and the diplomatic argumentation in the international organizations. There are several reasons for it, but all of them date back to the Kampuchean issue. First, Vietnam could no longer freely choose its own themes and subjects to present before these organizations, but it was obliged to respond to the Kampuchean question. Second, Vietnam was not mainly expressing its political orientation toward its allies and domestic public, but was now seeking to persuade as wide as possible an audience of its cause by using universal arguments based on moralistic, ethical, and juridistic principles. In this kind of argumentation, the Marxist standpoint was pushed into the background. Therefore, when the arguments of the Party cadres and leadership are compared with the Vietnamese diplomatic rhetoric vis-à-vis the global audience, it is difficult to discern any coherent doctrine on Indochina based on Marxist-Leninist theory.

The difference between the discussions of the Party cadres addressed to the public at home and the diplomatic parlance for the benefit of an international audience was equally evident when one compares the texts of the Vietnamese leadership at the 7th Non-Aligned Summit Conference in New Delhi in March 1983. Examination of an article by one Party analyst, Vu Hien, on the New Delhi Summit, which appeared in *Tap Chi Cong San,* is revealing. This article was strongly influenced by the Marxist-Leninist doctrine, the author having concentrated more on autocommunication than the transmission of information; and the theme of his rhetoric was the anti-imperialist struggle.[106] In view of the audience, the Communist Party cadres, Vu Hien was not obligated to deal in detail with the Kampuchean question, as the Vietnamese had to do at the Conference, but to concentrate on themes that upheld the doctrine. On the other hand, the aim of Hanoi's diplomacy in New Delhi was that the question of the Kampuchean seat in the Movement should not be raised. Vietnam tried, in the name of the Movement's unity, to prevent the discussion or at least limit it.[107] Following this line, Pham Van Dong did not deal in the general debate with the Kampuchean representation but concentrated on the general themes of nonalignment following the lines that the host country, India, had drawn in the draft of the political declaration.[108] However, the issue on the Kampuchean seat created a debate three days long at the Summit's ministerial meeting, where Foreign Minister Nguyen Co Thach had to argue in defense of Vietnam's policy in Southeast Asia.

Contrary to Pham Van Dong's address, the struggle between the two epithets concerning nonalignment, neutralism and anti-imperialism was a leading thought in Vu Hien's article. Interestingly enough, Dong touched upon the matter only slightly, following also here India's line. Vu Hien argued forcefully for anti-imperialism. He described it as "a heavy struggle between two trends," constituted on the one side by those who defend the anti-imperialist and anticolonialist policy, and on the other side by those "negative forces" whose policy of neutrality it is to keep the Movement "between the blocs," in order to lead the Movement "to make compromises with imperialist principles."[109] Dong dealt with this question in quite a different tone. He referred to Jawaharlar Nehru's definition of nonalignment as a positive aspect of peace, where colonialism is replaced by independent countries and international cooperation. He continued quoting Nehru further to the effect that "the nonaligned countries are not committed to the military blocs" without making any reservation that emphasis on this latter part of the definition would lead to a deviation of the movement, as he emphasized in his address at the 6th Summit Conference in Havana. On the other hand, he laid stress on the latter part by adding that noncommitment to the blocs means readiness to "welcome new horizons" and "the evolution of history."[110]

Despite the fact that Dong criticized American global policy and the collusion of U.S. with China, he avoided taking a strong pro-Soviet stance. In fact, he connected Soviet foreign policy to the broader phenomenon of lessening international tension, which was supported by neutral and nonaligned countries.[111] Similarly, his address lacked the formalist vocabulary that dominated his speech at the Havana Conference three years earlier. In contrast to Dong, who did not see the unanimity of the Movement in real danger, Vu Hien argued in his *Tap Chi Cong San* article that the Summit was a victory of the anti-imperialist trend over the neutralist deviation provoked by Beijing and Washington. This culminated in the issue of the Kampuchean seat, where Beijing's line of supporting the Coalition Government of Democratic Kampuchea (CGDK) under the leadership of Prince Sihanouk was defeated. From this, he reached a final conclusion along formalist lines according to which the success of the New Delhi conference based on the Movement's anti-imperialism and anticolonialism together with "the changes in the relation of the forces in the world, particularly the rise of the forces of national independence, democracy and the progressive forces in the Third World."[112]

If Foreign Minister Nguyen Co Thach's speech at the ministerial meeting of the Delhi Summit is compared with that of Pham Van Dong at the plenary meeting, there were differences in both the theme and the pattern of argumentation. Thach engaged in quiet talks with the ASEAN countries to prevent adoption of the theme, the Kampuchean question, for inclusion in the agenda. In fact, India had tried in earlier debate to force this item off the agenda, but this attempt was thwarted by the ASEAN countries to make it clear that no consensus existed on this issue.[113] Thach argued at the meeting both to contest the legitimacy of Pol Pot's government and the CGDK, and to defend the legitimacy of the Heng Samrin government by referring to the ethical aspects of the question. However, by defending the presence of Vietnamese troops in Kampuchea, he gave his argumentation a pragmatic turn. He justified Vietnam's presence in Kampuchea on the grounds of security. He stated that after failing to compel Vietnam to accept a status of dependence "China, on the one hand, has used the Pol Pot clique to unleash the war against Vietnam from its southwest and, on the other hand, launched a war of aggression on Vietnam at its northern border (...) In such a situation, Vietnam had a legitimate right to self-defense, and at the same time had the duty of helping the Kampuchean people to free themselves from the Pol Pot clique's genocide in response to the appeal of the National United Front for the Salvation of Kampuchea." Therefore, equally, the Vietnamese "volunteer troops" would "completely withdraw after China puts an end to its threats against the security of Kampuchea."[114]

Although Thach defended Cuba's course of action in Havana recommending leaving the Kampuchean seat vacant, he was unwilling to submit the Kampuchean question for deliberation on the basis of the two epithets of nonaligned, anti-imperialist struggle and noncommitment to the blocs. He asserted that the differences between the Non-Aligned Countries are "minor, local and temporary" if compared with the threat of "imperialism and reactionaries against the nonaligned."[115] Thus Thach, like Pham Van Dong, sought in his speech to prevent the issue from rising to major importance at the Conference. In this, again with the support of the host country, Hanoi was rather successful. This meant, however, that Hanoi could not raise the themes, which have a much closer affinity to the Marxist-Leninist doctrine, as Dong's speech proved. Its leading idea focused on a new international economic order broadly accepted by the Non-Aligned member countries and which did not assign Vietnam any special forerunner's role. Similarly, in order to avoid giving the impression of representing the policy of the socialist countries in the movement, the Vietnamese speeches did not draw on any formalist pattern and vocabulary. This separates them sharply from the Indochina doctrine formulated in the foregoing. This also points up the fact that the gap in foreign-policy rhetoric between the Party cadres and diplomatic parlance was widening further. The Marxist-Leninist formalism and the dominance of the doctrinal code had become prevalent and was even gaining strength among the Party cadres. On the other hand, the pragmatic foreign-policy argumentation, which had to respond to ideas emanating from outside the Marxist-Leninist doctrine, was further losing its grip on the doctrinal code and domestic mobilization.

THE INDOCHINA DOCTRINE AND REGIONAL DIPLOMACY

Vietnam's global role as a forerunner in the anti-imperialist struggle was largely lost, owing to the Kampuchean question. The connection of the Kampuchean question to the Great Power competition between the Soviet Union and China reduced the credibility of Vietnam's independent role among the Third World countries. The economic and diplomatic blockade imposed by the major Western powers forced Vietnam to ever-growing dependence on the Soviet Union, which increased Vietnam's reputation as a Soviet ally in Southeast Asia. This was heightened by the political and military support which Vietnam needed on account of the immediate threat of China. In the Indochina doctrine formulated above, the central element was the two camps struggle in Southeast Asia, where Vietnam's role was to defend the positions of the revolutionary forces and the socialist camp, headed by the Soviet Union. The doctrine was completed by the pragmatic argument about Vietnam's national security, which was threatened by Chinese expansionism. This chapter examines how this doctrine is applied in Vietnam's regional policy, together with its Indochinese partners, toward the ASEAN countries.

Although the political constellation that took shape during the late 1970s and early 1980s included several elements, all attempts to achieve a regional settlement started from the Kampuchean question. There were no official talks on the question at which the parties concerned would have negotiated with each other before the late 1980s. However, excepting a few informal meetings between Vietnam's foreign minister and his ASEAN counterparts, various one-sided diplomatic maneuvers took place, aimed at securing support in the multilateral diplomatic rivalries at the United Nations and in the Non-Aligned Movement. These included ministerial meetings of ASEAN as well as the conferences of Indochinese foreign ministers and the UN-sponsored conferences initiated by ASEAN, in which Indochina and its socialist allies did not participate. Among the few concrete political moves, the formation of the Coalition Government of Democratic Kampuchea, which was carried out through diplomatic maneuvres engaged in by China and the ASEAN countries, did not support the political solution during the 1980s.

Despite the fact that certain ASEAN leaders were eager to examine the power constellation from a rather simple model, there were still several trends in Southeast Asian politics that found their common denominator in the UN's voting on Kampuchea's credentials and the resolution. There existed different approaches toward Indochina among the ASEAN countries. Similarly, domestic politics, notably the military coup in the spring of 1980 in Thailand where Kriangsak Chomanand's government was replaced by one headed by General Prem Tinsulanoud, shifted ASEAN's policy toward new lines. These changes turned the ASEAN-Indochina constellation in many respects into a Vietnam-Thailand-China triangle, where the moderate ASEAN countries could not do anything else than follow the developments and proclaim the unity of ASEAN.

Owing to the security interests of Thailand, which were directly challenged by the Kampuchean developments, the policy line pursued by Bangkok was decisive in determining ASEAN's orientation. Therefore both Beijing and Hanoi directed their diplomatic activities in that direction. As far as Kriangsak's administration was concerned, Thailand tried to stay neutral vis-à-vis China and Vietnam, although the pressures to turn toward China were strong. However, the possibility that the Khmer Rouge would return to power in Kampuchea was not attractive, owing to the tense situation that existed on the Thai-Kampuchean border during Pol Pot's rule. Despite this danger, strong arguments were advanced to coordinate policy with China. First, the presence of Vietnamese troops at the Thai-Kampuchean border was a security problem, and to deal with this Thailand should seek the backing of a regional military force. The support of China depended on the possibility of the Khmer Rouge's using Thai territory as a sanctuary. China promised, however, to withdraw its support from Thailand's Communist guerrilla movement. Thus the danger that the Khmer Rouge and Thai guerrillas would join forces in a situation where Bangkok was striving to drive the Khmer Rouge out of Thailand was eliminated. In fact, with this support, Bangkok managed to crush the military organization of the Thai Communist Party at the beginning of the 1980s. Finally, the economic cooperation offered by Beijing proved to be quite beneficial; among other things, China sold crude oil to Thailand clearly under the market price. Thailand's hesitation between these benefits and neutrality in the Kampuchean question turned into a pro-Chinese orientation, which became dominant in Thai foreign politics when Prem came into power.[116]

Immediately after Prem Tinsulanoud's coup, Indonesia's President Suharto and Malaysia's Prime Minister Dato' Hussein Onn announced, after their meeting in Kuantan, Malaysia, an offer to Vietnam called the "Kuantan principle." It followed the outlines of the ZOPFAN concept in a move to lessen the influence of outside powers in the Southeast Asian region. The proposal intended, on the one hand, to help Vietnam break away from the Sino–Soviet power rivalry in Asia and to free it from

Soviet influence; and, on the other hand, it aimed at a political solution in the Kampuchean question. This solution was calculated to recognize Vietnam's security interests with respect to Kampuchea, i.e., to prevent the Khmer Rouge or any other pro-Chinese element from gaining power in Kampuchea.[117]

There were, however, two obstacles to a realization of the Kuantan formula. Two other members of ASEAN, Singapore and Thailand, had strong reservations. Although they did not condemn the principle, they declared that insofar as Vietnamese troops were in Kampuchea, ASEAN should give no signals of concessions to Hanoi.[118] Vietnam's new foreign minister, Nguyen Co Thach, on his visit to Malaysia in April, rejected the idea by refusing to discuss Kampuchea without the participation of the Heng Samrin government in these discussions. Hence he referred to the unity of Indochina and argued pragmatically that Vietnamese troops would remain in Kampuchea as long as the Chinese threat confronted Vietnam.[119] Thus Thach rejected the Kuantan principle in terms of both formal and pragmatic argument. But by referring to the Chinese threat, he admitted the assumption underlying the Kuantan formula to be correct. Simultaneously, by raising the ZOPFAN concept as a starting point for Indochinese relations with ASEAN, he tried to find the common denominator with the ASEAN countries. However, the emphasis on Indochinese unity reveals Hanoi's deviation from ASEAN's interpretation of the ZOPFAN concept.[120]

The Kuantan principle was finally dropped from the ASEAN-Indochina dialogue when armed Vietnamese units and Thai troops clashed in the Kampuchea-Thai border area in June 1980. This led Indonesia and Malaysia to revert to the common and tougher policy toward Vietnam. As a result of this new ASEAN orientation led by Singapore and Thailand, the two-bloc structure in Southeast Asia was strengthened. This constellation was further bolstered by the formation of the Coalition Government of Democratic Kampuchea (CGDK) on June 22, 1982, after nearly two years of negotiations between the Khmer factions and with the political support of Beijing, Singapore and Thailand. The essence of this coalition and the particular interests of Singapore and Thailand are too broad a subject to be discussed here. Generally, the common ASEAN background of this "government" was the growing Western criticism of the backing given Pol Pot at the United Nations and the threat that ASEAN would be left alone, together with China, at the front supporting Democratic Kampuchea.[121]

Interestingly enough, this development inside ASEAN coincided with the growth of the formalist tendency in Vietnamese Marxism-

Leninism. This tendency, as discussed earlier, connected Indochina to a part of the socialist world system. However, together with the open confrontation with China and the pursuit of a dialogue with the ASEAN countries, this forced Vietnam's foreign policy to reformulate its concepts and define the country's regional role.

The vocabulary of the first joint statement issued by the Indochinese foreign ministers, Phnom Penh's Joint Communiqué of January 1980, was indeed anti-imperialist and consistently adhered to the Marxist-Leninist doctrine. It stated that the events of recent years, in particular, showed that "American imperialism is the principal enemy of humanity," and "the expansionists and hegemonists of the Chinese big nation are the direct enemy" of Indochina. They both are "the enemies of peace, national independence and social progress in Southeast Asia."[122] The Indochinese foreign ministers did not hesitate to emphasize their relationship to the Soviet bloc, which permits the favorable balance of forces in Southeast Asia[123] When dealing with the ASEAN countries, the communiqué's vocabulary ignored the ZOPFAN and resembled Vietnam's foreign avant-garde policy toward Southeast Asia in the mid 1970s.[124]

After six months, the parlance of the Indochinese foreign ministers was, however, more modest. There were three important events that may have influenced this to some extent. Vietnam's old Foreign Minister Nguyen Duy Trinh had to step down from the top leadership, and he was replaced by the pragmatic and dynamic but pro-Soviet Nguyen Co Thach. In the second place, there was held the Kuantan meeting between Indonesia and Malaysia as well as Thach's visits to Thailand and Malaysia, which perhaps revealed to the Vietnamese the differences between the ASEAN countries. Finally, Vietnamese diplomacy had plenty of work to do explaining its positions after their military forces had clashed with Thai troops some weeks earlier.

In fact, the Vientiane Statement of July 18, 1980, concentrated on the situation at the Thai–Kampuchean border. It reserved the right of the troops of Vietnam and the Heng Samrin government to attack the Khmer Rouge forces along the border area and blame Bangkok for the clashes with Thai troops in the border area. Nevertheless, clear changes appeared in the statement's tone in general terms and in its stance toward the ASEAN countries. While the theme of the joint Phnom Penh communiqué was the anti-imperialist struggle, the Vientiane statement introduced the cause of peaceful coexistence in the context of two blocs in Southeast Asia. It would be realized, according to the statement, by both bilateral and multilateral treaties, which would stabilize the political system in Southeast Asia.[125] To express Vietnam's commitment to maintaining the existing political relations in Indochina, Hanoi always pointed up the equal position of Laos and the People's Republic of Kampuchea in the negotiations between Indochina and the ASEAN countries. In January 1981, the Indochinese foreign ministers proposed a mechanism to realize peaceful coexistence in Southeast Asia. This two-staged mechanism included, first, a regional conference "between the two groups – the Indochinese countries and the ASEAN countries – to discuss problems of mutual concern" in order to reach a treaty that includes, among other things, the "non-imposition of the will of one group on the other, and noninterference from the outside."[126]

This, along with what follows after, resembles much of the original idea of the ZOPFAN concept's realization. "Only" the essence, the existence of two groups in Southeast Asia differed from ZOPFAN. According to the Indochinese foreign ministers' proposal, this two groups system should be confirmed by a treaty and recognized and guaranteed by an international conference.[127] In order to emphasize the fact that the question was one of a treaty between two blocs and not between several individual countries, the proposal suggested that "there would be a preparatory meeting between a representative of the three Indochinese countries and a representative of the five ASEAN countries" before that conference.[128] Thus the détente toward the ASEAN countries adopted by Indochinese foreign ministers aimed at ASEAN's recognition of Indochina as a common bloc. This approach was even more strongly emphasized in the later joint statements issued by the Indochinese foreign minister's meeting. In the Phnom Penh Communiqué of July 20 1983, the ZOPFAN proposal was cleverly set in the context of the two blocs only by mention of Indochina and ASEAN. It stated that the Indochina group were "prepared to take the proposal of the ASEAN countries for a zone of peace, freedom and neutrality (ZOPFAN) as a basis for discussion between Indochina and ASEAN."[129] Simultaneously with this, the common Soviet vocabulary appeared more and more often, introducing clearly the Soviet approach to the Southeast Asian situation in these Indochinese statements. They included terms like international détente, peaceful coexistence between states of different socio-political regimes, and, as the statement of the 7th conference of Indochinese foreign ministers proved, socialist internationalism.[130]

Consistency is seldom the leading principle of political rhetoric. In the formalist Vietnamese Marxist-Leninist approach, there was a point that was clearly incompatible with the original Soviet approach to peaceful coexistence. The original idea of the Soviet doctrine was to avoid open war between the different political and social systems. Its

point of departure was a world clearly divided into two opposing camps.
The Vietnamese shared this view. However, there was a third factor in the
Vietnamese equation that is hard to fit into the original Soviet formula:
the role of China as a decisive factor in Southeast Asian relations.
Therefore the ASEAN countries were not only the regional counterpart
of the Indochinese countries but also, when China is added to Vietnam's
formula, potential allies or enemies of Vietnam. The problem for Vietnam
was that, in general, ASEAN's stand toward the Kampuchean question
was closer to that of China's than of Vietnam's. This was particularly true
as regards Thailand and Singapore, while Malaysia and, especially,
Indonesia were suspicious of China's regional role. This element was
always present in Vietnam's argumentation concerning the ASEAN
countries.

Naturally, from the retrospective point of view, this can be examined
as a pragmatic policy intented to divide the enemy. Nevertheless, in
actual situations, where the power constellation is never so clear as in
retrospective examination, the Vietnamese had to fit Marxist-Leninist
doctrine to the aim of persuading the ASEAN countries, or at least some
of them, for their sake, to oppose China. Therefore the concept of
peaceful coexistence, together with the ZOPFAN concept, was a crucial
element in Vietnam's attempt to find a common language in dealing with
the ASEAN countries.

In pursuing this policy, Vietnam used both its proposals of a regional
settlement and resisting China's threat to the whole of Southeast Asia. It
is difficult to estimate conclusively the success of this policy in the first
half of the 1980s, but the Vietnamese foreign minister's dynamic
diplomacy produced some interesting episodes and some confusion in
ASEAN's front against Vietnam on the Kampuchean issue. Similarly,
this pointed up the combination of pragmatic and formalist argumentation
in Vietnam's foreign policy. According to Hanoi's approach, ASEAN,
although it was recognized as a political reality, was not a homogeneous
entity. The ASEAN countries were divided into those that intended to
take an independent line vis-à-vis China and the United States, and those
that cooperated with China in the Kampuchean question. To the one
group belonged Malaysia, Indonesia and, sometimes, the Philippines.
The latter group, consisting of Singapore and Thailand, notwithstanding
the fact that their anti-Vietnamese attitudes often coincided, was not
homogeneous, either. Vietnam's foreign policy during Nguyen Co Thach's
period acknowledged this, but tried not to emphasize the role of this
group inside ASEAN.[131]

Nguyen Co Thach's style of rhetoric was indeed a pragmatic one. In fact, his argumentation followed in many respects the Kuantan principle and the idea of ZOPFAN, but it included also Vietnam's view of Indochina as a bloc. After his ASEAN tour, Thach acknowledged ASEAN's concern about the presence of the Vietnamese army in Kampuchea but added the reminder that Hanoi's concern was the Chinese threat.[132] In this respect, he was following the Kuantan formula excluding the Soviet factor emphasized by Malaysia and Indonesia. As regards the second point, contrary to ASEAN concern over the neutralization of Kampuchea, Vietnam stands, according to Thach, "for the neutralization of Southeast Asia. So these two requests must be met at the same time." The third point brought out the idea of the two-bloc structure in Southeast Asia behind his argumentation: "... they (the ASEAN countries) are concerned about the security of Thailand, while we are concerned about the security of Kampuchea, Vietnam and Laos. So both sides must meet each other's interests."[133]

The fourth problem discussed by Thach dealt with an international conference on the political solution of the Kampuchean question. Hanoi's stand was that Kampuchea had to be represented by the Heng Samrin government. To do otherwise would be interpreted as recognition of Vietnam's occupation of Kampuchea. To enter into official discussions on Kampuchea directly with Vietnam was one of the major premises of the ASEAN countries for talks on the political solution of the Kampuchean question. Thach did not give up on the principle of claiming participation by Heng Samrin's governments in the talks concerning Kampuchea, but gave the impression that there were several ways to dispose of this problem.[134]

Proof of Thach's ability to confuse common ASEAN lines on the Kampuchean question was given during the Non-Aligned Summit Conference in New Delhi. At this conference, the ASEAN front was kept united, but Malaysia's Foreign Minister Tan Sri Ghazali Shafie's report on his private talks with Thach during the Summit forced ASEAN to re-emphasize its unity and reject what Ghazali had considered as a tentative understanding with Vietnam. It is still unclear what kind of understanding was reached between Thach and Ghazali; but, according to Ghazali's report, some kind of understanding was reached that Vietnam and Laos without PRK would meet ASEAN to discuss the Kampuchean question.[135] Thach did not confirm this as such, but said that Vietnam was considering this possibility seriously.[136] However, after Thach's statement, the other ASEAN foreign ministers rejected Ghazali's formula and announced that

ASEAN was committed to the resolution adopted by the UN's International Conference on Kampuchea (ICK), where the main precondition for a political solution was the withdrawal of the Vietnamese troops. When the ASEAN foreign ministers met in Bangkok one week later, Ghazali did not publicly comment any more on his talks with Thach, and ASEAN's stand on the ICK's outlines were reaffirmed by a joint statement.[137]

Owing to ASEAN's abrupt break with the Ghazali talks, it never became clear how seriously the leadership in Hanoi was backing the direct negotiations without Phnom Penh. However, the Indochinese foreign ministers reiterated their readiness to examine the contents of the Thach–Ghazali talks,[138] and in July 1983 they confirmed that Phnom Penh had agreed to stand aside from the dialogue between "the two groups of countries."[139] The fact that at least some of the ASEAN countries benefited from an inflexible stance against Vietnam and supported the power constellation where the CGDK and also China were important elements was made clear to the Indochinese governments.[140] This was revealed during the Delhi Summit, where the ASEAN countries, with the strong support of China, had tried to get Kampuchea's seat for the CGDK by using the prestige of Sihanouk.

Despite the fact that Vietnam's regional policy included abundant formal elements, there equally remained a hard core of pragmatism in its rhetoric toward ASEAN. Hanoi tried to convince the ASEAN countries that acceptance of the presence of Vietnamese troops in Kampuchea was the only sure means to block China's influence in Southeast Asia.[141] This was done by pointing to the Chinese population in the Southeast Asian countries and to its influential positions in the national economies and the pro-Maoist movements in these countries. However, the most important argument was provided by China's war against Vietnam and its connection with the Kampuchean situation. This was the leading idea propounded by the Vietnamese in both the UN and the Non-Aligned movement, when it was defending its policy in Indochina. In this respect, there was some ASEAN response, as the Kuantan principle proved. The Chinese threat was connected to the presence of Vietnamese troops in Kampuchea and Phnom Penh; and Hanoi announced that Vietnam would withdraw when the danger of Pol Pot was eliminated.[142]

There occurred a parallel episode to the Thach–Ghazali Delhi talks, which caused obvious confusion on the Viet side. This was the proposal made by Thai Foreign Minister Sitthi Sawetsila when he returned from his visit to Beijing. In fact, this proposal was put forward by Malaysia earlier, in April of 1985. Thus renewed, it now turned into an ASEAN proposal for "proximity talks" between Vietnam and the CGDK. Now, the ASEAN countries allowed the Heng Samrin government to attend as part of the Vietnamese delegation. The proposal included, however, a preparatory list of the topics that the talks should deal with. The ASEAN countries emphasized that the talks would be exploratory in nature, and should include the following elements: a) withdrawal of foreign forces from Kampuchea, b) UN control and supervisory commission, c) national reconciliation and d) UN-supervised election and exercise of self-determination.[143]

In its immediate reaction, Hanoi rejected the proposal by both formalist and pragmatic arguments. The preparatory list of topics was interpreted as a precondition, which the Vietnamese had always opposed.[144] The Indochinese countries had submitted their proposal for a regional settlement in January, the main point being that the withdrawal of the Vietnamese troops was connected with the elimination of the Khmer Rouge forces. It contained the idea of general elections and international supervision of the agreement settling the Kampuchean question, thus approaching in some respects the ASEAN's proposals on Kampuchea. Nevertheless, it included also the doctrinal outlines of an overall settlement of the relations between the Southeast Asian countries, making impossible acceptance as such by the ASEAN countries. Thus the ASEAN countries rejected it as a proposal but were ready to discuss its technical points toward settling the Kampuchean issue.[145]

However, during these two years there had taken place a remarkable change in Vietnam's foreign-policy environment. The prolonged conflict had put Vietnam internationally into a more difficult position. Nevertheless, the reorientation taking place in Soviet foreign policy was dramatically shattering the basis of Vietnam's foreign policy. For Vietnam, the crucial question was: how did this reorientation affect Sino-Soviet relations and Vietnam's position there? The resolution of the Kampuchean question was a central precondition set by China as a way to normalize relations with the Soviet Union.[146] There were obvious signals that the Vietnamese would have to reconsider their relations by the time Yuri Andropov took charge in the Soviet leadership after Brezhnev,[147] but the real discussion on how the possible rapprochement in Sino–Soviet relations would influence Vietnam's regional role started when Mikhail Gorbachev continued, even more forcefully, Andropov's line of normalization of Sino–Soviet relations.[148]

The volte-face of Vietnam toward the proximity idea can be partly understood from this context. The reorientation of Soviet foreign policy did not favor dogmatic stances, but supported the Vietnamese foreign minister's pragmatism. The Indochinese Foreign Ministers took a positive stance toward the approach calling for indirect talks among the participants and direct talks with different Khmer factions. The elimination of Pol Pot's power and the status of the Heng Samrin government as a sovereign party in the negotiations were all that remained from the moral, formal and pragmatic arguments.[149] In fact, the formal argument can hardly be deciphered from Hanoi's diplomatic language, excepting a vague reference to peaceful coexistence as a basis for the relations in Southeast Asia. Consequently, it could hardly be said that the Vietnamese policy was following the lines of any particular doctrine on Indochina during the mid-1980s as opposed to the situation that prevailed during the early 1980s. Therefore examination of Vietnam's foreign-policy parlance reveals a widening gap from the doctrine and formal argumentation of the Party cadres, as it was already noticed in connection with Vietnam's argumentation in international forums. From this point of view, the important role that the discussion of foreign relations and foreign policy gained in the new political discourse that emerged in Vietnam during the 6th Party Congress in 1986 is quite understandable.

Part III
The Re-evaluation of
Vietnamese Marxism

6 Vietnam and Global Changes 1986–93

THE END OF DOCTRINAL UNITY

As revealed by examination of Vietnamese diplomatic parlance at the United Nations, in the Non-Aligned Movement and, to some extent, in regional diplomacy with the ASEAN countries, there was a widening gap between pragmatic foreign-policy rhetoric and the formalism that dominated the political programs of the Communist Party and the discussion engaged in by the Party cadres. Obviously, this was due to the dramatic change in Vietnam's international status from the forerunner of the anti-imperialist struggle to a regional power, which had to adjust its interests to those of the other countries in the region. Although the diplomacy had to respond without delay to this new situation, the Vietnamese Marxist-Leninist doctrine, with its general formal trend, left its basic presumptions about international relations and Vietnam's international role intact.

The first signs of the doctrinal reorientation of foreign relations could be seen in 1986, immediately after the 27th Soviet Party Congress and several months before the 6th National Congress of Vietnam's Communist Party. Evidently, the deadlock on the Kampuchean question – like Vietnam's dispute with China concerning the islands in the South China Sea and the continental shelf in particular, along with the political friction between them in general – promoted this reorientation. However, the discussion on foreign relations cannot be separated from the national and international reform movements of the other socialist states, which focused on Mikhail Gorbachev's politics in the Soviet Union. The domestic grounds for such reform lay in the desperate condition of Vietnam's national economy, the country's bad economic management, the prevailing corruption, and in the poor performance of the Party cadres – the bureaucracy and the political system as a whole could, in fact, be blamed.

The Vietnamese Communist Party cadres' discussion on domestic and foreign-policy issues, which began in the spring of 1986, did not follow the conventional style of presenting arguments, in which the Party decisions determine the general lines followed. In fact, the campaigns of criticism that preceded the 6th Party Congress – and continued as part of the renovation campaign after the Congress – created several distinct discourses.[1] The emergence of new vocabulary indicated the first doctrinal changes. Hence the most important area where the new vocabulary occurred was international relations. The changes mean the removal of certain old concepts, such as *ai thang ai* and three revolutionary currents and introduction of some new, mostly Gorbachevian terms, into the vocabulary of foreign policy. The new key words were the world's scientific-technological revolution *(cach mang khoa hoc – khi thuat te gioi)*, dependency *(su thuy thuoc)* and interdependence *(su le thuoc lan nhau)*, the trend of internationalization *(xu the quoc te hoa)* and an international order *(mot trat tu quoc te)*, which were all borrowed from the Soviet Unioin.

In order to shed more light on these new characteristics in the cadres' texts, I am presenting two different kinds of approaches as examples of the disintegration of the doctrinal unity. These two articles were published in the March and April 1986 issues of *Tap Chi Cong San* and both apparently pointed to the new political course.

The first, Hoang Tung's general account of the 27th Congress of the Soviet Communist Party, examined the new Soviet formulations of Marxism-Leninism and their relationship to the traditional Marxist-Leninist doctrine. The general idea brought out by Hoang Tung's account was that the basic premises and general application of the Marxist-Leninist doctrine, along with the appraisal of the international situation, had not changed. It was based on a class analysis of social relations and emphasized the common Marxist-Leninist way of mobilizing the masses, involving proletarian dictatorship and campaigns of criticism and self-criticism.[2]

With respect to international relations, the basic assumptions remained intact, although missing from the article was a certain central concept that had been intensively cultivated by the Vietnamese cadres. According to Tung, the underlying factors driving the international developments were the struggle between two economic and social systems and the second scientific and technological revolution. The developments generated by these factors were bound – as Hoang Tung maintained, keeping this Marxist-Leninist thesis unchanged – to lead to communism through the stage of socialism.[3]

There were certain revisions in Hoang Tung's analysis, compared with his writings in the early 1980s. Despite the second scientific-technological revolution, he paid heed to capitalism, which had survived and undergone remarkable changes since the turn of the century. Tung argued that the forms of capitalist exploitation had become more sophisticated and complicated, but as far as their political essence was concerned, they had became more reactionary in every respect. Therefore the threat to mankind of imperialism had not decreased.[4] Owing to these two factors, the scientific-technological revolution and the new characteristics of imperialism, he welcomed the new forms of the struggle and the new orientation of his government's foreign policy. The most central aspect of the situation was the fight for peace by the achievement of peaceful coexistence, which was "the new form of revolutionary struggle."[5]

In spite of the fact that these new emphases and the lack of certain established concepts indicated the changes in Vietnamese orientation in international relations, Hoang Tung's argumentation relied on a formal pattern. It included certain pragmatic tones emphasizing the role of wise foreign policy, which, however, was based on scientific deduction from the theory of class.[6] Obviously, the more moderate approach of the Soviet Union in international relations made him remove *ai thang ai* and the three revolutionary currents from his vocabulary. In particular, as far as the Soviet Union's international role and its relation to Vietnam were concerned, Tung declined to acknowledge the Soviets' own emerging lack of confidence in the formal doctrine's ability to deal with the complex questions of the future in international affairs. On the contrary, he concluded that with "the development of the first and greatest socialist country, the firm pillar of the new world, its people are transforming a wasteland into cultivated areas on their way to socialism and communism. This is closely related to the attainment of the destiny of all nations and, first of all, to the destiny of the socialist system and to our entire revolutionary doctrine."[7]

The general characteristic of the Marxist-Leninist doctrinal code is that it tends to mobilize the masses whether or not pragmatic or formal arguments are used. In this respect, there was a striking difference between Hoang Tung's article, in which the doctrinal code was obvious, and Luu Van Loi's article, which appeared one month later in the *Tap Chi Cong San*. Luu Van Loi was not such a high ranking cadre as Hoang Tung. One has also to bear in mind that Loi's article was an exception in the cadre's discourse at that time. Thus its political weight must be put into this context. However, comparison of these two articles reveals the extent of the doctrinal disintegration in Vietnam shortly after the Soviet 27th Party Congress.

Loi examined the exploitation of the maritime areas close to Vietnam. Evidently, his arguments were based on the realities of Vietnam's foreign relations. However, they departed radically from the old revolutionary pragmatism, where the goals determined the way reality was conceived. Loi's point of departure was that the existing reality should be defined before the goals are explicated. Thus he tried to put the premises of Vietnam's foreign policy on a more concrete basis. The implicit message of his article was that both the Marxist-Leninist doctrine and Vietnam's foreign policy had set goals that were impossible to realize. He did not outline any reality created by the class struggle or the friend/foe distinction, but by international law, by the declarations of the UN concerning the exploitation of oceans and ocean floors, and by technical capabilities, as well as by Vietnam's evident lack of them. His concrete subject matter related to Vietnam's offshore islands, particularly the Spratlys and Vietnam's continental shelf under the South China Sea. However, his rhetoric can also be viewed on a much more general level of Vietnam's foreign policy. Luu Van Loi wrote his article at a time when the new vocabulary was just crystallizing in Vietnamese Marxism, although the old Marxist-Leninist doctrine was the prevailing tendency among the Party cadres. Whether this was the reason for Loi's completely ignoring of the Marxist-Leninist vocabulary remains obscure. In any case, his historical and tradition-based analogies involved both pragmatic contemplation and a kind of argumentative modality, differing from the Marxist-Leninist doctrine.[8]

The background for Luu Van Loi's arguments can be seen to have been the Sino-Vietnamese dispute over the Paracel and Spratly islands, on which Hanoi had taken an inflexible stand by emphasizing its absolute sovereignty over both groups of islands. This emphasis on sovereignty was part of the Sino–Vietnamese relations after their breakdown in the late 1970s. At the same time, by delegating the rights to multinational companies, China started to exploit the mineral resources (crude oil, for example) in the South China Sea, notably in the areas close to the Spratly islands. Using the same argument of sovereignty, Vietnam had rejected the possibility of giving multinational companies the rights to exploit its soil. In fact, the economic blockade encircling Vietnam practically prevented this and simultaneously precluded the use of advanced technology for the utilization of Vietnam's natural resources. This issue was a sore one, particularly when it involved the mineral resources lying under the ocean floor.[9]

Vietnam's problem here was that it did not have the capabilities to utilize the resources of its territorial waters, let alone the areas contained in the economic zone. Loi's criticism was therefore directed at the empty claims of sovereignty (the island dispute with China) and at the declarations relating to the economic zone, in a situation where it had no possibilities to press its claims of sovereignty and no plans to exploit its economic zone. Luu Van Loi proposed concentrating its forces in the areas where the country could assert its sovereignty.[10]

What is interesting here is that Loi did not point to any either concrete or abstract goals but urged adoption of a national policy for the defining of goals with a practical basis. His arguments did not therefore champion any goal-oriented project, even on a limited scale, let alone on any ideological project with the function of mass mobilization. They concentrated purely on information having no self-motivating function. This was rather extraordinary in foreign relations at that time and, in fact, even later. A clear reference to a modality of argumentation deviating from the Marxist-Leninist doctrinal code is to be clearly seen in Loi's analogy to Vietnam's situation. He cited a Vietnamese proverb as a reminder: "The slow buffalo drinks muddy water *(trau cham uong nuoc duc)*." And he warned that in the current situation, involving natural resources, if the Vietnamese could not decide on their priorities in a reasonable way, "the 'slow buffalo' would not even have 'muddy water' to drink any more!"[11]

Evidently Hoang Tung's argumentation represented the main trend in the Communist Party. Despite some conceptual changes, the doctrinal code remained the same. Loi's rhetoric proved that Vietnamese pragmatism had both survived between the Party cadres and become transformed during the "orthodox" years of the early 1980s. Interestingly, the differences between the revolutionary pragmatism and Luu Van Loi's pragmatism indicate that pragmatic argumentation, in particular, might include some other cultural code usually covered by the Marxist-Leninist doctrinal code. Similarly, it reminds us that different types of arguments have different functions where the role of the code might vary.

The differences in argumentation between these two articles showed how radical were the changes that took place in Vietnamese argumentation in 1986. In the following chapters, the texts of the Vietnamese Party Cadres are examined both from a broader perspective and on the basis of a more detailed survey in order to answer the following questions: To what extent did the Vietnamese follow the Soviet approach? What new concepts did the Vietnamese introduce and what is their place in the doctrine? What kind of concepts were rejected and how did this change the argumentation patterns? Finally, according to the main theses put forward at the beginning of this study, the following questions on the doctrinal code can be presented: Did the Marxist-Leninist doctrinal code change or did it remain unchanged as a constant modality of argumentation in the Vietnamese political language in a situation where the whole international system changed dramatically? Did the doctrinal code disintegrate and did a rival code system appear? Or did the role of the doctrinal code diminish and did the other functions of the arguments presented become of primary importance in the Vietnamese foreign-policy argumentation?

SOVIET *PERESTROIKA* AND VIETNAMESE *DOI MOI* COMPARED

Following to a certain extent the 27th Party Congress of the Soviet Communist Party, the Vietnamese started campaigns involving criticism and self-criticism to correct the deviations in the economic and bureaucratic systems. The 6th National Congress of Vietnam's Communist Party encouraged further the expression of critical views of different social realms in order to improve the performance of the economy and the bureaucracy and to restore public confidence in the Party. In fact, the theoretical adjustment of Marxism-Leninism to Vietnam's current situation did not become a major issue at the Party Congress, the idea being to expose the flaws in the Party organization and in the functioning of the state system. Therefore, excepting the criticism of it, the Political Report depended heavily on formal Marxism-Leninism and its vocabulary. This was quite true also as regards the sections dealing with foreign policy, which adhered mostly to the established vocabulary.

However, some revisions were made in the vocabulary as it dealt with foreign relations, and they pointed to moderate changes compared with the 5th Party Congress. These developments were illustrative of the changes in the Vietnamese foreign-policy environment that had taken place between the late 1970s and the mid-1980s. Nevertheless, the changes in the expressions used and in the vocabulary discussing international relations in the 6th Party Congress's Political Report and, particularly, the new emphasis appearing after the Congress, referred primarily to the changes in the Soviet approach, which were then applied to the Vietnamese discussion. Although the Vietnamese did not parrot the Soviet vocabulary as such, a grasp of the Soviet "new thinking" on international relations was essential for a comprehension of the Vietnamese debate.

The reason that the Vietnamese gave to this Soviet vocabulary a new content was rather obvious. The Soviets dealt with international relations on the Great Power axis, whereas the Vietnamese tried to adjust mostly the same concepts to Vietnam's situation. The question as to whether these concepts indicated changes in the doctrinal code in these countries is much more complicated. The question seeks to find out, further, whether these new reforms were designed to change the basis of social and political rule or not. The Soviets connected the new thinking in international relations organically to the domestic *perestroika*.[12] The course of development in the Soviet Union showed that the reform movement really changed the basis of political rule. For Vietnam, the question is not so simple as that. Political developments did not proceed in the same way as in the Soviet Union since the Vietnamese Communist Party remained in political control.[13] However, despite the fact that the authority of the Communist Party was never challenged, the debate in Vietnam on international relations among the Communist Party cadres proved that foreign-policy argumentation lost its signifigance in self-motivation and autocommunication among the cadres. Therefore the doctrinal code was, at least partly, losing force in Vietnam's foreign-policy argumentation.

Insofar as the Soviet *perestroika* seemed to support the totalitarian method of political mobilization, the Vietnamese Party cadres enthusiastically repeated the new themes of the Soviet Communist Party. In fact, Gorbachev's policy in its early phase avoided interfering with the workings of Marxist-Leninist rule, but its aim was to restore the Leninist form of mobilizing the masses.[14] The Vietnamese Communists adjusted this idea to their old practices of emulation and campaigns of criticism. Thus "the organization and the mobilization of the masses to the emulation movements" were emphatically represented as the characteristics of the Communist Party's "revolutionary method of binding tightly the Party and the people."[15] Similarly, criticism and self-criticism were stressed at Vietnam's 6th Party Congress and the Political Report acknowledged the control function of mobilization: "All organizations, from those of the Party and the State to those of the masses, [and] all fields of activity ... must be placed under the control of the competent Party organization."[16]

However, when their reform reached the stage at which the Soviets started to re-evaluate their past, the Vietnamese did not follow Soviet suit. None of the previous Vietnamese leaders had been exposed to public criticism as in the case of the Soviet Union. Similarly, the VCP did not tolerate pluralism so far as it involved political activities outside the Communist Party. The Vietnamese were following rather the Chinese example, where the spontaneous stage of the mobilization organized by the Party was controlled by countermobilization. This was the practice particularly in China, but it made headway also in Vietnam. First, the Party organized campaigns to implement voluntary mobilization among the masses in order to revive the stagnated political mobilization. The campaign reached all the strata of society to activate the system and restore control. In Vietnam, the theme of *doi moi* (renew, renovate, renovation) infused all the efforts to vitalize the Marxist system. However, these campaigns tended to promote activities that went beyond the Marxist-Leninist rule. In Vietnam, the culminating point was the discussion on the subject of political pluralism, which was halted by the Party in 1989. Therefore the countercampaigns were needed to curb these negative phenomena, and the question of the *doi moi* of the political system was hardly touched upon among the Party cadres after 1989. In the Soviet Union, where Gorbachev leaned for support now on the radical reformers and now on the conservative Marxist-Leninists, the countermobilization could not be achieved and the *perestroika* resulted in ever-growing changes in the political system. In China and, particularly, in Vietnam, the campaigns were more tighty under Party control.[17]

Despite the fact that Hanoi officially supported Gorbachev's policy of *perestroika*, the Vietnamese, at a rather early stage, distinguished their *doi moi* from the Soviet *perestroika*. Although the Russian word *perestroika* may include the idea of "renovation" in its broad sense, it stands for "restructuring," and in the new Soviet vocabulary it referred particularly to "the restructuring of society."[18] The Vietnamese seemed to be fully aware of this.[19] They had a term equivalent to *perestroika* in the sense of "reorganizing," *cai to*, and sometimes "restructuring," *cau truc lai*.[20] The fact that *cai to* applied to the Soviet Union, and perhaps to the other socialist countries, and *doi moi* to Vietnam, was made clear. Thus *cai to* did not refer to the Vietnamese reform campaign. However, both *doi moi* and *cai to* did belong, together with all the reforms carried out in the socialist countries, according to a Vietnamese analysis, to the same historical trend and have developed from "the dialectics of history."[21] The political significance of this differentiation was later confirmed by Nguyen Co Thach in a situation where the Soviet *perestroika* and Vietnam's *doi moi* were already established on their own course. Thach argued for Soviet–Vietnamese cooperation as follows: "With the great undertakings of restructuring *(cong cuoc cai to)* in the Soviet Union and of the renovation *(cong cuoc doi moi)* in Vietnam, we have grounds to be optimistic about the relations of Vietnam's future cooperation with the Soviet Union and other socialist countries."[22] Therfore, by using the *doi moi* instead of expressions referring to the Soviet *perestroika*, the question was not merely "a new semantic twist,"[23] but indicated a different political orientation. Thus the *doi moi* promulgated by the Party contained the Marxist-Leninist doctrine, and all the destructive elements that might thwart the idea of totalitarian mobilization and control were discarded so far as possible. However, as Luu Van Loi's discussion on natural resources proved, not all the texts published even in the organ of the Party's Central Committee contained the elements of the Marxist-Leninist doctrinal code. This proved both a lessening of Party control over the cadres and the fact that the decisions of the Party leadership were not followed according to any single interpretation.

DOI MOI AND FOREIGN RELATIONS

The debate among the Party cadres on foreign relations under the general theme of *doi moi* is rather extraordinary in the history of the SRV. Among all the new concepts introduced into the Vietnamese political vocabulary, the debate presented different theoretical and even political views; and some of the articles published in *Tap Chi Cong San* and certain other major theoretical publications provided direct answers to questions and criticism of the discussants. This debate was also the first real discussion of Vietnamese foreign policy on a theoretical basis and as an independent theme.

As the *doi moi* campaign encouraged criticism of dogmatic presumptions and their unsuitability to current Vietnamese conditions, pragmatic argumentation re-emerged to the side of formal Marxism-Leninism. However, owing to the new concepts on international relations that the Vietnamese had adopted from the Soviet Union, both pragmatic and formal argumentation underwent a transformation so that theoretically, at least, there are four different kinds of patterns of argumentation on foreign relations: old pragmatic and old formal argumentation, based mostly on old concepts and employing new vocabulary only sparingly, and new pragmatic and new formal argumentation, which have adopted new concepts and have changed, to some extent, the basic presumption on international relations in the Vietnamese discussion.

In the Soviet Union, when Gorbachev tried, in the first steps of *perestroika,* to adjust his reforms to the old doctrine, the formalism was predominant in foreign policy.[24] However, when the reform policy progressed from its early phase, Gorbachev started to reinterpret the old concepts, only to ignore them and finally abandon most of them completely. For example, from the USSR Foreign Ministry Survey issued at the end of 1989 there can hardly be found any traditional Marxist-Leninist concepts. Only the concept of peaceful coexistence was mentioned, but only twice, and both cases are dealt with in the joint communique with

China.[25] This vocabulary relating to international relations reflected the new Soviet approach. The world was not examined on the basis of the simple model of two camps, but as a complicated system with different developing tendencies.[26] The key concept was the interdependence of the world. It represented a world that, though multipolar, has become a single entity. The reasons for this interdependence lay not only in the danger of nuclear war but involved environmental problems including the wasteful use of natural resources, as well as the possibilities of the scientific-technological revolution to resolve these issues and its impact on the world economy. These questions became also the main themes of the new Soviet approach.[27]

Inevitably, the new concepts led to the rejection of the old Soviet ideas, such as, first, the two camps idea and that of the international class struggle. As domestic (economic) needs were put forward as one of the leading issues of foreign policy, the "deideologizing" of Soviet foreign relations became a crucial principle. Thus the role of proletarian internationalism and socialist internationalism diminished gradually but inexorably. In fact, at the beginning of this new period, it seemed that peaceful coexistence would become a key concept, but its old linkage to the two camps theory made it difficult for it to become an universal principle. The new Soviet interpretation rejected the old view of peaceful coexistence as only another form of class struggle and turned it into the concept prevailing, for example, among the Non-Aligned countries, where it was bound to the cooperative approach, emphasizing the principles of legitimate interest, sovereignty and non-interference in international affairs. However, as the USSR Foreign Ministry Survey revealed, the attempts to bind peaceful coexistence to interdependence did not convince the Soviet partners in world politics, and therefore also the emphasis on peaceful coexistence decreased.[28]

As at the beginning of the Soviet *perestroika,* during the initial stage of Vietnam's reforms, the main Vietnamese trend in foreign relations revealed a commitment to the orthodox Marxism-Leninism. One Party cadre described the international situation in the first 1986 issue of *Tap Chi Cong San* as follows: "The most important feature of the international situation in 1985, which stands out in relief, is the strength of the three revolutionary currents, particularly the strength of the socialist system, with the Soviet Union in its center." In line with this optimistic mood, the writer was convinced that "the Soviet Union and the socialist countries, together with all the revolutionary forces, have a real capacity to prevent a new World War, guaranteeing the conditions for international peace for the great undertaking to construct socialism and communism."[29] A similar conviction on prefixed dogma of the revolutionary forces can be found from another article, where the author affirmed that "*the common strength of revolutionary and progressive streams are turning to the great current, concentrating its sharp point on the anti-imperialist struggle, which holds fast on peace, on national liberation, on democracy, and on social progress.* The class struggle is taking place all over the world, blazing hot and decisive according to its historical tendency" [italics by the author].[30] This presupposition made him draw the optimistic conclusion that "the offensive posture of the three revolutionary currents" would finally draw the the development in favor of Socialism. [31]

As Hoang Tung's article proved, the first Vietnamese estimations of the Soviet Communist Party's 27th Congress were based on the two camps struggle and the ever fiercer contradictions between capitalism and socialism. Besides, some analysts still included the idea of the three revolutionary currents in their appraisal of the international situation.[32] Interestingly enough, the foreign-policy section of the Political Report of the 6th Party Congress included only partly these estimations of the world situation as the basis for Vietnam's foreign policy. The Vietnamese counted themselves as part of the anti-imperialist and socialist forces of the world, but the Political Report lacked the optimism characterizing the foregoing appraisals of the world situation. The Report ignored the concept of the three revolutionary currents, and it hardly appeared in Vietnamese political parlance and did not belong to the Party cadres' general vocabulary after the 6th Party Congress. The Report continued to emphasize the special relationship among the Indochinese countries and socialist internationalism marketing the relations between Vietnam, the Soviet Union and the CMEA, and it mentioned proletarian internationalism in conjunction with the working-class movement. New emphasis was given to peaceful coexistence in Vietnam's foreign policy and to national concord in dealing with the Kampuchean question – both obviously as a result of Soviet influence.[33]

The political report did not contain such strong autocommunication as used to mark the language of the Party cadres. It did, however, contain the traditional Marxist-Leninist assumption of the world divided into two and the common Soviet vocabulary. Nevertheless, the new characteristic of the Vietnamese discussion after the 6th National Congress was that it was not bound to the Party Congress Political Report as happened after the 4th and the 5th Party Congress.

The rise of new formalism in foreign policy originated from the purpose of adjusting the Marxist-Leninist doctrine in response to the influences emanating from the Soviet Union and to the particular issues

of Vietnam's foreign policy and the *doi moi* campaign. Thus it belonged
to the part of the campaign to renovate the Marxist thinking and re-
evaluate some of its presumptions. This renovation of the thinking *(doi
moi tu duy)* in foreign relations also justified the pragmatic argumentation;
but as the idea of the renovation of thinking was to reformulate Marxism,
it emphasized quasi-logical argumentation from the Marxist-Leninist
premises.

The weight that was given in this situation to the concept of a
transitional period (to socialism) illustrates this attempt. The Vietnamese
were now ready to admit that this period would be longer than they had
supposed, and that the situation was more complex than the simplistic
versions of the two roads of the development. In their contemplation in
the philosophical quarterly *Tap Chi Triet Hoc*, Le Thi (1987) and Hoang
Nguyen (1987) tried to outline a materialistic basis for new thinking
about foreign affairs. Le Thi, particularly, concentrated on the concept of
a transitional period. Interestingly enough, his arguments approach some
main themes of western studies of international political economy, where
one's possibility to guide the political and economic development is
largely ignored. Le Thi notes that the world's scientific technological
revolution had advanced with unexpected speed, having different impacts
on both the capitalist and the socialist countries. This has created new
forces of production leading to an internationalized economy and changing
the political relations all over the world. Further, he remarks that the
focus of the struggle between capitalism and socialism has turned to the
Third World, when both the capitalists and the socialist countries try to
exploit the governments of the Third World countries to attract them to
their side in order to secure the global position of these systems.
Interestingly enough, Le Thi maintains that the interest of the
underdeveloped countries and the socialist countries do not always meet
and the real danger is that the Third World countries were left in the very
nucleus of this conflict. The third element which he pointed to was a
group of global issues, familiar already from Gorbachev's foreign policy
themes. This group includes the issues that equally affected both the
capitalist and the socialist countries: environmental problems, population
growth, famine, illiteracy, etc., which impede progress and raise the
danger of war.[34]

The foreign policy line which should be adopted at this stage of the
transitional period should be, according to Le Thi and Hoang Nguyen,
peaceful coexistence. This is not to acknowledge that the former policy
of revolutionary struggle had been wrong, but that the materialistic base
of this policy had changed. Hoang Nguyen argued that the concept of

three revolutionary currents represented all the relations of production and, owing to the fact that scientific-technological revolution has created new kinds of production and production branches, the materialistic basis of the currents has changed. He did not really explicate the role of the concept in Vietnam's current situation, but gave a more or less obscure estimation of its present signification. In fact, he seemed to refer through the concept rather to the past than to the present, when he analyzed the factors that had changed the world structure during recent decades. Particularly was this the case when he contemplated the development of the newly industrialized Asian countries (the NICs), where the main emphasis has been on the scientific-technological revolution.[35]

The crucial concept of "dependency" in the Soviet new thinking was introduced also into the Vietnamese vocabulary. Interestingly enough, the term dependency *su tuy thuoc* was used equally in both formal and pragmatic argumentation. In formal argumentation, it was connected to global themes, which had already been used in Gorbachev's vocabulary, and also to the intention to examine international affairs from the class standpoint.[36] For a pragmatic approach, the concept of dependency, which referred to the new structure of international relations, gave a justification for the setting of concrete aims, which were often economically motivated. Both patterns were based on acceptance of the fact that dependency meant that the possibilities for independent action were limited. The old starting point, whereby the two opposing camps were independent themselves without mutual interaction, was no longer valid. Accordingly, the new contradictions of the world have united it into a single entity.[37] This meant that whenever two opposing social and economic systems had common interests in dealing with global issues, they had to find "either a common language or various common activities" to solve these questions.[38]

Hoang Nguyen formulated these problems in two categories of foreign policy issues. The first consisted of "questions dealing with the establishment of a peaceful and stable environment" and the second "questions dealing with the success of building socialism in our country." In the first category, the crucial point was deciding how Vietnam could break the blockade of the capitalist countries and especially the ASEAN countries in order to be fully able to take advantage of the technological progress being made in these countries. The complexity here lay in the fact that Hoang Nguyen did not see much room for maneuver in the interest of Vietnam's security, since China's threat had not diminished. Similarly, he did not want to give up the ideological bonds between the Indochinese nations. He therefore recommended preserving the existing alliances and further developing them. He argued that "the power constellation of our international relations includes two points: to continue strengthening the relationship between Vietnam, Kampuchea and Laos and to create a closely bound and, moreover, the tightest possible relationship between Vietnam and the Soviet Union (as well as the other socialist brother countries)."[39] This basic orientation was explained by the second question, which takes the construction of socialism as a duty. In his answer to this question, Hoang Nguyen drew a most conventional conclusion. He emphasized that all the countries must make their choice between the socialist and capitalist systems in their endeavor to benefit from the new technology – but that the aim to cooperate with both groups of countries was doomed to failure. Interestingly enough, here he condemned all the attempts to approach ASEAN, obviously being contrary to the spirit prevailing at the Foreign Ministry in Hanoi: "The illusion of 'fishing from both sides' has always led to catastrophe, as in Yugoslavia. We should not by any means commit ourselves to the Western world, primarily our pro-Western neighbors in ASEAN, but we should make plain our strong leaning toward the Soviet Union and the other socialist countries."[40] Only on this basis, he argued, could Vietnam build its relations with the capitalist countries and exploit their technology and "even their experience in organizing work and the economy, for the sake of our prosperity."[41]

Notwithstanding this adherence to the Soviet bloc and the socialist road of development, the "new" formal argumentation made changes in the contents of the orthodox *ai thang ai* -concept. In his approach of joining old Leninist principles to the new thinking, Quoc Tuy did not give up the concept but amended it. He insisted that the class standpoint should be preserved in "international relations and foreign affairs without reverting to the outdated concept of dogmatism, which has been dominant with its class demand of discriminating friend from foe and use the class struggle for world revolution."[42] In a world of mutual dependence, the *ai thang ai* -concept was placed on a different level. He argued that in the existing situation, the questions of peace, national independence, democracy and social evolution were common denominators for the majority of the people, for the states and for the social classes, and coincided with the interests of the working class. In this struggle, the working class would have to take the leading role. It would have to be capable of uniting all the forces for their common sake. Surprisingly, Quoc Tuy reverted to the traditional vocabulary, when he drew the conclusion that the concept of the working class struggle showed how "to treat consciously the question of the friends and enemies of the class in the class struggle on the global scale. To us, it means the capacity to isolate clearly the small and warlike group of imperialists and reactionaries."[43] According to Hoang Nguyen, *ai thang ai* was part of the strategy of expanding the revolutionary forces, which included the military balance between the U.S. and the Soviet Union and the triumphs of national independence, including Vietnam's victory over the U.S. However, the scientific-technological revolution altered the situation, and continuation on the same road could result in failure if the socialist countries could not take advantage of this revolution.[44]

In line with this new formalist approach, the concept of peaceful coexistence became established in the Vietnamese Party cadres' vocabulary. Interestingly enough, real acceptance of the concept took place at the same time as the Soviet Union was changing the context and diminishing its importance. Thus the emphasis on peaceful coexistence in Vietnam reflected both recognition of the changes in Vietnam's international status and also its commitment to build socialism and establish the Marxist-Leninist rule. Despite the political expediency of preserving old concepts in the new vocabulary, it made this "new" formalism still more complex and inconsistent. Quoc Tuy, for example, just after he had abandoned the *ai thang ai* -concept as the basis of the class struggle, offered peaceful coexistence and proletarian internationalism (already discarded in the Soviet Union) as central elements in Vietnam's foreign policy. As he saw it, proletarian internationalism drew a border between the foreign policy of the socialist countries and the nations belonging to the other systems. Peaceful coexistence by no means replaced the principle of proletarian internationalism, but was "a particular form of class struggle during the transitional period."[45] He argued further obviously against the new Soviet interpretation of peaceful coexistence, which had also been adopted by certain Vietnamese cadres[46]: "Changing peaceful coexistence to a general principle that includes the relationships of the socialist countries with all countries signifies the rejection of proletarian internationalism and causes socialist foreign policy to abandon its offensive spirit of struggle; it changes the socialist countries' foreign policy of peace and turns it to conform to the lines of the pacifists and causes the socialist countries to take a defensive posture."[47] Similarly, the policy of peacuful coexistece suggested by Le Thi and Hoang Nguyen, is based clearly on the Marxist-Leninist doctrine of the two roads and not on the new preconditions offered by the scientific-technological revolution.[48]

Therefore the "new formalism" had difficulties theoretically connecting the concepts of dependence, class struggle and different social systems. For some, it was even difficult to acknowledge the incompatiblity of such concepts as "offensive posture" with mutual dependency, as Quoc Tuy's argumentation proved. Keeping this in mind, it is understandable that the concept of peaceful coexistence was so closely bound in formalist argumentation to the two camps theory. Thus the definition of the concept of peaceful coexistence as used by Le Thi resembles that in old Soviet textbooks where the concept involves both the class struggle and the ideological struggle.[49] As the concept denies only the direct use of arms to solve conflicts between states with different social systems, "it does not deny support of class struggle in different forms – armed, political, cultural and ideological."[50] Thus the Marxist-Leninist doctrinal code was an organic part of this form of the class struggle, especially when focused on the ideological struggle: "Its [ideological struggle's] contents should be rich, its forms and methods should be manysided, and it should mobilize the resources of knowledge in the natural and social sciences to realize this struggle."[51]

Evidently, the growing interaction with the ASEAN countries represented the practical need that prompted the Vietnamese to include the concept of peaceful coexistence in the Party cadres' vocabulary. There was a growing tendency in Hanoi to approach the ASEAN countries in order to prevent a closer alliance with China and the ASEAN countries. Obviously, application of the concept of peaceful coexistence was encouraged by Gorbachev's administration in its early stage, when it was formulating its new approach to international affairs. As far as the ASEAN countries were concerned, there existed among the Vietnamese Party cadres a strong view that the system in Southeast Asia was based on the two-bloc structure, with the Soviet Union guaranteeing stability.[52] This point of departure was, however, rejected by the ASEAN countries. Thus the concept of peaceful coexistence strengthened the old constellations rather than creating a new setting.

In brief, the inconsistency between some of the concepts in the new formalism was a consequence of the fact that the formalist rhetoric included this two-bloc structure, together with the Marxist-Leninist doctrinal code, which was difficult to fit into the new vocabulary, especially alongside the concept of dependence. The word "dependence" also belonged to the academic Marxist vocabulary; but instead of its negative connotation, Gorbachev's "new political thinking" turned it into a positive concept, emphasizing the possibilities in the situation. The pragmatic argumentation took heed of the relationship between the concrete goals, the methods and the structure of reality. In pragmatic argumentation the methods and goals tend to become entangled. This phenomenon in the "old" pragmatic argumentation represented a particular method of mobilizing the masses. However, the premises of Marxism-Leninism did not serve as the point of departure for pragmatic argumentation, although elements in it were used as foreign-policy goals. In the new foreign-policy debate, where the traditional Marxist-Leninist concepts lost their significance, this connection with the Marxist-Leninist doctrine became disengaged to an important extent.

I discussed this question earlier in the examination of Luu Van Loi's argumentation. His arguments against the fixed dogmas resembled that of a critic who had been prepared to oppose the orthodox Marxist-Leninist premises in economics during the *doi moi* campaign. The criticism encouraged by the Party in the *doi moi* campaign was therefore quite important from the standpoint of the re-emergence of pragmatism in the discussion of Vietnam's foreign policy. There were clear differences, however, from the pragmatism presented by Vo Nguyen Giap. These differences were due to the new concepts that appeared in the Vietnamese discussion after the 27th Congress of the Soviet Communist Party as well as to the different position of the Marxist-Leninist doctrinal code in argumentation. In "old" pragmatic argumentation, the goal of the Vietnamese Communists was predominant and adhered to the Marxist-Leninist vocabulary. In brief, it deviated from formalism by avoiding Marxist-Leninist premises as its starting point for argumentation; it examined the socialist countries from the *phan biet phan thu* point of view, where these Communists were considered as "strategic allies" on Vietnam's road of independence and socialism. Strong emphasis on self-reliance was connected to this, pointing up Vietnam's independence also from its socialist allies. By emphasizing the goal, which was entangled with the methods of organization and mobilization, the "old" pragmatic argumentation included the Marxist-Leninist doctrinal code.

The point of departure of the "new" pragmatic argumentation was the nature of international relations, under which all the concepts, theories, foreign-policy methods and goals, even, to some extent, domestic goals, should be subordinated. While in both "old" formal and "old" pragmatic argumentation the central concept in international relations was the "struggle" *(dau tranh),* the key concepts in the new pragmatism that characterized international relations and were also the starting points of argumentation were "dependence," "interdependence," and "order" *(trat tu).* Thus there were, also at the political level, completely different kinds of orientations in international relations. The old pragmatic approach emphasized that Vietnam could, by using correctly the international trends to take advantage of the international class struggle, build its socialism and to defend its independence mainly by its own resources.

The new pragmatic approach, when underlining the structure of international relations, differentiated these relations from the domestic political mobilization. Therefore in this argumentation, the role of the Marxist-Leninist doctrinal code was a minor one and seemed, in some cases, to disappear completely.

In interdependence resided both the limits and the possibilities of Vietnam's foreign policy. According to the pragmatic argumentation, the origin of interdependence was in the international division of labor. Therefore, the more developed the economy, the more developed is the division of labor. Thus, when developing its economy, Vietnam will face this question daily.[53] This characterization was evident already in Luu Van Loi's article. However, the new vocabulary of Gorbachev's new thinking, which was adopted in Vietnam, exposed clearly the structure of the "new" pragmatic argumentation in Vietnam's foreign policy. The use of the new concepts caused pragmatic argumentation to approach the "new" formalism; and sometimes they seemed to overlap each other. Similarly, the same addresser might use both patterns of argumentation, and it depended on emphasis whether the addresser could be classified as "pragmatist" or "formalist."

In his article "Some reflections on the renovation of thinking on foreign affairs," Phan Doan Nam took the changes in the global structure as his point of argumentation in an attempt to change Vietnam's foreign-policy thinking. The writer, by one estimation a close subordinate of Nguyen Co Thach's[54] and later editor-in-chief of the *Vietnam Courier*, presented the most radical theses so far on Vietnam's foreign policy in the February 1988 issue of *Tap Chi Cong San* from the pragmatic base and continued to develop them in 1991 just before and after the 7th Party Congress.

There were many common denominators in connection with the new formalist arguments. Similarly, Phan Doan Nam even used formal arguments when he pleaded to representing the class standpoint and the dynamic character of Marxism-Leninism in order to justify the new approach.[55] However, the premises of his rhetoric were the changes in international relations and Vietnam's international status, which had completely changed since 1975, and not the Marxist doctrine on class struggle. In conjunction with the growth of the world socialist system and the collapse of the colonialist system, according to Phan Doan Nam, the crucial qualifier that was determining the course of world developments, in which both the capitalist and the socialist countries were involved, was interdependence – the tendency of the countries to become linked together (Nam used the expression *su lien kiet*, which referred also to "solidarity" among the socialist countries). The particular characteristic of the capitalist countries – especially the imperialist countries – was mutual penetration *(xam nhap vao nhau)*, which had changed the nature of imperialist contradictions and forced the imperialists to curb their ambitions.[56] Interdependence, which touched every nation, was the consequence of the internationalization trend *(xu the quoc te hoa)*, and had "turned into a requisite *(tien de)* for the development of each country. This relationship is a yardstick *(thuoc do)* of the development level of the nation."[57]

Interestingly enought, Phan Doan Nam's arguments against the views on sovereignty and self-reliance tangle with the general discussion on integration and regionalism. Similarly, they challenge the views presented by, for example, Vo Nguyen Giap in his pragmatic argumentation, and the strong emphasis on self-reliance which had persisted in Vietnam, as Luu Van Loi pointed out in his article. Thus Phan Doan Nam agreed with Loi: "Over the years ... we have emphasized the spirit of independence and sovereignty *(tinh doc lap tu chu)*, but have continuously failed to see fully the dependence of our national development on the general developmental trend in the world. The new thinking does not deny the spirit of independence and the sovereignty of each country, but it emphasizes the reciprocal influence of independence and sovereignty in each country and the general developmental trend of our time."[58]

Despite the fact that the starting point of the new pragmatism called for a re-evaluation of the concepts of sovereignty and independence in foreign policy, it generally avoided infringing on the domestic sovereignty of the Communist Party. The crucial question was rather one of how the Vietnamese should react to the changes in its foreign-policy environment in order to maintain political stability in their country. Thus Phan Doan Nam's aim was to develop foreign-policy thinking as an independent exercise, without doctrinal connections with Marxist-Leninist theory. The most radical point in his approach was the proposal of rejecting the idea of *phan biet phan thu* and its links to the concept of peaceful coexistence. His argumentation proved that he had adopted a new interpretation of peaceful coexistence; he argued both against the class standpoint in connection with this question and also against the narrow view of national interests. Nam therefore emphasized that the question of peaceful coexistence can not be linked to the issue of *phan biet phan thu*. He argued that "peaceful coexistence ... is an international order in which countries of different sociopolitical systems can live as friendly neighbors and cooperate in all areas, economic, scientific-technological and so forth."[59] This interpretation of peaceful coexistence was rejected by the formalists, who stressed peaceful coexistence as a particular form of class struggle, as proved by Quoc Tuy's argumentation. However, Phan Doan Nam's attack was not directed solely against the formalist premises, but also against the old pragmatic ideas of attaining the goals by all possible methods. Therefore he criticized the pragmatic dogma of "negotiating while fighting" as incompatible with the existing international situation.

The important issue here was Phan Doan Nam's neutral concept of order, which enabled him to ponder calmly the possibilities of determining what kind of international order was going to evolve and how Vietnam would have to respond to it. Nam contemplated this in his article in the issue of *Tap Chi Cong San* that appeared in September 1991 following several remarkable changes in the context of Vietnam's foreign-policy discussion: first, an attack by the top leadership against the new pragmatic approach, which started from the revanche of orthodox argumentation included in Party leader Nguyen Van Linh's speech at the Communist Party Plenum in August 1989. In a sense, Phan Doan Nam was defending his position against a formalist attack. In the second place, the collapse of Marxist-Leninist state systems in East Europe was already a reality, as were likewise the new roles of the United Nations and the United States, which were clearly revealed in the Gulf War. Finally, the unsuccessful coup d'état of the old Communists in Moscow followed by the diminishing power of the Soviet Communist Party left the Vietnamese Communist ideologically alone.

From the point of view of the great changes taking place constantly in Vietnam's foreign-policy environment, Nam outlined four scenarios of the future world order. The first scenario was a world order based on U.S. dominance, where the U.S. would be "the most equal among equals." The second possible world order was based on a structure of three poles, where the world would be dominated by three capitalist centers, the United States, West Europe and Japan. The third scenario was a world order based on the five members of the UN Security Council, where the relationship between the U.S. and the Soviet Union constituted the most important factor. Finally, he outlined a scenario that Vietnam and other nations should aim to realize. It was based on the idea of a world community built by independent, sovereign and equal states, which would be united by common goals of cooperation.[60]

Phan Doan Nam's contemplation of the open development of the international structure deviated from formalist Marxist-Leninist argumentation that took global development toward socialism, although troublesome from time to time, as a fact. He turned to the Marxist tradition by analyzing the basic contradictions *(cac mau thuan co ban)* of the world, though using them in a rather unorthodox manner. In spite of the end of the Cold War, the contradiction between socialism and capitalism had not disappeared. Nam turned the concept of three revolutionary currents upside down when he ventured to consider that capitalism was advancing and the socialist countries, national movements and workers' movements were declining. He pointed out that the reactionary forces which predicted the collapse of socialism "are realistic in the sense that the new world order is not going to follow the model of the October Revolution." The contradiction between capitalism and socialism was not going to appear only as an armed and ideological struggle, but would take place in every sector of social life as well as between different countries involving the conflicts between the socialist countries.[61] In this, the similarities with Gorbachevian "new thinking" and the themes that Western studies on international political economy have presented on the nature of international society are obvious.

Nam argued that the current crisis of the socialist countries was not the result of imperialist sabotage, but of the disagreements between the socialist countries, which made the economic, scientific and technological factors of prime importance. Similarly, there were no stereotypic contradictions between the developed capitalist countries and the developing countries considered by Phan Doan Nam to be basic, but rather the contradiction between the seven most industrialized capitalist countries and the most underdeveloped countries. This contradiction manifested itself in the control maintained by the developed countries over these underdeveloped countries. Interestingly enough, Nam tended to emphasize the contradiction between the capitalist centers, the U.S., West Europe and Japan, as a decisive contradiction in the process of formation of the new world order. He predicted that this contradiction would not lead to war, but to the alienation of these centers from each other. Finally, the fourth contradiction was to be found in the immediate security interests of the world power centers, primarily those of the United States and the Soviet Union. These contradictions appeared in the existing situation to be a primary factor in the regional conflicts and thus their peaceful settlement was important.[62]

According to Nam, the resolution of these contradictions would determine the form of the new world order. Thus he did not make any prediction as to what kind of order would prevail. This kind of acceptance of an open future was one characteristic of the "new" pragmatic argumentation in foreign policy.[63] Notwithstanding the contradictions, he pointed to certain tendencies that are bound to stabilize developments.

He argued that the most important tendency, namely, the economic, scientific and technological competition, would not eliminate the basic contradictions but would nevertheless have a deep influence on their resolution. First of all, when the importance of the factors at work is fully understood, the arms race must turn, on account of the scantity of resources, to peaceful competition in the scientific, technological, and economic sectors. This line of development calls for growing interaction between the countries and thereby interdependence will become one dominant tendency in the new world order. Phan Doan Nam considered that Vietnam's possibilities, despite its lack of economic resources, lay in an educated population, which would be capable of responding to scientific-technological progress and to its economic consequences.[64]

Notwithstanding this interdependence between states, Nam emphasized along the old lines of pragmatic argumentation that the global power constellation was one of the decisive factors in the development of the present world order. Hence the crucial thing was that now all the states were claiming the status that belonged to them according to their potential. He therefore argued that the new world order was totally different from what it was after World War II. In spite of the fact that the United States was the most powerful, there were several poles, several power axes as well as regional power groups, that determine the course of development. Among the aforementioned power centers, Phan Doan Nam took heed of the development of Sino–Soviet relations, and the development of China, Japan and, particularly, the Asia–Pacific region. Here the role of Vietnam was one of wait and see, and then try to work into the general developmental trend. The important question affecting Vietnam's choices here involved the consequences of the crises in the socialist countries.[65]

Characteristic of Vietnamese political thinking, the concept of power and the possibility of violence had not disappeared in the "new pragmatism." Discussing the nature of present and future wars, Tran Trong Thin drew a Clausewitzian conclusion: "The present wars are still basically the continuation of politics *(ngay nay chien tranh ve vo ban van la su ke tuc chinh tri)*, although in the near future politics may add new colors."[66] However, as opposed to the old revolutionary pragmatism, the new pragmatist rejected the idea of attaining the set goal by rationalist calculation and action. The order might be better called disorder, where any fair estimation of the world's political, military, and economic changes, even in the middle range, can hardly be made.[67]

Despite the fact that the concept of order was accepted in this pragmatic argumentation, this did not mean that any kind of order whatsoever and, particularly, any kind of control that interdependence might bring along could be accepted.[68] This called for a definition of independence and sovereignty[69] and special attention to regional conflicts[70] as well to the regional possibilities.[71] In this, when dealing with interdependence, Nguyen Co Thach introduced the concept of regionalism *(chu nghia khu vuc)* to describe these possibilities. He discussed the difficult equation of the present, when the most developed and, in a sense, the most independent countries were the most dependent on cooperation with other countries. Thus "regionalism is developing more and more to the significance attainable by economic cooperation and endeavors in terms of favorable geographical conditions across political and military alliances. This is the new specific trait of an international division of labor."[72] Therefore Vietnam's chances of survival may lie in regional cooperation better than in the conventional strategy of alignment with ideologically motivated friends.

This international cooperation with different political and economic systems did not mean that the pragmatic argumentation, though giving up the old Marxist-Leninist concepts and ideas on international relations, was directed against the Communist Party rule in Vietnam. In fact, among the articles included here, the demand for the democratization of political life was even stronger in formal argumentation, whereas the sovereignty of the Communist Party was not touched upon in the pragmatic contemplation of foreign relations. The main pragmatic argument for new thinking about foreign policy insisted that Vietnam should adapt to the international trends in order to maintain political stability. Vietnam could not, however, answer all the questions with this kind of thinking. Therefore the readiness of the armed force as the ultimate instrument of politcs should be maintained.[73]

Nevertheless, the waning of the Marxist-Leninist doctrine in the pragmatic approach obviously caused the reaction of orthodox Marxism-Leninism against the new thinking in foreign policy. The most important attack against the new thinking in foreign policy and, particularly, against the pragmatic arguments was made by the Communist Party's general secretary Nguyen Van Linh in his speech at the 7th Plenum of the Party's 6th Central Committee in August 1989. In his speech, the Vietnamese party leader rehabilitated the old formal Marxist-Leninist vocabulary, all of which had been already explicitly rejected by Phan Doan Nam (1988). This involved the two camps theory, the *ai thang ai* concept, the doctrine of four fundamental contradictions: the contradiction between the capitalist camp and the socialist camp, the contradiction between the working class and the bourgeoisie in the capitalist countries, the contradiction between colonies, national movements, and imperialism and the contradiction between the imperialist countries themselves. The denial of these old teachings, asserted Nguyen Van Linh, "has led certain persons to believe mistakenly that the essence of imperialism has changed." He therefore concluded that "as long as imperialism exists and as long as the socialist revolution has not yet achieved victory on a world scale, the theoretical points of Leninism have still kept their original value."[74]

Evidently, Linh's speech was part of a campaign to direct and limit the *doi moi* movement and, particularly, to curb pluralism, which had been raised from the demand for democracy in political life.[75] The focus on international relations proved that at least a part of the Party leadership considered foreign policy exceedingly important to the Marxist-Leninist doctrine and political mobilization.[76] The extravagant emphasis on the concepts of socialist internationalism and proletarian internationalism just before the collapse of the people's democracies in East Europe and dogmatic commitment to "the class struggle to solve the *ai thang ai* - question between socialism and capitalism on a world scale" revealed this connection between foreign policy and domestic rule.[77] However, the fact that the evaluations and attempts to develop new thinking appeared after the Party leader's speech in the Party's main theoretical journal proved that in the Party leadership there also existed a strong tendency to move away from the old positions in foreign policy.

INTERNATIONALIZATION AND THE RE-EVALUATION OF MARXIST DOCTRINE

In examining the disintegration of the Marxist-Leninist doctrine in the Party cadres' discussion on foreign relations, three factors provoking opposite tendencies should be taken into consideration. First, there is the development of Vietnam's international position, in which the regional development of Southeast Asia was crucial. Second, there is the fall of the Soviet Communist Party from power, which led to the disintegration of the Soviet Union as a whole. The third factor is the discussion encouraged by the Party leadership to fit the Marxist-Leninist doctrine into the renovation campaign and into the one-party power system, which also reflected the discussion of international relations.

As regards the first question, concerning the regional development in Southeast Asia, Vietnam's gradual disengagement from Kampuchean affairs played a central role. The initiative for this development was not taken by the Vietnamese, but by the Soviets with their strong encouragement of Hanoi to start peace talks on Kampuchea with the Southeast Asian countries in order to move one obstacle out of the way to the normalization of Sino–Soviet relations. However, Vietnam tried to take all practical advantage of the regional talks between Indochina and the ASEAN countries in the years 1987–1989. Despite the fact that the formal arguments regarding Vietnamese policy toward Kampuchea persisted during this period, the growing interaction with the ASEAN countries and Vietnam's practical need to break down its isolation emphasized the pragmatic arguments.

The formal arguments in the regional negotiations dealt very much with the presence of Vietnamese troops in Kampuchea and the role of Vietnam in settling the Kampuchean question. Vietnam's stance was that its troops in Kampuchea were fulfilling Vietnam's international duty and acting in response to a call from the Phnom Penh government. Accordingly, Kampuchea was depicted as an independent agent, which could not be passed over in the negotiations. Moralistic arguments were presented as Vietnam's precondition for a Kampuchean settlement, with the Vietnamese troop pullout to be linked to "the prevention of the recurrence of the genocidal policies and practices of the Pol Pot regime." The first Vietnamese claim was formally circumvented by the structure of the Jakarta Informal Meetings in July 1988 and February 1989. There the (Kampuchean) "parties involved," the Phnom Penh government and the Coalition Government of Democratic Kampuchea, including all three resistance factions, held their first meetings. After that, "the parties concerned," Vietnam, the ASEAN countries and Laos, participated in the later sessions together with the Kampuchean parties. Owing to the strictly regional nature of these discussions, Hanoi's main pragmatic argument relating to its Kampuchean policy, the threat posed by China, could not be dealt with in these negotiations. Therefore the attempt to eliminate the Khmer Rouge faction from the Kampuchean settlement reflected this.[78]

However, the regional negotiations offered Vietnam a method of breaking out of its international isolation in Southeast Asia. In this respect, the ZOPFAN concept, which was connected with the negotiations agenda, clearly served Vietnam's interests. This was supported also by the volte-face of Thai policy, which turned, after Chatichai Choonhavan's government came to power in August 1988, to Indochina from its previous antagonistic policy.[79] The significance of this aspect in the regional talks was emphasized when compared with the main issue, the resolution of the Kampuchean question, which could not be brought to a conclusion until the great powers found common ground in the UN

Security Council during the Gulf Crisis in the fall of 1990. Naturally, Vietnam's unilateral decision to withdraw its troops from Cambodia[80] in September 1989 served both the solution of this regional issue and Vietnam's policy of stronger involvement in Southeast Asian affairs. Of course, the signing of the Paris Peace Accords on Cambodia on October 21, 1991, was decisive for the new trend and opened up prospects for Southeast Asian cooperation.

After the Cambodian peace settlement, the interaction between Vietnam and the ASEAN countries, primarily in the economic but also in the political sphere, started to accelerate. As regards politics, the emphasis on ZOPFAN was switched, after the terms of neutrality changed in the period following the collapse of the Soviet Union, over to the Bali treaty of Amity and Cooperation in Southeast Asia. The adoption of the Bali treaty offered to Vietnam a new channel for closer cooperation and for a gradual progress toward membership in ASEAN. Thereby, Hanoi would also be more closely involved in the other Asia–Pacific arrangements, such as the ASEAN free trade area and, more broadly, in the Asia-Pacific Economic Cooperation (APEC). Together with its new policy in Southeast Asia, Vietnam started to proceed to normalize its relations with China and the United States, though it was keeping a lower profile in these directions.[81]

All this seemed to support pragmatic argumentation on foreign relations that lacked Marxist-Leninist premises. However, the opposite tendency of falling back on formalist argumentation seemed to follow in the wake of domestic difficulties and the collapse of the Marxist-Leninist governments. The reason why the pragmatic approach could not take advantage of this development was obvious: there was an urgent need for the Communist Party to find theoretical premises to support its power in a new situation. This question was emphasized even more when the Soviet Union disintegrated at the end of 1991.

This theoretical re-evaluation connected with the political reaction was quite evident already in Nguyen Van Linh's address at the 7th Plenum of the Central Committee in August 1989. Its connection with the events in Beijing in June 1989 was also obvious. Nevertheless, Linh's speech was not an attempt to develop the Marxist-Leninist doctrine in order to respond to the changes that had already taken place in international relations, but to restore discipline to the discussion among the Party cadres. In the political debate before and after the 7th Party Congress, and in the Congress documents themselves, a clear intention emerged to reformulate the Marxist-Leninist premises to fit the current international situation in order to justify the prevailing political system in Vietnam.

The central issue in this fairly abstract and formal discussion was the question of the period of transition (to socialism). Although the concept itself was rather remote from the reality of international developments, it was very important for formal argumentation and the survival and continuity of the Marxist-Leninist doctrinal code in foreign-policy argumentation. Similarly, it linked internal security issues and international relations tighter together. Characteristically, before the 7th Party Congress, the discussion on the concept of the basis of the Draft Program was led by academics, who dealt with both the name of the concept itself, its content and its applicability to the current international situation. The discussion was even reflected in the name of the Political Program of the Congress, which was named the "Political Programme for National Construction in the Period of Transition to Socialism." According to the Vietnamese media, there existed mutual understanding of the necessity for the concept, but there was disagreement on how to apply it in Vietnam's present situation. Although the theoretical evaluations of the transitional period were not dramatic if the 7th and the 6th Party documents are compared, the concept was emphasized far more at the 7th Party Congress.[82]

In the Political Report of the 6th Party Congress, the transitional period was linked to *ai thang ai* between the two roads of development. Although the political program had moved many steps away from the orthodox Marxist-Leninist interpretation of the 5th Party Congress' Program, it held firmly on to both proletarian dictatorship and socialist industrialization. The notion expressed in the Political Report of the 6th Party Congress that the transitional period was at its initial stage allowed more flexibility for the economy to move in the direction of a small-scale market. Accordingly, Vietnam could "advance directly to socialism from small-scale production, bypassing the stage of capitalist development, because our revolution is taking place in a period of transition to socialism on a global scale."[83] As the Vietnamese line of development was seen as part of a general trend, the concept took on a strong autocommunicative function.

The political program of the 7th Party Congress could no longer share a strong belief in this kind of international development. Vietnam's transition to socialism was, according to this program, taking place "at an international juncture characterized by great and profound changes," with socialism "now facing numerous difficulties and challenges." Although the transition was now taking place in Vietnam, in the general international arena "imperialist forces have stepped up a ruthless counteroffensive with a view to wiping out the socialist countries."

However, the program drew the formalist conclusion that "finally mankind will certainly advance to socialism, for this is the law of historical evolution."[84]

In brief, the program included the main premises of Marxism-Leninism, such as class struggle, where "the contradictions between socialism and capitalism are unfolding fiercely," i.e., the idea of two roads of development and the struggle between these roads. However, the collapse of socialism in East Europe raised the possibility that also socialism might lose this struggle. This brought along a certain revision to the concept. First, history had passed the people's democratic stage, although many developments were left to be accomplished. Similarly, the idea of transition to socialism via large-scale industrialization controlled by the state had to be abandoned. The new policy was now directed toward "a socialist-oriented mixed economy." As the transition to socialism became more a domestic project for Vietnam, the idea of self-reliance was re-established in the Vietnamese vocabulary. Both proletarian dictatorship and the principle of democratic centralism remained important principles during the transitional period.[85]

The concept of a transitional period was crucial also when the multiparty system was rejected in Vietnam. The idea of the multiparty system operating along the socialist path was incompatible with the idea of the struggle between two roads of development during the transitional period. Interestingly enough, Nguyen Van Linh used pragmatic rather than formalist arguments when he turned down pluralism at the Congress. He argued that "in the context of this country, there was no objective need to establish a pluralistic political system, a multiparty system with opposition parties." He warned that recognition of a multiparty system with opposition parties would allow "forces of reaction and revenge living in the country or returning from abroad to act against our homeland, our people, and our regime."[86] The obvious reason why Linh used arguments referring to Vietnam's political realities, rather than to the theoretical premises of Marxism-Leninism, lay in his intention to avoid direct criticism aimed against the political developments taking place in the Soviet Union.

However, despite the strong emphasis on the concept of the transitional period, this was not directly reflected in the foreign policy sections of the Party Congress documents. The transitional period entered the foreign-policy discussion several months later. The discussion on international relations, which started in 1986, was noted in the documents of the Congress. Interestingly enough, it lacked both the Marxist-Leninist vocabulary and formalist reasoning. Foreign relations were dealt with strictly within the limits of current international relations. Nevertheless, the Party tried to limit the discussion to international affairs when it seemed to threaten the superiority of Marxist-Leninist dogma. This tendency was also reflected in the Party leadership, where the foreign-policy delineations of Nguyen Co Thach had been too radical for the Politburo. After Thach's resignation from his post, the nomination of a new foreign minister was delayed and the emphasis of the foreign-policy discussion turned in some degree to the defense ministry, a circumstance that stimulated the re-evaluation of formal arguments. This can be clearly noted in the discussion following the Party Congress. The new foreign minister, Nguyen Manh Cam, had been a career diplomat and thus had less room to move than his predecessor.

Notwithstanding the absence of Marxist-Leninist vocabulary on international relations from the 7th Party Congress documents, formal Marxism-Leninism did not abandon its concepts even after the collapse of the socialist countries, including the disintegration of the Soviet Union. Certain concepts were even "rehabilitated," involving a combined attack on the new pragmatism and an attempt to develop the formal arguments in foreign policy in the same manner as at the 7th Party Congress when dealing with domestic affairs. In the discussion preceded by the 7th Party Congress, some cadres argued that the crisis in the socialist countries did not signify a crisis of the Marxist-Leninist doctrine, but was due to the mistakes in their theoretical perceptions and applications of the doctrine.[87] They claimed that in political thinking one had to return to the theoretical premises of Marxism-Leninism: "We consider that Marx and Lenin, when they used the method of dialectical materialism and when they explained as well as examined the economy, created the grounds for an economic and political doctrine in order to explain the world and society and in order to create the grounds for the Marxist doctrine of scientific socialism. ... Thus Marxism-Leninism is an impressive scientific project; its nucleus has to be studied, its heart had to be found, i.e., the method of dialectical and historical materialism, which is the Marxist conception of the world and the Marxist outlook on life."[88]

By pleading on behalf of these premises, Nguyen Van Duc argued in the Party's and the defense ministry's theoretical review *Quoc Phong Toan Dan* against the key concept of "order" in pragmatic argumentation by posing a question about "the new world order or the new form of the struggle." He continued questioning in the formalist manner: "Thus, is the substance of the new world order possible? If expressed in a positive way, could there ever exist in a class society, in a class struggle, and in a national struggle a world order that represents the correct meaning of freedom, even in a relative sense?"[89] The author then rejected the whole idea of order by referring to history, where the existence of imperialist systems had led to major wars. In fact, the two-bloc structure that was created by the socialist revolution all over the world was, according to him, closer to the idea of order than the previous and present systems. Chaos, rather than order, described better the current system. However, the author presented another model: "Therefore there is no new world order, but only, no more and no less, the new form of the struggle between two antagonistic social forces."[90]

Owing to the decline and collapse of the Soviet Union, Nguyen Van Duc admitted that the revolutionary forces were on the defense, but refused to admitted that the meaning of socialism had disappeared from the globe. He emphasized the role of the remaining socialist countries, thus implicitly referring to a possible, at least ideological, alliance with China, and the combined ability of these countries to reform and keep to their Marxist-Leninist rule.[91] Duc concluded that at the present stage the struggle for peaceful coexistence was the best way for the revolutionary forces to solidify their ranks; but this peaceful situation should not amount to a "peaceful and humiliating surrender. Therefore war can break out anywhere, anytime, and at any level."[92]

The general characteristic of the emerging formal argumentation was that it tried to make the connection with the theoretical premises of the socialist state system and its foreign policy. Nearly all the formal approaches endeavored to find an answer to the critical question of why socialism had collapsed in the Soviet Union, in the "motherland of the world's socialist revolution." The answer obtained by these surveys can be condensed as follows: The question of *ai thang ai* during the transitional perioid is a crucial law that determines whether the society is developing toward socialism or capitalism. The socialist road of development can be maintained only if the proletarian class holds the political power. The threat to this power is posed by the imperialists, who are eager to use the reactionary circles inside their country. The conclusion of this was that imperialism took advantage of the reform process for "peaceful evolution" *(dien bien hoa binh)* to break up the Communist Party in the Soviet Union. Therefore the collapse was due to the subjective failures of the Party leadership in their evaluations of class struggle during the transitional period. The lesson for Vietnam was that the Vietnamese should stick firmly to the basic premises of Marxism-Leninism to prevent imperialism from conquering Vietnam peacefully.[93] Thus the concept of "peaceful evolution" tried to bind the transitional period, *ai thang ai,* the external enemy and mobilization together. Although this had much to do with internal security issues, the criticism directed by formalism at the "new political thinking" focused also on international relations.[94]

Although the concept of peaceful evolution was loudly echoed by the conservatives in the Communist Party and the persons affiliated with security and defense matters, also pragmatic orientated foreign ministry officials repeated it routinely. Besides the fact that the term linked Vietnamese vocabulary to the rhetoric of Beijing, it also comes close to the principles which some Southeast Asian leaders have advocated in order to resist liberal Western ideas of democracy as a phenomenon totally alien to Asian societies.[95]

The most extreme claims of formalism still involved the restoration of the central theoretical elements of political mobilization by utilizing foreign relations. These are: the doctrine of the contradictions between socialism and capitalism, the reasoning to justify proletarian dictatorship, proletarian internationalism and the national liberation movements. These are combined with "the doctrine of defending the fatherland and socialism and the new model of the working-class party."[96] However, the formal argumentation did not only conserve the old concepts, but there were attempts to elaborate the Marxist-Leninist doctrine for the new situation. One of the most interesting approaches appeared in Hong Ha's article in the December 1992 issue of *Tap Chi Cong San,* in which he tried to redefine some of the central concepts. As his evaluation was rather close to actual foreign policy, he used pragmatic arguments too. A particular color to the examination of his ideas was brought out by the fact that Hong Ha was a member of the Secretariat of the Central Committee and head of its foreign relations committee. At that time, Nguyen Manh Cam, the foreign minister, was only a member of the Central Committee, together with 146 other members.

In his attempt to re-evaluate the Marxist-Leninist doctrine on international relations, Hong Ha used both arguments based on the structure of reality and arguments drawn through formal deduction. He accepted the concept of order and admitted that the old world order did not exist anymore while socialism was declining, but the new world order had not yet determined its form. Accordingly, "the international chessboard *(ban co quoc te)* is rearranging."[97] The materialistic basis for this rearrangement was the internationalization of the forces of production and scientific-technological progress. However, when pondering what factors were driving future developments, Hong Ha fell back on rather conventional premises of the doctrine on contradictions. In fact, he contented himself with only a moderate reformulation of the old idea of four fundamental contradictions. Hence, characteristically, the author tried to bind these contradictions more tightly to both the domestic and the international position of Vietnam. He pointed to six contradictions: "The contradiction between socialism and capitalism; the contradiction between the ever-rising tendency to socialize the forces of production and the system based on private capitalist ownership; the contradiction between workers and capitalists, between national sections and the bourgeois class; the contradictions and the competition between the developed capitalist countries; the contradiction between the developing countries and the developed countries inside the capitalistic system; and the contradiction between imperialism and the developing countries that had gained their national independence."[98]

Hong Ha argued that these contradictions provoke animosity also in the Southeast Asian–Pacific area despite the fact that this area was, at the moment, in an active phase of economic development. He asserted that these contradictions showed up in all kinds of actions and interventions between different states. Therefore "the national and the class struggles of the people continue strenuously." However, the ideal of socialism has held fast all over the globe, rallying peoples to the front to solve these contradictions.[99] Here he clung faithfully to the same deduction as that made by Le Duan twenty-two years before[100] from the four contradictions of the world to the three revolutionary currents. Hong Ha argued that the way to resolve these contradictions depended largely on three trends influencing the foreign policies of different countries. He distinguished them as follows: 1) The rising consciousness which underlies independence, freedom, self-reliance and commitment to "the struggle against foreign imposition and intervention, for peace, independence, and development." 2) The trend of the socialist countries, the Communist and workers' parties, and all the revolutionary and progressive forces to continue firmly in their struggle against hostile and reactionary forces, and the strong commitment of these progressive forces toward the ideals of socialism. 3) The trend of competition in the context of peaceful coexistence; this competition takes place in the economic sphere and it determines for better or worse the place of different countries in the world system.[101]

Hong Ha's theses were a mixture of formalism and pragmatism. The emphasis on the contradictions between socialism and capitalism as a basic point of view could be clearly traced to Marxist-Leninist formalism. Similarly, the first and second trends, which he deduced from the contradictions, harked back to this. These trends also included autocommunication, with its attempt to connect Vietnam and its social system to the general global trends. The lineages to Marxist-Leninist formalism were further strengthened in his conclusion. He maintained that the line of development, which might be unstable and quite complex, and might undergo remarkable vicissitudes, is still governed by these laws, i.e., the aforementioned contradictions and the developmental trends.[102]

Hong Ha's theses also contained strong elements of revolutionary pragmatism. He listed a group of contradictions that cannot be derived from the contradiction between capitalism and socialism. Among these kinds of contradictions are those of racial, ethnic and religious origin and those produced by famine and civil wars. Thus these contradictions can be understood to form the reality for Vietnam's foreign policy. Similarly, the third trend can hardly be deduced from the starting points of class struggle. The most evident characteristic of his theses, which pointed up the lineages of revolutionary pragmatism, was his argument that Vietnam's foreign policy must be conducted by observing the aforementioned laws and the international vicissitudes caused by them.[103] Revolutionary pragmatism also involved the intention both to secure the political rule in Vietnam by linking security policy and foreign policy, and to attempt to take advantage of the developments taking place in the proximate region. Evidently, Hong Ha's mixture of formal and pragmatic arguments was intended to answer to questions concerning domestic and foreign affairs, but theoretically this equation would be difficult to form.[104]

In fact, the documents of the 7th Party Congress did not advocate any formal approach to Vietnam's foreign policy despite the formal tendency of the Congress in general. However, certain formal expressions could be seen in Vietnam's appraisal of international relations. Stronger formal tones were used when "the imperialist counteroffensive" was linked to the downward course of the world's socialist system. Both Nguyen Van Linh's speech at the Party Congress and the Political Programme included moderate expressions on foreign relations. The tasks and objectives of Vietnam's foreign policy were limited, clearly to serve Vietnam's interests without any commitments to "international duties." Although the documents reiterated the importance of Vietnamese-Soviet relations, the focus on foreign policy was turning in other directions. Linh stated : "With a wide open foreign policy, we declare that Vietnam wishes to befriend all countries in the world community and to strive for peace, independence and development."[105] The Political Programme lacked autocommunication when dealing with Vietnam's foreign policy. On the other hand, the uncertainty of the future was pointed out, and this uncertainty complicates the making of appropriate foreign policy decisions.[106] Similarly, the Political Report exposed a rather extraordinary attitude when it admitted that the Party had been guilty of failures and made wrong assessments in arriving at foreign-policy decisions.[107]

However, the pragmatism no longer formed any uniform pattern. Rather are the different vocabularies and argumentation patterns being built on top of each other. However, the most important qualifier in Vietnamese foreign-policy argumentation was the existence or absence of the Marxist-Leninist doctrinal code. The doctrinal code did not as such determine political orientation, although a strong doctrinal code seemed to prevail in the arguments of the circles close to Vietnam's military forces, whereas in the argumentation of persons closely associated with the Foreign Ministry the doctrinal code quite often completely disappeared. But from this there cannot be derived the conclusion that neglect of the Marxist-Leninist doctrinal code might also mean rejection of the political system in Vietnam. On the contrary, Phan Doan Nam, for example, used purely pragmatic arguments that were not molded by the doctrinal code when he dealt with questions of security, national defense and foreign policy. His formulation of the question as to how to secure the political order when the foreign policy and foreign trade had to be opened approached that of the security and military circles. His demand for combining security, national defense and foreign policy can be even seen as part of a campaign for removing Nguyen Co Thach from the Party leadership and restoring control of foreign policy to the collective leadership.[108] But he did not deduce his contemplation from formal premises, such as *ai thang ai* and peaceful evolution, but from the need to maintain stability in Vietnam.

Interestingly enough, the expression "peaceful evolution," which appeared once in the Political Programme, was not put into the frames of formal argumentation. Similarly, the communiqué of the 3rd Plenum of the 7th Party Central Committee in June 1992, to which the orthodox Marxist-Leninist arguments referred, did not formulate peaceful evolution from the quasi-logical deduction. The communiqué clearly included the Marxist-Leninist doctrinal code, but its argumentation was based on revolutionary pragmatism, including goal, mobilization and auto-communication.[109]

Correspondingly, the absence or existence of the doctrinal code in Vietnamese arguments on international relations did not necessarily show Vietnam's orientation in foreign politics. On both formal and pragmatic grounds, with or without the Marxist-Leninist modality of argumentation, the same conclusion was drawn regarding foreign-policy orientation. Near unanimity prevailed in Hanoi that, following the collapse of the Soviet Union, Vietnam's main foreign-policy interest was the regional cooperation in Southeast Asia. For pragmatic argument, the main emphasis was on economic cooperation with Southeast Asia. This would boost Vietnam's economy and help the country to take part in ASEAN's cooperative endeavors, and it would politically support Vietnam's position vis-à-vis China.[110] For formal argument, the fact was crucial that cooperation in the East Asian region did not threaten Vietnam's internal stability, as this threat was seen in relations with the Western powers.[111]

In spite of the obvious consensus on foreign policy, the arguments in which the Marxist-Leninist doctrine dominates seem to prefer closer cooperation with China and with the other remaining Marxist systems in contrast to arguments that have a different modality of argumentation. However, despite this different orientation, a more interesting question concerns the disintegration of the doctrinal code in argumentation on international relations. The presence of the Marxist-Leninist doctrinal code in the political argumentation of the Party circles involves the question of the power of the Communist Party in Vietnam. The growing absence of the doctrinal code from Vietnam's foreign-policy parlance raises a new question about the modality of argumentation. Inside the Party, argumentation continues that retains remnants of the vocabulary of Soviet new thinking, but the argumentation can not be connected to the Marxist-Leninist doctrine. Obviously it also reflects Vietnam's approach to Southeast Aasian cooperation, which has led to the adoption of a new political vocabulary.[112]

Here it might be asked whether the revolutionary pragmatism in Vietnam has contained other structural rules of argumentation alongside the Marxist-Leninist doctrinal code, which has now emerged in a new situation. If the connection of revolutionary pragmatism to other code systems can be shown, reference could be made, at least in a limited sense, not only to disintegration, but also to the development of the Marxist-Leninist doctrinal code.[113] In any case, the absence of the doctrinal code indicates that the Vietnamese arguments and representations concerning foreign policy at the beginning of the 1990s had a rather different function from before. Autocommunication, which used to dominate Vietnamese statements and arguments, has turned increasingly into a means of promoting and developing Vietnam's foreign relations.

7 Conclusion: The Disintegration of the Marxist-Leninist Doctrine

The admission of socialist Vietnam to a capitalist organization in Southeast Asia, ASEAN, in July 1995, dramatically shows the changes that have taken place in Asia. Similarly, it shows a different course of development compared with the European experience after the collapse of the socialist world system. In Europe, the socialist and Marxist-Leninist state systems collapsed and a change over to the capitalist and pluralistic democratic system began. In the Far East, however, both the former Soviet allies and other Marxist states have continued their political rule and state ideology, although most of them have made remarkable changes in their economic system and foreign-policy orientation.

These differences between European and Asian developments during the radical changes taking place in the world system are clearly brought into focus by Vietnam's political course. Vietnam, in many respects, lay in the center of these changes. In the cold war situation, the Vietnam conflict showed how the Vietnamese Communists stood at the forefront of the world's revolutionary forces. The Sino–Soviet conflict also reflected Vietnam's position inside these forces, finally leading Vietnam into the Soviet bloc and involving it in the new armed conflict in Indochina in the late 1970s and 1980s. Even the solution of the Kampuchean question at the beginning of this decade reflected Vietnam's position on the superpower axis and in the changing international system. But after the disintegration of the Soviet Union, Vietnam no longer followed the Soviet pattern of political and social development, but turned to its Asian neighbors, particularly the Southeast Asian countries. Although this line of development in Asia, supported strongly by the growing economic weight of this region in global affairs, was no surprise to those closely watching the Asian scene, it calls for re-evaluation of some old beliefs and concepts regarding political culture, political doctrine and foreign policy.

Ostensibly, the same political doctrine persisted in Vietnam during the period of great upheavals in the international system between 1975 and 1993. Vietnam's commitment to the Marxist-Leninist vocabulary after the spring victory of 1975 was understandable: for the Vietnamese

Communists, this victory proved the superiority of the Marxist-Leninist doctrine. The Sino–Soviet rift soon made evident the limits and possibilities of Vietnam's political vocabulary, and the collapse of the world's socialist system finally placed into doubt the justification of the Marxist-Leninist theory of international relations. However, the fact that the political doctrine has survived the radical changes in both the international system and Vietnamese society indicates that the Vietnamese Communists have managed, so far, to combine different elements in their doctrine without totally abandoning Marxism-Leninism.

The main aim of the present study has been to answer the broad question of how Vietnam's political doctrine developed and responded to these radical changes in its international environment. The research material, which emphasized the features of Marxist-Leninist parlance but concealed the more detailed contemplation behind foreign-policy decisions and political doctrine, called for an orientation that would concentrate on Vietnamese political argumentation. However, with respect to political culture, the cultural aspects of the doctrine are in the present study looked upon as a dynamic element. As far as political language and political rhetoric are concerned, they may contain several different vocabularies. In the case of the present scrutiny of Vietnam's foreign-policy language, attention was paid to two most obvious vocabularies: that of revolutionary pragmatism, with its obvious origins in the Vietnamese literati class argumentation and its deep attachment to Asian pragmatism; and that of formal Marxism-Leninism, which was adopted by Vietnam in a rather orthodox form, owing to the close contacts between the Vietnamese Communists and the Soviet Communist Party.

On this basis, more accurate questions and presumptions about Vietnamese political argumentation and change of doctrine, with special emphasis on international relations, were put forward. Concerning the structural rules of Vietnamese Marxist-Leninist argumentation – the Marxist-Leninist doctrinal code – four presumptions were presented. One was the stability of the doctrinal code; that is to say, while the audience and the situation of argumentation might vary, the doctrinal code remains constant both in pragmatic and formal rhetoric. Another dealt with the development of the doctrinal code, which refers to the possibility that new elements might appear and/or old elements disappear from the structural rules of argumentation. The third concerned the possible disintegration of the doctrinal code, and the fourth, the diminishing of the doctrinal code – which means that the structural rules lose their significance and the other patterns of communication gain more weight.

A general observation is that the doctrinal code was quite prominent in the Party cadres' argumentation between 1975 and 1985. As far as foreign relations are concerned, it was the dominant element of argumentation, displacing the other elements. Moreover, the significance of the doctrinal code was more central in formal than in pragmatic argumentation. In diplomatic parlance, the code appeared first when Vietnam emphasized its role in the Third World's developments, and then when the Vietnamese attached themselves to the Soviet foreign-policy line. Despite the importance of the doctrinal code in Hanoi's diplomatic parlance, the examination of this parlance revealed that, with their rhetorical themes and political vocabulary (phrases and concepts), the Vietnamese made clear their own line vis-à-vis the other socialist countries, particularly the Soviet Union and the PRC, between 1975 and 1977. Similarly, the Sino–Soviet rift set preconditions in the other fields of foreign policy; and this tended to emphasize the pragmatic arguments presented in 1975 and 1977, and to weaken the doctrinal code.

The emergence of the Kampuchean issue widened this obvious gap between the Party cadres' discussions and Hanoi's diplomatic parlance. In the domestic discussion, Vietnam's regional role was defended by arguments that loudly echoed the central elements of the Brezhnev doctrine. However, the pragmatic tones that appeared in Vietnam's "Indochina doctrine" – Vietnam's geopolitical security interests and the endeavor of self-reliance – diverted the Vietnamese approach from the Soviet doctrine. In the most conspicuous example of Vietnam's diplomatic argumentation, which was presented during the Non-Aligned's 1983 Conference in New Delhi, the tendency to sidestep formal arguments was particularly apparent. In fact, a similar development occurred on a larger scale in the United Nations, where Vietnam was forced to defend its occupation of Kampuchea. Similarly, in Vietnamese dealings with the ASEAN countries, pragmatic arguments came to the fore. Yet, at the same time, the Vietnamese stance toward Southeast Asia, which was based on the two camps theory up to 1985, stressed, however, the formal Marxist-Leninist point of view. Therefore, in brief, the Marxist-Leninist doctrine did not disappear from Vietnamese diplomatic rhetoric between 1975 and 1985 but served more or less effectively as a link between foreign policy and domestic politics.

The Vietnamese diplomatic efforts to break out of international isolation had, however, weakened the Marxist doctrine in their diplomatic rhetoric. With respect to the discussions engaged in by the Vietnamese Party cadres, the new Soviet approach to international relations, which started to emerge in 1985, was highly significant. The obvious move to renovate Marxism-Leninism led to the cultivation of political jargon intended in foreign policy to separate the domestic political system from international cooperation. Pragmatic arguments re-emerged with very weak links to the doctrine. Although the doctrinal code and formalist arguments remained in the rhetoric of a number of Party cadres, the widening gap between the discussion of international relations and the debate on domestic rule and mobilization became more obvious. Therefore, as far as foreign relations are concerned, there is little doubt that the Marxist-Leninist doctrinal code both disintegrated and diminished in Vietnam's foreign-policy argumentation during the period 1986–1993.

The gap between the argumentation of the Party cadres and the diplomatic argumentation that emerged particularly after the rise of the Kampuchean question could be seen in an interesting light in the application of foreign-policy themes. Immediately after the fall of Saigon, themes derived from the doctrine became important while Vietnam was formulating its foreign policy. The theme of the anti-imperialist struggle emphasized Vietnam's aspiration to be identified as avant-garde in the Third World's struggle against the industrialized capitalist world; and, by means of the theme of proletarian internationalism, it tried both to deal with the Sino–Soviet rift and to emphasize the overall orientation of the government's foreign policy. Similarly, both themes linked the domestic and international lines of the Communist Party. After the internationalization of the Kampuchean question and the outbreak of hostilities with China, Vietnam was largely obligated to give up these themes in its diplomatic parlance. In order to gain as wide an audience as possible, Vietnam had to use more universal (moral) and more pragmatic arguments than was offered by the Marxist-Leninist doctrine. This coincided with the downward trend of the doctrinal code in diplomatic argumentation.

As a brief answer to the question about the doctrine's capability of responding to the changes in Vietnam's international environment, the following summation can be made: Vietnam used both pragmatic and formal rhetoric within the limits of its doctrine in order to harmonize the demands of international relations and domestic political rule. During the most remarkable changes in international relations since the Second World War, from 1986 to the disintegration of the Soviet Union, the Marxist-Leninist doctrinal code in Vietnamese foreign-policy argumentation both disintegrated and diminished as it lost its ability to connect international developments with political power in Vietnam. This meant that international relations no longer had any self-motivating function for the Vietnamese Communists. In this new situation, "new pragmatism" emerged in foreign-policy argumentation for the purpose of responding to the new situation. Its links to revolutionary pragmatism are clear, but it is detached from the Marxist-Leninist doctrinal code.

In the new pragmatism, which appeared in 1986, it is questionable whether one can find the new structural rules of argumentation in foreign-policy texts comparable to the decisive role that the Marxist-Leninist doctrine played. Thus, without falling into improper generalizations, we may conclude that the pragmatic formula of political argumentation, in which the division between friends and foes – or even between oneselves, friends and foes – is made, is a special national characteristic of Vietnamese Marxism-Leninism. From this point of view, the traditional argumentation displayed similarities to the Marxist-Leninist doctrinal code. It is understandable that revolutionary pragmatism, using a similar argumentation pattern, was adopted in the early phase of the Indochina Wars. Owing to the same pragmatism, the Vietnamese seem to be able to adapt to the present situation with their Southeast Asian neighbors. However, on the basis of the present study, I am inclined to emphasize that the emergence of revolutionary pragmatism and "new pragmatism," in particular, developed from the challenges generated by international conjunctures and the domestic situation. Internationally, the turn taken by Marxism in the Soviet Union during the 1980s is crucial to an understanding of the development of Vietnamese discussion. On the other hand, domestic difficulties forced the Vietnamese Communists to seek a balance between the practical needs of society and the formal premises of Marxism-Leninism.

Formal Marxist-Leninist argumentation in Vietnam was borrowed mostly from the Soviet Union. It followed both Stalin's vocabulary and the general Soviet parlance from the 1960s and the 1970s, and tried to make a connection between the domestic politics of a Marxist-Leninist state and its foreign policy. The formal argumentation reflected an aspiration to establish and maintain Marxist-Leninist rule in every domain of society, following the Soviet model. By their formal argumentation, the Vietnamese also showed their foreign-policy orientation. This occurred especially during the 1970s and the early 1980s. The commitment to orthodox Marxism-Leninism brought, as we have seen, most difficult theoretical and practical questions to formal argumentation when international relations started to change rapidly in the late 1980s and the early 1990s. Despite attempts to develop a Marxist-Leninist theory corresponding better to changing international relations by introducing a new, largely Soviet-based vocabulary, the formal arguments lost their dominance in dealing with the international issues involving Vietnam. Significantly enough, however, formal parlance did not disappear from Vietnam's foreign policy. It linked the country's political structure to domestic and national security issues generated by the growing internationalization of Vietnam's relations. Hence, the formal arguments relating to foreign policy, presented mainly by the Vietnamese security forces, came close to those of the Chinese after the suppression of the democracy movement in June 1989. These arguments bound Vietnam's independence closely to the political power of the Communist Party.

A new foreign-policy vocabulary is again becoming established, but this does not mean that the old vocabularies are being totally neglected. They are rather building on top of each other. In the present situation, the Vietnamese foreign-policy argumentation might include relics of Marxist-Leninist formalism, together with pragmatic contemplation originating from older rhetoric, combined with the concepts of the Gorbachevian "new thinking." A brand-new foreign-policy vocabulary is also emerging. ASEAN's concepts of regionalism and resilience, for example, reflect Vietnam's new approach. The adaptation of ASEAN's old slogan of "unity in diversity" also reflects this approach,[1] but it also shows how distant is the old concept of socialist unity, which was previously enthusiastically advocated by the Vietnamese, and in which diversity was not accepted even nominally.

If the different sectors of Vietnamese political language and the different kinds of textual material are dealt with, their multistory character might be emphasized even more: They might even include more different vocabularies, such as those adopted from the Chinese and other Eastern philosophical ways of thinking and those adopted from the French and other Western political and humanistic traditions.

The crucial notion of two argumentation patterns in Vietnamese Marxism-Leninism, and their disintegration during the 1980s and early 1990s, is of great significance in gaining an insight into Vietnamese political parlance. Nonetheless, it is equally important to emphasize their mutually complementary roles in Vietnamese Marxism. Some Party cadres might be called "pragmatist" or "formalist," but, irrespective of the fact that, during the latest developments, the Foreign Ministry seemed to use pragmatic arguments while the Defense Ministry rested its foreign-policy arguments more on formal Marxism-Leninism, this division has not been decisive in Vietnamese politics. Argumentation patterns have been closely related to the current situation and the audience, as well as to the theme of argumentation. Moreover, different arguments are often mixed in the same texts. However, it is probable that in time the formal Marxist-Leninist arguments will disappear even in the justification of the Communist Party's power, and the Vietnamese will turn to the pragmatic style of arguing for the monopoly of the single party, as has happened in most of Vietnam's Southeast Asian and Asian capitalist neighbors, many of which are organized according to semitotalitarian ideologies. Thus Vietnamese political argumentation may include in the future a code to mobilize the masses, but it is questionable whether this code would cover foreign-policy argumentation. All this does not necessarily mean that formal argumentation with some Marxist-Leninist coloring will totally disappear from Vietnamese political parlance. On the contrary, it is highly likely that Marxism-Leninism will leave its traces in the Vietnamese political language even in case the Communist one-party system is formally abandoned.

It can be argued that Vietnamese political language is rhetorical by nature and cannot therefore be automatically assumed to provide the cognitive elements for the Vietnamese Communists. Hence the word "doctrine" in the doctrinal code refers to the fact that, in order to show their loyalty to the Communist Party, the Party cadres must follow the Marxist-Leninist parlance. Thus the only thing that can be predicted is the stability or change of the political parlance. Similarly, the approach according to which the cognitive structure can be derived from certain political concepts is equally vague. First, the Marxist-Leninist concepts have not remained untouched; their contents have changed and new concepts have been introduced, while other ones have been discarded. The changes in foreign-policy concepts have always coincided with changes in Vietnam's international environment. Accordingly, the repetition of certain concepts and phrases need not indicate that they are crucial in the decision-makers' cognition,[2] but simply that they are an important part of the political mantra – autocommunication for mobilizing the masses.

The Marxist-Leninist doctrinal code provides a certain way to build arguments. As the doctrinal code is connected to the key method of gaining and establishing political power for the Communist Party, its basic structure has not changed. The fact that in the long run the doctrinal code's significance was diminishing and was partly disregarded at the end of the period examined here has something to do with the gradual changes in the political system, particularly the decreasing importance of the Communist Party as the overall organizer of Vietnamese society.

The motives and intentions of the Vietnamese in their foreign-policy decisions and alignments are beyond the scope of the present study. In the case of the Soviet Union, painstaking research in the Soviet archives for the purpose of comparing the conclusions arrived at relating to the operational code, the foreign-policy doctrine, and the outlook on the world, all of which has been based on the public material left by the Soviet leadership, would show to what extent these concepts can explain the cognitive basis of political behavior. In Vietnam, such material is not available. Therefore I suggest that in the case of Vietnam, as well as in every other case involving public material, the approaches to political argumentation should be developed.

The cognitive approach to doctrine studies seeks to predict future decision-making, or at least the possible reaction of the state to the different options faced by its foreign policy. The study of doctrine based on the study of political language does not aim at making such predictions, but at exploring the connection between political language and political power. Thus changes in the political system can radically alter this language. In the case of Vietnam, these changes do not, however, depend solely on Vietnamese political choices, but on general developments in the Asia–Pacific area. Hence, the question of how the Vietnamese succeed in taking advantage of the Asia-Pacific region's growing importance on a global scale will also show their ability to adapt the new political vocabulary to their own political tradition.

The new developments in Asia and Vietnam's efforts to integrate into them have made questionable the role of the Marxist-Leninist doctrine in the field of Vietnam's foreign policy. The "unity in diversity" prevailing in Southeast Asia has so far helped the Vietnamese Communist Party to maintain its role in domestic affairs and to fit its foreign policy into the regional context. This disintegration of the doctrine raises new questions about the relationship of the domestic affairs, foreign policy and political culture of the whole Southeast Asian region. It likewise calls for approaches to political language, international relations and foreign policy that might lead to a better understanding of the important developments taking place in this part of the world.

Notes and References

1 INTRODUCTION: MARXISM-LENINISM AND GLOBAL CHANGE

1 Kautsky 1973, p. 141; see also Ionescu 1972 and White et al. 1982.
2 See Scalapino and Dalchoong Kim 1988.
3 Leites 1953, pp. 15–25. Interestingly enough, Leites was engaged in Vietnamese studies when he made a report for the RAND Corporation on the Viet Cong and its political culture in the late 1960s. See Lucian W. Pye (1985, pp. 59 and 244). Pye shares Leites's broad generalizations on the cultural aspects of the Vietnamese consciousness. Douglas Pike's (1966) study on the organization and communication practices of the National Liberation Front of South Vietnam follows in many respects Leites's study-program, including the cultural elements in the Vietnamese consciousness.
4 George 1980 and Pike 1971.
5 Pye and Verba 1965, Eckstein 1988.
6 Brodin 1977 and Heradstveit and Narvesen 1978.
7 Holsti 1977, pp. 373–374; Triska and Finley 1968, pp. 112–113, 115; and Mitchell 1982.
8 Berry 1972, Brodin 1977; and Mouritzen 1981.
9 Brodin 1977, p. 278.
10 See also Berry 1972, pp. 2–3.
11 See Rosenberg and Wolfsfeld 1977.
12 Mouritzen 1981, p. 36.
13 Leites 1953, pp. 16–20, Berry 1972, pp. 2–3, Hoffman and Fleron 1980, pp. 91–100, Ulam 1980, Daniels 1980, pp. 156–157 and Mitchell 1982, p. 3.
14 Leites 1953, pp. 18 and 22.
15 Porter 1981, 1985, 1990a, Thayer 1984 and 1985.
16 See Marr 1971 and 1981, Woodside 1976, Huynh Kim Khanh 1982.
17 See Fitzgerald 1972.
18 Marr 1981, pp. 2, 130–135 and 413–415.
19 Marr 1981. pp. 402– 403, and Huynh Kim Khanh 1982.
20 Ho Chi Minh, the founder of the ICP and President of the DRV until his death in 1969, was a product of Confucian education as he belonged to an earlier generation. Pham Van Dong, the DRV and SRV's long-time premier, Vo Nguyen Giap, military leader and defense minister (officially dropped from the Politburo at the 5th Party Congress in 1982), Truong Chinh, secretary general of the Communist Party 1941–1956 and president of the SRV 1981–1986, and Le Duc Tho, a Political Bureau member with important positions in the Party organization, have a Confucian family background. See Trinh Van Thao 1990, pp. 38–57. Pham Van Dong, Truong Chinh and Le Duc Tho did not step aside from the Party leadership until the 6th Party Congress in December 1986.
21 See Eckstein 1988.

22   *Quoc ngu* (national language) script, the romanized Vietnamese script, is
      used in this study without diacritical marks.
23   Eco 1976, pp. 13–14.
24   Edmondson 1984, pp. 5–8, Barilli 1989, pp. 21–22, Summa 1990, pp. 184–
      186.
25   Perelman and Obrechts-Tyteca 1971, p. 154.
26   Ibid., p. 149.
27   Ibid., p. 163.
28   Bernstein 1971, p. 122.
29   Halliday 1984, pp. 5–6, see also Halliday 1978, pp. 24–27.
30   Halliday 1984, p. 6.
31   Jakobson 1986, pp. 150–153.
32   Lotman 1990, p. 14.
33   Ibid., p. 15.
34   Vietnamese political language and the semantics of political words developed
      gradually during the colonial and postcolonial periods, and there was no
      such attempt as in Democratic Kampuchea (1975–78) to change the whole
      language to serve the revolutionary system. As regards Vietnamese language
      development, see Marr 1981, pp. 167–175, on Democratic Kampuchea,
      Chandler 1976.
35   See Susiluoto 1990, pp. 69–75.
36   Lotman 1990, Broms and Gahmberg 1983; and Broms 1988
37   Susiluoto 1982 and 1990.
38   Tu dien triet hoc, pp. 158–161.
39   Ibid., p. 159.
40   See Ricoeur 1988.
41   Minoque 1989.
42   Arendt 1953, 1967, Lefort, 1978, 1979, 1988, and Marcuse 1969.
43   Minoque 1985, pp. 1–7.
44   Lefort 1988, p. 48.
45   Arendt 1967, p. 470 and Lefort 1978, pp. 234–239.
46   Trinh Van Thao 1990, pp. 158–162, 287–288.
47   Perelman and Obrechts-Tyteca 1971, pp. 193–198.
48   Ibid., pp. 261–274.
49   Ibid., see also p. 198.
50   See Susiluoto 1982, p. 149, and 1990, p. 70.
51   Lotman 1990, pp. 32–33, Broms 1988, pp. 133–134.
52   Perelman and Obrechts-Tyteca 1971, pp. 15, 65–66, Perelman 1982, pp.
      21–23.

2   TWO APPROACHES OF VIETNAMESE MARXISM-LENINISM

1   Trinh Van Thao (1990, pp. 287–288) calls them the two versants of
     Vietnamese Marxism.
2   The general secretary of Vietnam's Communist Party from 1960 until his
     death in 1986.

3   Vo Nguyen Giap 1961, pp. 85–86, Truong Chinh, SW, pp. 24–25.
4   Lich Su Dang Cong San I, pp. 226–227. Also History of the August Revolution, pp. 111, 116, 129. The opportune moment contains the political and military situation on both sides; see Van Tien Dung 1977, pp. 22–25.
5   Lich Su Dang Cong San IV, p. 68.
6   See Starr 1973, pp. 24–26.
7   Lich Su Dang Cong San I, p. 224.
8   Truong Chinh, SW, pp. 619–621. See also Lich Su Dang Cong San VI, p. 55.
9   Lich Su Dang Cong San I, pp. 224–225 and Truong Chinh, SW, p. 620.
10 Vo Nguyen Giap 1961, p. 33.
11 Vo Nguyen Giap 1975, pp. 69–70, 197–198, 309–314, Giap 1961, p. 93 and Truong Chinh, SW, pp. 620–623. Also Huynh Kim Khanh 1982, pp. 84–85 and 265–269.
12 See also Huynh Kim Khanh 1989, pp. 14–15.
13 See History of the Communist Party of Vietnam, 1986, p. 55.
14 Vo Nguyen Giap 1961, pp. 22 and 27.
15 Ibid., pp. 47 and 55–56, 59–60.
16 Vo Nguyen Giap 1975, p. 65.
17 See the discussion on this in the next chapter.
18 History of the August Revolution, pp. 52–53.
19 Truong Chinh, The Resistance Will Win, SW, p. 131–133; also Le Duan, OSRV III, pp. 42–43 and Truong Chinh, Marxism and Vietnamese Culture, SW, pp. 280–282. See also Marr 1981, pp. 402–403.
20 Le Duan, OSRV I, p. 25, and Le Duan 1976, p. 75.
21 Le Duan 1976, pp. 74–75.
22 Ibid., pp. 51–54 also Vo Nguyen Giap 1971, pp. 134–138.
23 Vo Nguyen Giap 1971, pp. 38–39.
24 See also Turley 1980, pp. 178–181.
25 Le Duan 1976, pp. 60–61.
26 Le Duan, OSRV III, pp. 53–61.
27 Tu dien triet hoc, p. 909.
28 Ibid., pp. 909–910.
29 See Ho Chi Minh, Appeal for Patriotic Emulation, Aug. 1, 1949, OR, pp. 193–196. Ho Chi Minh extended emulation to all daily activities. Ibid, p. 195. During the developmental stage of Marxist-Leninist rule in the DRV, these campaigns gained strength drawn purely from the Marxist-Leninist doctrine. See Statute of Vietnam Workers' Party, in Turner 1974, p. 396.
30 Le Duan 1976, p. 81.
31 Lich Su Dang Cong San IV, p. 191.
32 Ibid., pp. 191–192.
33 Le Duan 1976, p. 65.
34 Ho Chi Minh, OR, p. 245 and also Le Duan 1976, p. 58.
35 See e.g. Triet Hoc Mac - Le-nin 1978 and Chu nghia duy vat bien chung 1985.
36 For example, Mot tac pham soi sang 1970, p. 17.
37 This was observed also in Leites's (1953) classical study, pp. 28–30.
38 Tran Con 1983 and 1984, Ho Van Thong 1984 and Pham Nhu Cuong 1984.
39 Tran Con 1983, pp. 46–47.

40 Ho Van Thong 1984, p. 107.
41 See Tran Con 1983, p. 45.
42 Ibid., p. 46.
43 Mot tac pham soi sang 1970, p. 20 and Tran Con 1984, p. 124.
44 Hoang Tung 1983, p. 86.
45 Ibid., pp. 34 and 39–44.
46 Nguyen Hong Phong 1977, pp. 241–249, 270–271, Dang Xuan Ky 1978 and Nguyen Tho Chan 1986, p. 29. In spite of the fact that "a new socialist man" was crucial in Soviet Marxism, there is an interesting connection to a traditional Confucian idea. Hence, the parallelism can be seen with the Vietnamese concept of *quan tu* (superior man), which refers to the ideal goal of the Confucian educational system (see Trinh Van Thao 1990, pp. 131 and 167).
47 To nghien cuu lich su chien tranh 1972b, p. 51.
48 To nghien cuu lich su chien tranh 1972a, p. 24.
49 Ibid., p. 25.
50 Ibid., p. 26.
51 To nghien cuu lich su chien tranh 1972b, p. 43.
52 Ibid., p. 53.
53 Ibid., p. 50.
54 Hoang Tung 1983, see particularly pp. 8, 132, and 164–165.
55 Ibid., p. 23.
56 Ibid., p. 81.
57 Ibid., p. 82.
58 Ibid., pp. 39–43.
59 Ibid., p. 126.
60 Ibid., p. 82. Similarly, over 20 years before Hoang Tung's essays, Truong Chinh linked the *ai thang ai* struggle to the national reunification campaign and to "the rousing of patriotic feelings and the intensification of the hatred for the U.S.-Diem clique with education for socialist labour and socialist construction and the building of a new life in North Viet Nam." Third National Congress, Vol. III, p. 15.

3 VIETNAM AND THE WORLD'S REVOLUTIONARY FORCES

1 As Truong Chinh's appraisal of the world situation at the 2nd Party Congress, held in 1951, demonstrated, the basic structure, which survived up to the 1980s, existed as early as the beginning of the 1950s. Similarly, the appraisal of the world situation changed hardly at all during this period. See Truong Chinh, SW, pp. 301–322.
2 See Donnell and Gurtov 1968; Smyser 1980.
3 Thayer 1989a, pp. 62, 66–67, 102.
4 Donnell and Gurtov 1968, pp. 24–38; Smyser 1980, pp. 7–8, 53, 60–65.
5 Donnell and Gurtov 1968, pp. 39–43.
6 See, e.g., Vo Nguyen Giap 1971, p. 29.
7 For interesting pragmatic contemplation on foreign relations, see Le Duan OSRV I, pp. 49–50; also Le Duan OSPIP, pp. 20 and 27–28.

8 Le Duan 1970b.
9 See Nguyen Duy Trinh 1975 and Huong Nam 1976.
10 Le Duan 1970a, 1970b and Truong Chinh 1972.
11 Tu dien triet hoc, p. 159.
12 Le Duan, OSPIP, pp. 91–92.
13 Le Duan 1970a (English translation exists in Le Duan SW, pp. 163–329) and 1970b.
14 See Truong Chinh 1972, p. 12.
15 Le Duan 1970a, p. 37 and Le Duan 1970b, pp. 5–6.
16 Le Duan 1970b, p. 5.
17 Hong Chuong 1981, p. 48, Do Tu 1980, p. 49, also Le Duan OSPIP, p. 25.
18 Le Duan 1970b, p. 7, Vo Nguyen Giap 1971, pp. 75–76.
19 Do Tu 1980, p. 51.
20 Hong Chuong 1981.
21 Le Duan, OSPIP, p. 28.
22 Third National Congress, Vol. I, p. 171.
23 Le Duan, OSPIP, p. 17.
24 Ibid., p. 19.
25 Ibid., pp. 39–47, 77.
26 "Tasks at the present stage of the struggle against imperialism and united action of Communist Parties and all anti-imperialist forces." IMCWP 1969, p. 21.
27 Leonid Ilyich Brezhnev, IMCWP 1969, pp. 157–159.
28 See Chan 1994, pp. 84–90.
29 Editorial Department of "Renmin Ribao" 1977, pp 11–17.
30 Ibid., pp. 27–28.
31 Ibid., pp. 20, 27.
32 Ibid., pp. 12–13, 17–18.
33 See Pham Van Dong 1958.
34 Le Duan 1970a, pp. 105–106 and Le Duan 1970b, pp. 7–9. See also Thayer 1985, pp. 57–58.
35 Pham Van Dong in Hanoi Aug. 31, 1971, and VNA Sept. 1, 1971, SWB, FE/3777/A3/7.
36 Text of joint statement signed in Hanoi on Oct. 7, 1971, by Le Duan and Podgorny, SWB, FE/3809/A2/2.
37 Full text of Pham Van Dong's speech at the banquet of Nov. 21, 1971, SWB, FE/3846/A3/11.
38 Nhan Dan, according to VNA's English broadcast April 22, 1970, SWB, FE/3361/A2/5–6.
39 Gen. Giap Speaks on Dien Bien Phu Anniversary, May 6, 1974, SWB, FE/4594/A3/3–4 and Thanh Tin 1974, p. 79.
40 CPV: 4th National Congress, pp. 245–247.
41 See Thayer 1984, Thayer 1985 and Porter 1990a.
42 Le Duan 1970b, p. 9.
43 Thanh Tin 1974, pp. 78–79, Tinh hinh the gioi dau thap ky 80, p. 70, and Phuc Cuong 1980, pp. 40–41.
44 Le Duan 1970a, pp. 105–108.
45 Le Duan 1975, pp. 20–21, and Tinh hinh the gioi dau thap ky 80, p. 69.

46   CPV: 5th National Congress, p. 158; see on this, Vietnam Social Sciences 1/1984, pp. 8, 120.

47   Pham Xuan Nam 1977, pp. 166, 172.

48   Chu Huy Man 1980, pp. 33–34 and Mot giai doan phat trien, p. 6.

49   Nguyen Duy Trinh 1977, p. 4; also Nguyen Duy Trinh 1979, p. 315.

50   Pham Xuan Nam 1977, p. 201; also pp. 174, 199–200.

51   Le Duan, OSPIP, p. 12.

52   Nguyen Duy Trinh 1979, pp. 283–285.

53   See Perelman and Obrechts-Tyteca 1971, p. 275. Nathan Leites (1953, p. 101) calls this "the fear of goal-fulfillment." According to him, there is, in Marxist-Leninist thinking, "a tendency to preserve the future as the time of consummation."

54   Nguyen Duy Trinh 1979, p. 315.

55   See Huynh Kim Khanh 1982.

56   Tu dien triet hoc, p. 762 and Do Tu 1980.

57   Do Tu 1980, p. 52.

58   Tu dien triet hoc, pp. 762–763.

59   Do Tu 1980, p. 53.

60   Quoc Tuy 1989, p. 15.

61   Konstantinov 1968, pp. 3–7, Sanakoyev 1969, pp. 51–52, Tsapanov 1972; pp. 20–22. Also Kubálková-Cruickshank 1985, p. 95.

62   Le Duan OSPIP, pp. 47–54.

63   Pham Xuan Nam 1977, p. 169.

64   See Thayer 1989a, pp. 66–67.

65   Le Duan OSPIP, p. 22–23, also p. 34.

66   Ibid., p. 171.

67   Ho Chi Minh, Third National Congress, Vol. I, pp. 175, 179.

68   Le Duan 1970b, p. 13.

69   See Van Hien 1978, p. 99; Le Thuc 1978, p. 102; Phuc Cuong 1981, pp. 32, 34.

70   Third National Congress, p. 170.

71   La Con 1976, p. 78.

72   Ibid.

73   Pham Nhu Cuong 1979, pp. 9–10.

74   CPV: 4th National Congress, p. 144.

75   Nguyen Duy Trinh 1979, pp. 279, 313; Tinh hinh the gioi dau thap ky 80, pp. 68–69; Vu Tien 1982, pp. 85–86, 91, 93; Hoang Chi 1986, pp. 47 and 50.

76   Pham Xuan Nam 1977, p. 169.

77   Vo Nguyen Giap 1974, pp. 20–26.

78   Nguyen Duy Trinh 1975, pp. 5, 6 and 7.

79   Ibid.

80   Ibid., p. 13.

81   Ibid., pp. 8–9.

82   Ibid., pp. 9–10, 11.

83   Ibid., p. 6.

84   Ibid., p. 12.

85   Vietnamese media reported Nguyen Duy Trinh's displacement at the end of

January 1980; see, SWB, FE/6333/i. Vo Nguyen Giap's dismissal became public at the 5th Party Congress in March 1982. According to Thai Quang Trung (1985, p. 81), also Giap had to leave the top leadership in the winter of 1980.

86 Nguyen Duy Trinh 1975, p. 9.
87 Ibid., p. 19; see also p. 6.
88 Le Duan 1970b, pp. 10–12.
89 Ibid., p. 12.
90 Huong Nam 1976, p. 59.
91 Ibid., p. 60.
92 Ibid., p. 62.
93 Ibid., pp. 63–65.
94 CPV: 4th National Congress, pp. 142–152, 245–250.

4   THE STRIVING FOR AVANT-GARDE FOREIGN POLICY 1975–78

1   For an overall review of Vietnam's regional and international challenges, see Tønnesson 1992, also Porter 1993, pp. 185–215, Thayer 1984 and 1989b.
2   Leonid Ilyich Breznev, IMCWP 1969, p. 171. For more detail, see Rakowski 1976, pp. 96–99.
3   Horelick 1974, pp. 269–273, see also Longmire 1989, p. 112.
4   See NCNA Oct. 9, 1973, SWB, FE/4395/A2/2, Peking Radio June 1, 1975, SWB, FE/4919/A1/2 and NCNA Sept. 2, 1975, SWB, FE/4998/A1/2.
5   NCNA April 25, 1975, SWB, FE/4888/A3/2, NCNA April 30, 1975, SWB, FE/4893/A3/9–10, NCNA May 23, 1975, SWB, FE/4913/A2/1 and Radio Peking June 1, 1975, SWB, FE/4919/1–2.
6   CPV: 4th National Congress, p. 149.
7   Nguyen Trong Vinh in Peking, SWB, FE/4894/A3/17.
8   Ibid, SWB, FE/4894/A3/15.
9   Vietnam's representative at the UN General Assembly's discussion on "Deepening and consolidation of international détente" on Dec. 19, 1977, A/32/PV.106.
10 Ross 1988, pp. 86–93, Chanda 1986, pp. 176–185.
11 See Pao-min Chang 1986, pp. 20–25, Duiker 1986, p. 72 and Chen 1987, pp. 45–47.
12 See NCNA Nov. 26, 1975, SWB, FE/5072/A3/6.
13 Hanoi Radio May 6, 1975, SWB, FE/4898/A3/9.
14 See PRC's Foreign Minister Huang Hua's foreign policy address for the cadres of July 30, 1977, in Chen 1979, p. 273. This took place during Pham Van Dong's visits to China in April and June 1977. According to this source, Beijing refused to negotiate on the islands. As early as in July 1976, the editor-in-chief of Nhan Dan leaked information to a Swedish journalist that Vietnam was ready to make a deal with China on the island question. See Stockholm Radio July 6, 1976, SWB, FE/5254/A3/1, also Duiker 1986, p. 73.

15 Nhan Dan editorial as broadcast by Hanoi Radio July 20, 1977, SWB, FE/ 5519/B/2–3.

16 VNA June 2, 1977, SWB, FE/5530/A3/2.

17 See Willetts 1978, pp. 17–45.

18 VNA May 21, 1977, SWB, FE/5519/A2/2.

19 Report from the Kampuchean 2nd anniversary in Peking, April 17, 1977, SWB, FE/5490/A3/3.

20 See Ross 1988, pp. 133–138.

21 Truong Chinh Nov. 5, 1977, Hanoi Radio, Nov. 6, 1977, SWB, FE/5663/ A2/2–3.

22 "Full text" of the speech at the banquet by Hua kuo-feng, NCNA, Nov. 20, 1977, SWB, FE/5673/A3/3–4.

23 "Full text" of Le Duan's reply, NCNA, Nov. 20, 1977, SWB, FE/5673/A3/ 6.

24 See SWB, FE/5663/A2/2 and SWB, FE/5673/A3/4–5.

25 SWB, FE/5673/A3/3.

26 SWB, FE/5673/A3/6, see also Ross 1988, p. 149.

27 Hanoi Radio in English, Jan. 27, 1978, SWB, FE/5726/A3/6 and Hanoi Radio in Thai, Jan. 28, 1978, SWB, FE/5726/A3/7.

28 SWB, FE/5747/A3/1–2.

29 Pao-min Chang 1982, p. 16. See also Stern 1985 and Vo Nhan Tri 1990, pp. 66–72, on the position of the Hoa capitalists in the South's economy after the fall of Saigon.

30 Stern 1986, p. 66.

31 Hoang Tung 1983, p. 87.

32 Vo Nhan Tri 1990, p. 66.

33 Pao-min Chang 1983, p. 17.

34 Ibid., pp. 9–28.

35 NCNA, April 30, 1978, SWB, FE/5802/C2/1–3, NCNA, May 24, 1978, SWB, FE/5822/C/1–3. See also Amer 1991, pp. 57–67.

36 The statement by the spokesman of the SRV Foreign Ministry "regarding the Chinese distortions on the Vietnamese Government's policy towards the Hoa people in Vietnam," VNA in English May 27, 1978, SWB, FE/ 5825/A3/9.

37 As broadcast by Hanoi Radio May 28, 1978, SWB, FE/5825/A3/10.

38 Hanoi Radio June 18. 1978, SWB, FE/5846/A1/1–5.

39 Ibid.

40 Porter 1981, p. 106.

41 Vo Nguyen Giap 1979, pp. 14–15 (this article was originally published in October 1978), also Nhan Dan July 15, 1978, SWB, FE/5866/A3/5.

42 Quyet Thang 1978, p. 18.

43 CPV: 5th National Congress, p. 172.

44 Porter 1981, p. 105. See also Quyet Thang 1978.

45 CPV: 4th National Congress, p. 35.

46 CPV: 5th National Congress, p. 30.

47 Chu Huy Man 1980, p. 31.

48 Pham Van Dong 1978, pp. 7–9.

49 Van Tao 1980, pp. 4–8.

50 Ta Ngoc Lien 1979, pp. 162–180, Truong Khue Bich 1979, pp. 65–80.

51   Truc Xuyen 1979, p. 48.
52   Nhan Dan's and Giai Phong's editorials (Nov. 7, 1975) as broadcast Nov. 6 and 7, SWB, FE/5056/A2/3–4 and Suslov's speech at VWP's 4th Congress, Dec. 15, 1976, SWB, FE/5392/C/12–13.
53   See CPV: 4th National Congress, pp. 64–73, 91–96, Hoang Tung 1983, pp. 11, 88–90.
54   Pike 1987, pp. 189–190.
55   Ross 1988, p. 66, Pike 1987, pp. 128–129, Thayer 1989b, pp. 136–137, Thakur and Thayer 1992, p. 194, and Vo Nhan Tri 1990, pp. 98–99.
56   See Vo Nguyen Giap's article in May 1976, SWB, FE/5217/C/11.
57   SWB/FE/5392/C/13. See also Chanda 1986, pp. 185–187.
58   See CPV: 4th National Congress.
59   VWP Message on Albanian Party Anniversary, Nov. 7, 1976, SWB, FE/5359/A2/2.
60   Pike 1987, pp. 129–133.
61   VNA March 23, 1977, SWB, FE/5471/A2/1.
62   See Suslov's speech of Dec. 15, 1976, SWB, FE/5392/C/13.
63   Nhan Dan's editor-in-chief to Swedish correspondent, Stockholm Radio, July 6, 1976, SWB, FE/5254/A3/1.
64   Nhan Dan, July 2, 1978, SWB, FE/5855/A3/2.
65   See Suslov's speech, Dec. 15, 1976, SWB, FE/5392/C/13.
66   Hiep uoc giua Viet nam va Lien xo, Dieu 6. For the English version of the treaty, see UN document November 8, 1978, A/33/362.
67   Hiep uoc giua Viet nam va Lien xo, Dieu 5. The paragraph on peaceful coexistence was included in the SRV-GDR Treaty of Friendship and Cooperation, Dec. 4, 1977; see SWB, FE/5686/A2/1–3.
68   Mot giai doan phat trien, p. 7.
69   Hiep uoc giua Viet nam va Lien xo, Dieu 7.
70   Mot giai doan phat trien, p. 6.
71   Pike 1987, pp. 172–176.
72   Bui Dinh Thanh 1977, p. 292.
73   Ibid., p. 293, see also Nguyen Hong Phong 1977, pp. 269–271.
74   Hong Chuong 1981, p. 50.
75   Do Tu 1980, p. 51.
76   Quan Doi Nhan Dan, Nov. 17, SWB, FE/5975/A3/3.
77   Ibid., SWB, FE/5975/A3/1–2.
78   Huynh Kim Khanh 1982.
79   Brown - Zasloff 1986, Brown 1988, and Stuart-Fox 1986.
80   Heder 1979, Vickery 1986. On NLF-Khmer Rouge relations, see Carney 1989.
81   Thang loi vi dai cua cach mang Lao, p. 10.
82   Ibid., p. 12.
83   Ibid., p. 11.
84   Ibid.
85   Ibid., p. 13.
86   Excerpts from Nhan Dan, Dec. 4, 1975, on Hanoi Radio, SWB, FE/5078/A3/2–3, also DRV leaderships' message to Lao President and Premier, SWB, FE/5079/A3/2–3.
87   Hanoi Radio, Dec. 4, 1975, SWB, FE/5079/A3/2–3.

88   DRV leaderships' message to Lao President and Premier, SWB, FE/5079/ A3/3.

89   For early use of the term, see Lao party leader's message to Le Duan on the VWP anniversary, Feb. 3, 1976, SWB, FE/5127/A3/2.

90   The joint statement on the delegation's visit, signed by Le Duan and Kaysone Phomvihan Feb. 11, 1976, SWB, FE/5133/2–5.

91   Kayson Phomvihan, Feb. 7, 1976, SWB, FE/5131/A/3/2–3.

92   See Souphanouvong's reply to Podgornyy, Dec. 30, 1975, SWB, FE/5102/ A2/2 and Vientiane Radio Feb. 24, 1976, SWB, FE/5144/A2/4. For the Soviet view, see Suslov, Dec. 15, 1976, SWB, FE/5392/C/13.

93   Tuyen bo chung Viet-nam–Lao, p. 90.

94   Hiep uoc giua Viet-nam va Lao, Dieu 1.

95   Ibid., p. 96.

96   Ibid., Dieu 5.

97   Tuyen bo chung Viet-nam–Lao, pp. 84–90.

98   Dien van cua dong chi Pham Van Dong, July 16, 1977, Tinh nghia Viet–Lao, p. 61.

99   CPV: 4th National Congress, p. 151, the Draft Political Programme of Vietnam Fatherland Front, Feb. 4, 1977, SWB, FE/5432/C/4.

100 Dien van cua dong chi Le Duan, July 15, 1977, Tinh nghia Viet–Lao, p. 22.

101 Tinh nghia Viet–Lao, p. 6, also Tuyen bo chung Viet-nam–Lao, p. 92.

102 Pham Van Dong's speech at banquet, NCNA, Nov. 21, 1971, SWB, FE/ 3846/A3/6.

103 DRV Leaders' Message to Sihanouk, Penn Nouth and Khieu Samphan, April 17, 1975, SWB, FE/4882/A3/4.

104 See Phnom Penh Radio, Aug 2, 1975, SWB, FE/4973/A3/1, and Sihanouk's Message to the DRV President and Premier, April 30,1975, SWB, FE/4893/ A3/12.

105 Khieu Samphan's interview, Radio Phnom Penh, Aug. 13, 1975, SWB, FE/ 4982/B/3–4.

106 Phnom Penh Radio, May 10, 1975, SWB, FE/4902/A3/9.

107 Sihanouk's Message to the DRV President and Premier April 30, 1975, SWB, FE/4893/A3/12.

108 Message from Cambodian revolutionary organization to the VWP Central Committee, Dec. 1, 1976, SWB, FE/5398/C/4.

109 See Khieu Samphan's interview, SWB, FE/4982/B/3–4 and the interview of Pol Pot with the VNA, July 28, 1976, SWB, FE/5273/C/3–4. On Pol Pot's speech in Beijing, SWB, FE/5628/A3/6–13.

110 VNA Sept. 29, 1977, SWB, FE/5629/A3/2–3.

111 NCNA Nov. 20, 1977, SWB, FE/5673/A3/6.

112 Huu Nghi 1975, pp. 56–57.

113 On China's policy, see Duiker 1988 and Pao-min Chang 1985.

114 Hua Kuo-feng's speech, Sept. 28, 1977, SWB, FE5628/A3/3–5.

115 For a more detailed account of the conflict, see Heder 1981, Evans & Rowley 1984, pp. 84–128 and Chanda 1986.

116 See the statement by the spokesman for the Ministry of Information and Propaganda of Democratic Cambodia, Jan. 3, 1978, SWB, FE/5704/A3/1– 2, Radio Phnom Penh Jan. 3, 1978, SWB, FE/5704/A3/2–3. Also Phnom Penh Radio, Jan. 23, 1978, SWB, FE/5722/A3/2–4.

117 See Duncanson 1978.
118 Mitchell 1972, pp. 191–192.
119 VNA Jan. 6, 1978, SWB, FE/5708/A3/12.
120 Ibid., SWB, FE/5708/A3/3.
121 Ibid., SWB, FE/5708/A3/11, see also Hanoi Radio Jan. 13, 1978, SWB, FE/5713/A3/8.
122 Hanoi Radio Jan. 11, 1978, SWB, FE/5711/A3/5–6.
123 Hanoi Radio Feb. 1, 1978, SWB, FE/5730/A3/5–6, Hanoi Radio Feb. 15, 1978, SWB, FE/5741/A3/2–3.
124 Ngo Dien, assistant to the Foreign Minister, April 7, 1978, SWB/FE, 5783/A3/2–3.
125 Shee Poon-Kim 1977, Irvine, Roger 1982, Suh 1984, Nair 1986, pp. 1–20, Tilman 1987, pp. 33–34.
126 Shee Poon-Kim 1977, pp. 755–757, Irvine, Roger 1982 and Suh 1984.
127 The ASEAN Declaration, Bangkok, Aug. 8, 1967, ADS, p. 23, also Huxley 1985, pp. 1–10.
128 The ASEAN Declaration, ADS, p. 23.
129 Zone of Peace, Freedom and Neutrality Declaration, Kuala Lumpur, Nov. 27, 1971, ADS, p. 30.
130 Hänggi 1991, pp. 23–24.
131 Allison 1988, pp. 133–134. See also Longmire 1989, pp. 112–113, 116–117.
132 Choudhury 1982, pp. 235–242.
133 Declaration of ASEAN Concord, Bali, Feb. 24, 1976, ADS, pp. 32–34.
134 Tenku Rithauddeen March 20, 1976, FAM, March 1976, pp. 69–71.
135 Treaty of Amity and Cooperation in Southeast Asia, Bali, Feb. 24, 1976, Article 18, ADS, p. 37.
136 See Nguyen Giao Hien 1976, p. 65.
137 Binh luan 1976, pp. 74–75.
138 Ibid., p. 75.
139 Ibid., p. 74–75.
140 The joint statement on the delegation's visit, signed by Le Duan and Kaysone Phomvihan Feb. 11, 1976, SWB, FE/5133/A3/2–3.
141 Tuyen bo chung Viet-nam–Lao, p. 87.
142 The joint statement on the delegation's visit Feb. 11, 1976, SWB, FE/5133/A3/3.
143 Political Declaration, Algiers, September 5–9, 1973, CDNAC Vol. I, p. 201.
144 The speech of Souphanouvong, see The Colombo Conference, p. 334.
145 The speech of Pham Van Dong, see The Colombo Conference, p. 230.
146 The speech of Souphanouvong, ibid.
147 See Nair 1986, p. 63.
148 See next chapter.
149 Minister of Foreign Affairs Phoune Sipaseuth, CDNAC, Vol. II, p. 935.
150 See Malaysia's reservations, CDNAC, Vol. II, p. 937, and that of Indonesia, ibid. pp. 931–932.
151 See also Hänggi 1991, pp. 39–40.
152 Binh luan 1976, pp. 75 and 76, 77–78.
153 Ibid., p. 76.

154 Ibid., p. 78.
155 Ibid. See Porter's (1985) analysis of this article, in which he emphasized this angle as a starting point for Vietnamese policy toward the ASEAN countries.
156 Hanoi Radio Aug. 3, 1975, SWB, FE, 4974/A3/1. See also the statement by the DRV Foreign Ministry spokeman May 6, 1975, SWB, FE/4898/A3/9 and the Thai Statement on the talk with the Delegation of the Ministry of Foreign Affairs of the Provisional Revolutionary Government of the Republic of South Vietnam May 19, 1975, FAB, Vol. XV, No. 2, 1975, pp. 56–57; and the Joint Press Statement between Thailand and Vietnam issued on the official visit of H.E. Phan Hien, Vice-Minister of Foreign Affairs, to Thailand, ibid., p. 66.
157 See next chapter on Vietnam's policy in the UN on the Question of East Timor.
158 Tuyen bo chung Viet-nam–Lao, p. 87.
159 CPV: 4th National Congress, p. 151.
160 Nguyen Duy Trinh 1974, p. 16.
161 See the next chapter.
162 See, for example, *Singapore Bulletin*, Aug. 1978, p. 12.
163 Nguyen Giao Hien 1976, p. 66.
164 *Singapore Bulletin*, Aug. 1978, p. 12.
165 See Weatherbee 1985, p. 9; and Hänggi 1991, p. 40, who followed him.
166 See the Joint Communiqué issued by Thailand and Vietnam on the establishment of their diplomatic relations, Hanoi Aug. 6, 1976, FAB, Vol. XVI, No. 3, p. 44 and the Joint Communiqué between Thailand and Vietnam issued on the official visit of Mr. Bhichai Rattakul to Hanoi, Aug. 6, 1976, ibid., pp. 41–42.
167 "Full text" of the 5th July VNA interview with Nguyen Duy Trinh, SRV Vice-Premier and Minister of Foreign affairs (VNA's translation), SWB, FE/5252/A3/4. For the Vietnamese version, see Le Thuc 1978, p. 102. Interestingly, in the Thai version, the English translation states: "for the benefit of genuine independence, peace and neutrality in Southeast Asia," FAB, Vol. XVI, No. 3, p. 44.
168 "Full text," SWB, FE/5252/A3/4.
169 *New Nation* (Singapore) Nov. 4, 1977.
170 See the speech of Malaysian Prime Minister Datuk Hussein Onn, Oct. 4, 1977, FAM Dec. 1977, p. 5; also Singaporean Prime Minister Lee Kuan Yew, the *Straits Times* (Singapore), Sept. 23, 1976.
171 Malaysian Minister of Home Affairs Tan Sari M. Ghazali Shafie in Kuala Lumpur, Oct. 25, 1975, FAM, Dec., p. 80; Minister of Foreign Affairs YBM Tengku Ahmad Rithauddeen, April 1, 1977, FAM, June 1977, p. 105; and Rithauddeen, Nov. 24, 1977, FAM, Dec. 1977, pp. 39–40.
172 See Prime Minister Lee Kuan Yew, the *Straits Times*, Sept. 23, 1976, and Singapore foreign minister's speech in New York, Oct. 4, 1977, *Speeches*, Nov. 1977, Vol. I, No. 5, pp. 31–40.
173 Joint Communiqué issued on the occasion of the official visit of H.E. Nguyen Duy Trinh, foreign minister of the Republic of Vietnam to the Republic of Indonesia from Dec. 28 to Dec. 31, 1977. DLN, p. 77.

174 Van Hien 1978, p. 99; see also Le Thuc 1978, p. 105.
175 Speech by the minister of foreign affairs, YBM Tenku Ahmad Rithauddeen, Kota Kinabalu, Nov. 24, 1977, FAM, Dec. 1977, pp. 39–40.
176 Vietnam's representative, Mr. Cu Dinh Ba, A/S-10/PV.27.
177 Malaysia's representative, Mr. Zaiton, A/S-10/PV.11. See also Rithauddeen's appraisal for the necessity of an extraregional aspect in ZOPFAN, FAM, Dec. 1977, p.40.
178 Porter 1981, p. 107. On the formulation of the joint statements, see, for example, Joint Statement by H.E. General Kriangsak Chomanan, prime minister of the Kingdom of Thailand and H.E. Mr. Pham Van Dong, prime minister of the Socialist Republic of Viet Nam, Sept. 10, 1978, FAB, Vol. XVIII, No. III, 1978, p. 11.
179 See Joint Statement issued on the occasion of the official visit of H.E. Pham Van Dong, prime minister of the Socialist Republic of Vietnam to the Republic of Indonesia, Sept. 20–23, 1978, DLN, July–Sept. 1978, p. 79; and Joint Statement by Kriangsak Chomanan, Pham Van Dong, Sept. 10, 1978, FAB, Vol. XVIII, No. III, 1978, p. 12.
180 On the development of membership in the movement, see Jankowitsch and Sauvant, Introduction in CDNAM, Vol I, pp. xxxii–xliii.
181 See Singham's (1978) appraisal of Vietnam's role at the Colombo Conference, pp. 224–225.
182 Allison 1988, p. 49. See also the Cairo Conference's (1961) criteria of non-alignment in CDNAC, Vol I, p. 41.
183 See 1. Declaration, Belgrade, Sept. 1–6, 1961, the Belgrade Conference, pp. 3–7; see also Indonesia's Sukarno's speech at the Belgrade Conference, ibid., pp. 26–27.
184 Fourth Conference or Heads of State or Government of Non-Aligned Countries: Political Declaration, Algiers, Sept. 5–9, 1973. CDNAC, Vol. I, pp. 191–201.
185 LeoGrande 1980, pp. 41–42; see also Allison 1988, pp. 49–52 and the Political Declaration in CDNAC, Vol. I, especially p. 194, and the Economic Declaration, ibid., pp. 214–226. Re the interest of the Soviet Union and China in the Non-Aligned Countries, see Larrabee 1976.
186 Jankowitsch and Sauvant, Introduction in CDNAM, Vol I, pp. xxxviii–xliii; and Willets 1978, pp. 36–41.
187 Hanoi Radio, Oct. 10, 1975, SWB, FE/5037/A1/1–2.
188 Nguyen Nhu Lien 1975, p. 88.
189 Ibid., p. 89.
190 Remarque de la delegation de la Republique Democratique du Viet-Nam sur le point 7 du programme de Lima, CDNAC, Vol. III, p. 1286.
191 Political Declaration and Strategy to Strengthen International Peace and Security and to Intensify Solidarity and Mutual Assistance Among Non-Aligned Countries, Lima Aug. 25–30, 1975, CDNAC, Vol. III, p. 1217.
192 See Meetings of the Coordinating Bureau of Non-Aligned Countries at the Ministerial Level: First Meeting, Algiers, March 19–21, 1974, CDNAC vol. III pp. 1381–1385 and Third Meeting, Havana, March 17–19, 1975, ibid. pp. 1424–1435; see also Malaysia's foreign minister's answer, April 1, 1977, in Parliament to the question about the failure of ZOPFAN in Colombo, FAM, June 1977, p. 105.

193 Political Declaration and Strategy to Strengthen International Peace and Security and to Intensify Solidarity and Mutual Assistance among Non-Aligned Countries, Lima Aug. 25–30, 1975, CDNAC, vol. III, p. 1215.

194 For the Soviet side, see Bondarevsky and Sofinsky 1976 and Orestov 1976; for the Chinese side, see NCNA, July 6, 1976, SWB, FE/5228/A2/2.

195 Bondarevsky and Sofinsky 1976, p. 55.

196 NCNA, July 6, 1976, SWB, FE/5228/A2/2.

197 Speech by Pham Van Dong, the Colombo Conference, p. 229.

198 Political Declaration, Colombo, Aug. 16–19, 1976, CDNAC, Vol. II, pp. 773–774.

199 See *VNC* No. 75, Aug. 1978, p. 29.

200 See Chanda 1986, pp. 136–160.

201 UNGA; 32nd Session, Plenary Meetings, A/32/PV.3.

202 Ibid.

203 Ibid.

204 Ibid.

205 See Hanoi Radio June 2, 1975, SWB, FE/4920/A3/2–3, on the talks between Vietnam and the U.S. on the normalization of their relations; see Chanda 1986, pp. 136–160.

206 Vietnam's representative in the UN, Dinh Ba Thi, in the discussion concerning the Report of the Economic and Social Council A/32/PV.34.

207 UNGA; 32nd Session, Plenary Meetings, A/32/PV.3.

208 Vietnam's representative Vo Anh Tuan at the Fourth Committee, A/C.4/32/SR.15.

209 Ibid.

210 Dinh Ba Thi at UNGA Plenary Meeting, A/32/PV.83 and Vo Anh Tuan before the Fourth Committee, A/C.4/32/SR.18.

211 Vietnam's representative Ha Van Lau before the Fourth Committee, A/C.4/33/SR.26.

212 Dinh Ba Thi, A/32/PV.83.

213 See UNGA Plenary Meetings, A/30/PV.2187, A/30/PV.2188, A/30/PV.2439, and the Fourth Committee, A/C.4/32/SR.20.

214 Cf., Singapore's representatives' statements in the Fourth Committee during the 33d and 34th sessions, A/C.4/33/SR.20, and A/C.4./34/SR.15.

215 Yen Van 1976, p. 76.

216 Ibid., p. 77.

217 Ibid., p. 78.

218 Vo Anh Tuan, A/C.4/32/SR.15.

219 Ibid.

220 Nguyen Duy Trinh, A/33/PV.21.

221 Vietnam's representative Nguyen Linh Quy at UNGA Plenary Meeting, A/33/PV.34.

222 Nguyen Duy Trinh, A/33/PV.21.

223 Nguyen Duy Trinh, A/32/PV.3.

224 Nguyen Duy Trinh, A/33/PV.21.

225 Ibid.

5   ISOLATION AND FORMALISM 1979–85

1   Radio Hanoi Jan. 18, 1979, SWB, FE/6026/A3/9.
2   Voice of the Cambodian People Dec. 5, 1978, SWB, FE/5988/A3/1–2. See also Nayan Chanda's (1986) presentation on Vietnam's role in the establishment of the KNUFNS, pp. 338–341.
3   See Chen 1987, pp. 105–113; Chanda 1986, pp. 356–358.
4   Vo Nhan Tri 1990, pp. 72–109; Porter 1993, pp. 49–51.
5   See Thai Quang Trung 1985, pp. 63–93.
6   Vo Nhan Tri 1990, pp. 128–140.
7   Chu Huy Man 1980, p. 25. The Communist Party history raises this as a main theme. See Lich su Dang cong san IV, pp. 5–26. This was based obviously on the interpretation adopted at the 5th Party Congress.
8   Vo Nguyen Giap 1979. The book includes the following essays: Ca nuoc mot long, bao ve vung chac to quoc Viet Nam xa hoi chu nghia, (originally published in *Tap Chi Cong San*, October 1978), pp. 9–46; Giuong cao mai mai la co "quyet thang", san sang xa than vi nuoc, bao ve vung chac to quoc xa hoi chu nghia va xay dung thanh cong chu nghia xa hoi (a speech in honor of the 34th anniversary of the Vietnamese People's Army and in honor of the 32nd anniversary of the beginning of the nationwide resistance war), pp. 47–60; Nhan dan Viet Nam nhat dinh that bai (originally published in Tap chí Cong san, March 1979), pp. 62–82; Chien tranh Nhan dan bao va to quoc trong ky nguyen moi (a lecture held on the occasion of the 25th anniversary of the Dien Bien Phu victory), pp. 83–144; Thang loi vi dai cua hai cuoc chien tranh bao ve to quoc va nhiem vu ca toan dan va toan quan ta trouc tinh hinh moi (a report made at the 5th meeting of the fourth National Assembly), pp. 145–212.
9   Thai Quang Trung 1985, p. 81.
10   See Thayer 1984 and Thai Quang Trung 1985. The memoirs of Bui Tin (1995, pp. 131–135) supports Thai Quang Trung's view on disagreements between Vo Nguyen Giap and Le Duan, together with Le Duc Tho. Bui Tin (p. 131) also mentions Giap's and other Party leadership's disagreements over Vietnam's policy toward Kampuchea.
11   Vo Nguyen Giap 1979, pp. 71, 74, 88, 99, and 186.
12   Ibid., p. 208.
13   Ibid., pp. 173–174.
14   Ibid., p. 135.
15   Ibid., p. 136.
16   Ibid., p. 108, also pp. 126–127.
17   Ibid., p. 129.
18   Ibid., pp. 186–212.
19   Ibid., pp. 207–210.
20   CPV: 5th National Congress, p. 155.
21   Hoang Van Thai 1983, p. 8.
22   Ibid., p. 10, see pp. 9–10.
23   Ibid., p. 52.
24   Ibid., p. 39.
25   Ibid., pp. 38–45.
26   See Hoang Van Thai 1982, p. 17.

27   See Phuc-Cuong 1980, p. 42.
28   Hoang Van Thai 1983, pp. 47, 64 and 76.
29   See, for example, Lien-xo - tru cot 1982.
30   CPV: 5th National Congress, p. 135.
31   See, for example, Tran Quynh 1983, who used the concept in the title of his article but ignored it in the text and used proletarian internationalism to illustrate Soviet–Vietnamese relations.
32   See Le Thi 1979, p. 59, and Hoang Tung 1983.
33   CPV: 5th National Congress, p. 38; Vu-Tien 1982, pp. 85–86.
34   Hoang Van Thai 1983, pp. 52–56.
35   CPV: 5th National Congress, p. 138.
36   See Truc-Xuyen 1979; Hong Tien 1979, pp. 71–80; Pham Huy Chau 1979, p. 123; also Le Thi 1979, and Vu-Tien 1982, pp. 91–92.
37   See Pham Nhu Cuong 1979b, pp. 7–21, Van-Trong 1979, and Nguyen Ngoc Minh 1979.
38   CPV: 5th National Congress, pp. 144–145.
39   Le Thuc 1978, p. 105.
40   CPV: 5th National Congress, p. 136.
41   Phuc-Cuong 1981, p. 32.
42   See Nguyen Huy Hong 1983, p. 260.
43   Phuc-Cuong 1981, p. 34.
44   Cuc dien the gioi, pp. 66–68.
45   Pham Binh 1984, p. 84, and Nguyen Huy Hong 1983, pp. 259–261, 264.
46   Nguyen Huy Hong 1983, pp. 257–258.
47   Ibid., pp. 258–259.
48   Pham Binh 1984, pp. 82–84.
49   Ibid., p. 83.
50   Nguyen Huy Hong 1983, p. 266.
51   Ibid.
52   See Thai Quang Trung 1985, p. 81.
53   "Full text" of the February 2 speech by Le Duan, VNA in English, Feb. 2, 1980, SWB, FE/6337/C1/18.
54   Ibid., SWB, FE/6337/C1/17–20.
55   Ibid., SWB, FE/6337/C1/10
56   CPV: 5th National Congress, p. 135.
57   CPV: 6th National Congress, p. 122.
58   Statement of the Summit Conference of Laos, Kampuchea and Vietnam, DKP, p. 167.
59   Ibid., p. 168.
60   The Text of the Joint Statement of Nov. 4, VNA, Nov. 4, 1983, SWB, FE/7484/A2/2–4.
61   Hanoi Radio, Feb. 18, 79, SWB, FE/6047/A3/9–11; 'Nhan Dan' editorial, VNA in English, Feb. 18, 79, SWB, FE/6046/A3/16; Excerpts from the speech by Le Duan, VNA in English, Dec. 21, 79, SWB, FE/6308/A3/4.
62   Treaty of Peace, Friendship and Cooperation between the Socialist Republic of Vietnam and the People's Republic of Kampuchea, SWB, FE/6047/A3/14–16.
63   See the 'Nhan Dan' editorial on Chinese aggression, VNA in English Feb. 18, 79, SWB, FE/6046,/A3/15–16; Giap's Message to Ustinov on Soviet

Armed Forces' Day, VNA, in English Feb. 22, 79, SWB, FE/6051/A2/1; General Giap's interview with 'Rude Pravo', VNA, in English Oct. 31, 79, SWB, FE/6261/A3/1–2, Excerpts from Le Duan's speech VNA, in English Dec. 21, 79, SWB, FE/6308/A3/3–7.

64 "Full" text of article by Truong Chinh, "On Kampuchea," published in the Hanoi press on Nov. 24, and read in English by the VNA Nov. 24, 1979, SWB, FE/6283/A3/4.

65 Ibid., SWB/FE/6283/A3/4–6, 8.

66 See, for example, DKP, p. V.

67 Kampuchea Dossiers III, and see UNGA document of Dec. 21, 1978, A/33/546.

68 Pao-min Chang 1985, p. 134.

69 Statement by the Indonesian foreign minister as chairman of the ASEAN standing commitee on the escalation of the armed conflict between Vietnam and Kampuchea. Jakarta, Jan. 9, 1979, ADS, p. 446.

70 See Joint Statement, Special Meeting of ASEAN Foreign Ministers on the Current Political Development in the Southeast Asian Region, Bangkok, Jan. 12, 1979, DKP, p. 74, and Joint Communiqué issued at the 12th ASEAN Ministerial Meeting, DKP, pp. 77–78.

71 Willets 1981, pp. 9–18.

72 Ibid., p. 13.

73 See Address by President Tito in General Debate, RIA, Vol. XXX, No. 707, pp. 15–16; Address by Josiph Vrhovec, Yugoslav Federal Secretary for Foreign Affairs, Ibid., pp. 16–17; Petkovic 1979; Tengku Ahmad Rithauddeen, Minister of Foreign Affairs, Malaysia, Havana Addresses, pp. 449–451; and Sinnathamby Rajaratman, Minister of Foreign Affairs, Singapore, Havana Addresses, particularly pp. 642–644.

74 Speech by Pham Van Dong at the Sixth Conference of Heads of State and Government of the Non-Aligned Countries, NT, No. 38, 1979, p. 29.

75 Ibid.

76 Ibid., p. 29.

77 Ibid., p. 31.

78 Ibid.

79 Willets 1981, p. 15.

80 See Ibid., p. 16, *Straits Times*, May 26, 1979, June 10, 1979, June 11, 1979, June 30, 1979; *New Nation*, June 11, 1979.

81 Willets 1981, p. 16, *Straits Times*, Sept. 5, 1979, and FEER, Oct. 26, 1979.

82 Political Declaration, 12 §, The Non-Aligned in Havana, p. 81.

83 Political Declaration, 135 §, ibid., p. 105.

84 Political Declaration, 136 §, ibid.

85 Phan Hien, A/34/PV.13.

86 Ibid.

87 See Ha Van Lau A/34/PV.34

88 See A/34/500 and A/34/PV.2.

89 A/34/500, A/34/L.2 and A/34/L.3.

90 A/34/PV.3 and A/34/PV.4, also Amer 1990, pp. 52–53. During the following decade, Democratic Kampuchea's support grew steadily in the voting on Kampuchea's credentials. See Amer 1989, pp. 16–19, and Amer 1992, pp. 89–108.

91 Ha Van Lau, A/34/PV.3.
92 Ha Van Lau at the GA discussion 1980, A/35/PV.39.
93 Ha Van Lau, A/35/PV.39.
94 Ha Van Lau, A/34/PV.3.
95 Resolution adopted by the General Assembly 34/22, DKP, p. 126.
96 Document A/34/L.7 and Document A/34/L.7/REV.1 and REV.1/ADD.1.
97 Document A/34/191.
98 Document A/34/L.13/REV.2.
99 A/34/PV.62.
100 See statements by Singapore's (A/34/PV.62), Indonesia's (A/34/PV.65), and Thailand's (A/34/PV.66) representatives.
101 Document A/35/L.2/REV.1 and REV.1/ADD.1.
102 See Document A/34/L.7 and Document A/34/L.7/REV.1 and REV.1/ADD.1.
103 Phan Hien A/34/PV.13.
104 Document A/34/L.38.
105 See the voting records in DKP, pp. 138–141, and the changes in voting patterns in Amer 1989, pp. 31–36, and Amer 1992, pp. 124–149.
106 Vu Hien 1983.
107 SRV Foreign Minister Interviewed on Non-Aligned Summit and Cambodia, Hanoi Radio March 15, 83, SWB, FE/7284/A3/1–2.
108 Pham Van Dong 1983.
109 Vu Hien 1983, p. 68.
110 Pham Van Dong 1983, p. 7.
111 Ibid., p. 10.
112 Vu Hien 1983, pp. 69–70.
113 FEER, March 3, 1984; *Straits Times*, March 7, and March 19, 1983.
114 Texts of Thach's Address, Hanoi VNA in English March 4, 1983, FBIS-APA, March 7, 83, p. K 1.
115 Ibid., p. K 4.
116 See Huxley 1985, pp. 46–51; Sukhumbhand Paribatra 1987, pp. 20–33; Chang 1983; and Chang Pao-Min 1985, pp. 118–120.
117 Kuala Lumpur radio, March 27, 1980, SWB, FE/6383/A3/3 and FEER, April 4, 1980. See also Kroef 1981, pp. 516–517; Saravanamutu 1984, pp. 189–190; and Nair 1986, pp. 128–130.
118 See Nair 1986, p. 129, also Singapore's Prime Minister Lee Kuan Yew, Sept. 22, 1980, *Speeches*, Oct. 1980, Vol. 4, No. 4, p. 16.
119 FEER, May 16, 1980, pp. 12–13.
120 Ibid., p. 13.
121 See Chang Pao-Min 1985, pp. 119–121; Bekaert 1983, pp. 176–178; and Kroef 1983.
122 Phnom Penh Joint Communiqué, Jan. 5, 1980, DKP, p. 144.
123 Ibid., p. 144, see also p. 146.
124 Ibid., p. 147.
125 Vientiane Statement, July 18, 1980, DKP, p. 149.
126 Ho Chi Minh Statement, Jan. 26, 1981, DKP, p. 154.
127 Ibid.
128 Ibid.
129 Phnom Penh Communiqué, July 20, 1983, DKP, p. 175.
130 See Vientianne Communiqué, Feb. 17, 1982, DKP, p. 160, Statement of

234   *Notes and References*

Summit Conference of Laos, Kampuchea and Vietnam, DKP, pp. 167–169.
131 See SRV Foreign Minister's Interview on Results of SE Asia Tour, Hanoi Radio, Aug. 5, 1982, SWB, FE/7099/A3/1–2.
132 Ibid., FE/7099/A3/1.
133 Ibid.
134 Ibid. See also on this stand, *New Straits Times* (Kuala Lumpur) 28, Feb. 1983.
135 Kuala Lumpur Radio March 14, 1983, FBIS-APA, 16 March 83, p. O 2.
136 SRV Foreign Minister Interviewed on Non-Aligned Summit and Cambodia, Hanoi Radio March 15, 83, SWB, FE/7284/A3/3; see also *Asiaweek*, March 25, 1983, and FEER, March 31, 1983.
137 See 'Text' of ASEAN minister's statement issued, AFP, March 23, 1983 FBIS-APA, March 23, 83, p. J 1; Bangkok Radio March 21, 83, FBIS-APA, March 22, 83, p. J 2; and *Asiaweek*, April 8, 1983.
138 Phnom Penh Communique April 12, 1983, DKP, p. 171.
139 Phnom Penh Communique July 20, 1983, p. 175.
140 Phnom Penh Communique April 12, 1983, DKP, p. 171.
141 See Thayer 1983, pp. 321–322; Buszynski 1984, p. 30.
142 Nhan Dan July 15, 85, as read in French in VNA's report, July 15, 85, SWB, FE/8004/A3/9.
143 Joint Statement by ASEAN Foreign Ministers on the Kampuchean Problem, Kuala Lumpur, July 8, 1985, DKP, p. 112.
144 VNA in English, July 5, 85, SWB, FE/7997/A3/4, and Nhan Dan, July 15, 85 read VNA's French report July 15, 85, SWB, FE/80004/A3/8–9.
145 See Ho Chi Minh Communiqué, Jan. 18, 1985, DKP, pp. 185–187, and the ASEAN response to it; see Jakarta Radio, April 6, 85, SWB, FE/7921/A3/2–3.
146 See, for example, Interview with Chinese International Affairs Adviser, Hongkong, 'Wen Wei Po," June 22, 85, SWB, FE/7985/C/1–2; and 'Chinese Foreign Minister Comments on Remarks by Gorbachev and Le Duan', Xinhua, in English, June 29, 85, SWB, FE/7991/A3/3.
147 See Vietnamese Foreign Minister Interviewed, Kyodo, in English, Dec. 22, 83 SWB, FE/7524/A3/1–2.
148 See Le Duc Tho's interview with AFP, April 6, 85, SWB, FE/7921/A3/1–2.
149 Communiqué of the 11th Conference of the Foreign Ministers of Kampuchea, Laos and Vietnam, issued at Phnom Penh on Aug. 16, 1985, DKP, p. 188.

6 VIETNAM AND GLOBAL CHANGES 1986–93

1 See Huynh Kim Khanh 1988.
2 Hoang Tung 1986, pp. 16–17.
3 Ibid., pp. 13–14.
4 Ibid., p. 19.
5 Ibid., p. 20.
6 Ibid., pp. 19–20.
7 Ibid., p. 21.
8 Luu Van Loi 1986.

9   Ibid., p. 60.
10   Ibid., pp. 60–61, 55.
11   Ibid., p. 61.
12   Shevardnadze 1990, p. 7.
13   Thayer 1991, pp. 209–214, and Thayer 1992a.
14   See Sakwa 1990, pp. 102–125, and Yan Sun 1994, pp. 42–43.
15   Nguyen Tho Chan 1986, p. 29.
16   CPV: 6th Party Congress, pp. 167–168.
17   For a comparison of the development of reforms in the Soviet Union and China, see Yan Sun 1994. For the development of *doi moi*, see Huynh Kim Khanh 1988, Thayer 1992a, also Wurfel 1989. Particularly as regards *doi moi* and pluralism, see Porter 1990b, pp. 85–88, and Porter 1993, pp. 96–100.
18   Pyykkö 1992, p. 30.
19   In that sense, Paul Evans errs when he claims that "*perestroika* had not been translated into Vietnamese as of the summer of 1988" (Evans 1989, p. 46). The Vietnamese did not use the word *perestroika*, but the Vietnamese equivalent. This did not, however, deviate from the normal Vietnamese practice, as all Marxist key terms have their Vietnamese equivalents, and the direct loans are rarely used.
20   For example, Hoang Nguyen 1987, p. 71; Le Thi 1987, p. 23; Van Tao 1988, p. 74; Nguyen Co Thach 1989, p. 7; and Quoc Tuy 1989, p. 13.
21   Van Tao 1988, p. 74.
22   Nguyen Co Thach 1989, p. 7.
23   Evans 1989, pp. 46–47.
24   For an analysis of Soviet foreign relations theory during the early years of *perestroika*, see Light 1988, pp. 294–314.
25   The USSR Foreign Ministry 1989, pp. 11 and 71.
26   White 1991, pp. 187–188.
27   Butler 1989, p. 372; Sakwa 1990, pp. 317–320; White 1991, pp. 185–213.
28   See Sakwa 1990, pp. 316–330; the USSR Foreign Ministry 1989; Nagorniy 1990, pp. 183–186; Duncan and McGiffert Ekedahl 1990, pp. 76–79.
29   Phan Doan 1986, p. 103.
30   Hoang Chi 1986, p. 44.
31   Ibid., p. 46.
32   See Nguyen Than Le 1986, pp. 90–93.
33   CPV: 6th National Congress, pp. 118–130.
34   Le Thi 1987, pp. 22–25.
35   Hoang Nguyen 1987, pp. 67–72.
36   Quoc Tuy 1989, p. 13.
37   Van Tao 1988, p. 72.
38   Quoc Tuy 1989, p. 13.
39   Ibid., p. 75, see pp. 73–76.
40   Ibid., p. 77.
41   Ibid.
42   Quoc Tuy 1989, p. 13.
43   Ibid., p. 13.
44   Hoang Nguyen 1987, p. 71.
45   Quoc Tuy 1989, p. 16.

46   See Phan Doan Nam's interpretation of peaceful coexistence later in this
      chapter.
47   Quoc Tuy 1989, p. 16.
48   Le Thi 1987, pp. 28–30 and Hoang Nguyen 1987, pp. 73–76.
49   Le Thi 1987, p. 28.
50   Ibid., p 29.
51   Ibid., p. 30.
52   See, Hoang Hien 1987, p. 97.
53   Nguyen Co Thach 1989, p. 3.
54   This estimation is presented by Porter 1990a, p. 9.
55   Phan Doan Nam 1988, pp. 52–53.
56   Ibid., p. 52.
57   Ibid., p. 53.
58   Ibid., p. 54.
59   Ibid., pp. 54, 79.
60   Phan Doan Nam 1991b, p. 55.
61   Ibid., p. 56.
62   Ibid., pp. 56–57.
63   See also Tran Trong Thin 1991 and Nguyen Trong Thu 1991.
64   Phan Doan Nam 1991b, p. 57.
65   Ibid., pp. 58–59.
66   Tran Trong Thin 1991, p. 59.
67   Ibid., pp. 57, 59.
68   Nguyen Trong Thu 1991, p. 59, and Phan Doan Nam 1991a, p. 30.
69   Tran Trong Thin 1991, p. 57.
70   Nguyen Trong Thu 1991, p. 60.
71   Phan Doan Nam 1991a, p. 31.
72   Nguyen Co Thach 1989, p. 3.
73   Phan Doan Nam 1991a, p. 31.
74   Nguyen Van Linh 1989, p. 6.
75   Ibid., p. 11.
76   The connection between the anti-pluralist campaign and new foreign-
      policy thinking was emphasized when Tran Xuan Bach, the director of the
      Communist Party's Foreign Affairs Department and known for his radical
      reformist views, had to resign from the Political Bureau in March 1990. See
      Thayer 1992a; also Porter 1993, p. 100, and Kolko 1995, p. 17.
77   Nguyen Van Linh 1989, p. 9.
78   On the Kampuchean peace process, see, for example, Palmujoki 1990, Than
      1991, Yeong 1992 and Leifer 1993.
79   Palmujoki 1990.
80   The new name for Kampuchea, "the State of Cambodia," was announced on
      April 30, 1989.
81   See Duong Quoc Thanh 1991, Nguyen Vu Tung 1993 and Hoang Anh Tuan
      1993, Frost 1993, Leifer 1993, and, particularly, the Vietnamese addresses
      in Interaction for Progress 1991.
82   CPV: 7th National Congress, p. 45. On the debate on the transitional period,
      see Nhan Dan, Dec. 10, 1990, JPRS-SEA-91-003, pp. 30–32, and Saigon
      Giai phong, May 8, 1991, JPRS-SEA-91-017, pp. 15–16.
83   CPV: 6th National Congress, p. 31, see pp. 43–44.

84 CPV: 7th National Congress, pp. 48–49.
85 A report presented by Nguyen Van Linh at the Congress on June 21, 1991, in CPV: 7th National Congress, pp. 9–17.
86 Ibid., p. 23.
87 Do Minh 1991, p. 56.
88 Ibid.
89 Nguyen Van Duc 1992, p. 57.
90 Ibid.
91 Ibid., pp. 59–60.
92 Ibid., p. 61.
93 See the discussion in *Tap Chi Cong San*, Doan Cuong 1992, Song Tung 1992, Le Xuan Luu 1992, Tran Ba Khoa 1993 and Bui Phan Ky 1993.
94 Following the formalist delineation (Le Tinh 1992, p. 59), the "new political thinking" is a new manifestation of the convergence theory which rejects class struggle and makes compromises with imperialism.
95 Le Thinh 1993 and Nguyen Manh Cam 1993; see also Thayer 1992b, p. 402.
96 Le Xuan Luu 1992, p. 3.
97 Hong Ha 1992, p. 10.
98 Ibid.
99 Ibid.
100 See Le Duan 1970b.
101 Hong Ha 1992, p. 11.
102 Ibid., pp. 10–11.
103 Ibid.
104 Ibid., pp. 12–13.
105 A report presented by Nguyen Van Linh at the Congress on June 21, 1991, in CPV: 7th National Congress, p. 43.
106 CPV: 7th National Congress, p. 133.
107 Ibid., pp. 90–91.
108 Phan Doan Nam 1991a, p. 30, in particular.
109 Thong bao 1992, pp. 3–4.
110 Dinh Nho Liem 1992, pp. 60–61, Nguyen Manh Cam 1993, pp. 12–13, 15 and Vu Khoan 1993.
111 Le Tinh 1993, p. 60.
112 See, Dinh Nho Liem 1992, Nguyen Manh Cam 1993 and Vu Khoan 1993.
113 Another question is the Vietnamese discussion on foreign policy in other than Party circles. The Vietnamese articles appearing in international publications follow their standards of argumentation and no particular trait reflecting Vietnamese political culture can be observed. See Duong Quoc Thanh 1991, Nguyen Vu Tung 1993 and Hoang Anh Tuan 1993.

7 CONCLUSION:
THE DISINTEGRATION OF THE
MARXIST-LENINIST DOCTRINE

1 See, Nguyen Ngoc Truong, "Vietnam's New Home," FEER, July 29, 1995.
2 Brodin 1977, follows this idea of Leites; see her methodological discussion, pp. 294–295.

Bibliography

VIETNAMESE DATA

Binh luan (1976) "Tuong lai cua cac nuoc Dong-Nam A phai doc lap, hoa binh va trung lap that su," *Hoc Tap*, 5, 74–78.

Bui Dinh Thanh (1977) "Su ket hop nhuan nhuyen chu nghia yeu nuoc va chu nghia quoc te vo san trong Cach mang Viet Nam," Uy ban Khoa hoc Xa hoi Viet Nam, Vien su hoc: *Cach mang thang Muoi va Cach Mang Viet Nam*. Ha Noi: Nha xuat ban khoa hoc xa hoi, 283–327.

Bui Phan Ky (1993) "May suy nghi ve chien luoc quoc phong trong boi canh quoc te moi," *TCCS*, 5, 58–62.

Chu Huy Man (1980) "Duong loi cach mang xa hoi chu nghia va su nghiep bao ve to quoc xa hoi chu nghia," *TCCS*, 6, 23–34, 67.

Chu nghia duy vat bien chung (1985) *Triet Hoc Mac - Le-nin, chu nghia duy vat bien chung. Chuong trinh cao cap.* Truong dang cao cap Nguyen Ai Quoc, Khoa triet hoc. Ha Noi: Nha xuat ban sach giao khoa Mac - Le-nin.

CPV: 4th National Congress. Communist Party of Vietnam. *Fourth National Congress, December 14–20, 1976, Documents*. Hanoi: FLPH 1977.

CPV: 5th National Congress. Communist Party of Vietnam. *5th National Congress, March 27–31 1982, Political Report*. Hanoi: FLPH 1982.

CPV: 6th National Congress. Communist Party of Vietnam. *6th National Congress, December 15–18, 1986, Documents*. Hanoi: FLPH 1987.

CPV: 7th National Congress. *Communist Party of Vietnam. 7th National Congress, Documents*. Hanoi: FLPH 1991.

Cuc dien the gioi. "Cuc dien the gioi hien nay," *TCCS*, 1. 1982, 63–70.

Dang Xuan Ky (1978) "Ve nhung phuong thuc va bien phap xay dung con nguoi moi," *TCCS*, 8, 57–65.

Dinh Nho Liem (1992) "Viet Nam trong xu the chung cua Chau A – Thai Binh Duong," *TCCS*, 3, 60–61.

Do Minh (1991) "Co nen lay chu nghia Mac-Le-nin lam nen tang tu tuong hay khong?" *TCCS*, 5, 56–57.

Do Tu (1980) "Ve moi quan he giua giai cap, dan toc va quoc te," *TCCS*, 7, 49–54.

Doan Chuong (1992) "Bai hoc thoi dai," *TCCS*, 2, 5–9.

Hiep uoc giua Viet Nam va Lao. "Hiep uoc huu nghi va hop tac giua nuoc Cong hoa xa hoi chu nghia Viet-nam va nuoc Cong hoa dan chu nhan dan Lao," *Tinh nghia Viet–Lao mai mai vung ben hon nui hon song*. Ha Noi: Nha xuat ban Su that 1978, 95–101.

Hiep uoc giua Viet Nam va Lien-xo. "Hiep uoc huu nghi va hop tac giua nuoc Cong hoa xa hoi chu nghia Viet-nam va Lien bang cong hoa xa hoi chu nghia Xo-viet," *Tap Chi Quan Doi Nhan Dan*, 11. 1978, 1–4.

History of the August Revolution. Hanoi: FLPH 1979.

History of the Communist Party of Vietnam. Compiled by the Institute of the History of the Communist Party of Vietnam under the Institute of Marxism-Leninism. Hanoi: FLPH 1986.

Ho Chi Minh (OR) *On Revolution. Selected Writings, 1920–66*. Ed. by Bernanrd B. Fall. London: Frederick A. Praeger 1967.

Ho Van Thong (1984) "May van de chung trong nhan thuc tu tuong ve thoi ky qua do hien nay o nuoc ta," Truong Dang Cao Cap Nguyen Ai Quoc, Khoa triet hoc: *Quan triet nghi quyet dai hoi lan thu V cua Dang. Vao giang day va nghien cuu triet hoc*, Ha Noi: Nha xuat ban sach giao khoa Mac - Le-nin, 101–122.

Hoang Chi (1986) "Tinh hinh the gioi va chinh sach doi ngoai cua Dang va nuoc ta," *TCCS*, 8, 44–51.

Hoang Hien (1987) "Cung ton tai hoa binh giua hai nhom nuoc ASEAN va Dong Duong," *TCCS*, 3, 94–98, 106.

Hoang Nguyen (1987) "Doi moi tu duy trong cong tac doi ngoai," *TCTH*, 2 (57), 6, 66–78.

Hoang Tung (1983) *May van de ve cong tac chinh tri va tu tuong trong chang duong hien nay cua cach mang xa hoi chu nghia*. Ha Noi: Nha xuat ban Su that.

Hoang Tung (1986) "Mot van kien ly luan sang tao va mang y nghia thoi dai," *TCCS*, 3, 13–21, 30.

Hoang Van Thai (1982) "Ve quan he hop tac dac biet giua ba dan toc Dong-Duong," *TCCS*, 1, 11–17, 24.

Hoang Van Thai (1983) *Lien minh doan ket chien dau Viet nam–Lao–Cam-pu-chia*. Ha Noi: Nha xuat ban Su that.

Hong Ha (1992) "Tinh hinh the gioi va chinh sach doi ngoai cua ta," *TCCS*, 12, 10–13.

Hong Chuong (1981) "Quan he bien chung giua nhan to dan toc va nhan to quoc te," *TCCS*, 7, 47–53.

Hong Tien (1979) "Chu nghia banh truong dai dan toc va ba quyen nuoc lon Trung Quoc, mot quai thai cua thoi dai," Pham Nhu Cuong (chu bien), *Phe phan chu nghia banh truong va ba quyen nuoc lon cua gioi cam quyen phan dong Bac Kinh*. Uy ban Khoa hoc xa hoi Viet Nam. Ha Noi: Nha xuat ban Khoa hoc xa hoi, 62–85.

Huong Nam (1976) "Chinh sach doi ngoai cua nuoc Cong hoa xa hoi chu nghia Viet-nam," *Hoc Tap*, 9, 59–66.

Huu Nghi (1975) "Cuoc khang chien chong My, cuu nuoc cua nhan dan Cam-pu-chia da gianh duoc thang loi hoan toan," *Hoc Tap*, 5, 48–57.

La Con (1976) "Phong trao giai phong dan toc va su that bai cua chu nghia thuc dan cu va moi," *Hoc Tap*, 8, 69–79.

Le Duan (OSPIP) *On Some Present International Problems*. Hanoi: FLPH 1964.

Le Duan (OSRV) *On Socialist Revolution in Vietnam I–III*. Hanoi: FLPH, 1965–1967.

Le Duan (1970a) "Duoi la co ve vang cua Dang. Vi doc lap, tu do vi chu nghia xa hoi tien len gianh nhung thang loi moi," *Hoc Tap*, 2, 27–111.

Le Duan (1970b) "Chu nghia Le-nin soi sang muc tieu cach mang cua thoi dai," *Hoc Tap*, 6, 1–16.

Le Duan (1975) "Dang Lao dong Viet-nam, nguoi lanh dao va to chuc moi thang loi cua cach mang Viet-nam," *Hoc Tap*, 2, 12–27.

Le Duan (1976) *This Nation and Socialism are one. Selected Writings of Le Duan*. Ed. by Tran Van Dinh. Chicago: Vanguard Books.

Le Duan (SW) *Selected Writings*. Hanoi: FLPH 1977.

Le Thi (1979) "Chu nghia dan toc phan dong cua bon banh truong Bac Kinh la su doi lap hoan toan voi chu nghia quoc te vo san." Pham Nhu Cuong (chu bien), *Phe phan chu nghia banh truong va ba quyen nuoc lon cua gioi cam quyen phan dong Bac Kinh*. Uy ban Khoa hoc xa hoi Viet Nam. Ha Noi: Nha xuat ban Khoa hoc xa hoi, 32–61.

Le Thi (1987) "Tu duy moi ve cuoc dau tranh tu tuong, dau tranh bao ve hoa binh, chong chien tranh hat nhan hien nay." *TCTH*, 4 (59), 12, 21–31.

Le Thuc (1978) "Mot chinh sach ngoai giao dung dan va kien dinh," *TCCS*, 11, 101–106.

Le Tinh (1992) "'Tu duy chinh tri moi' la gi?" *TCCS*, 4, 57–59.

Le Tinh (1993) "The gioi nam 1992 co gi moi?" *TCCS*, 1, 57–60.

Le Xuan Luu (1992) "Ban chat cach mang va khoa hoc cua chu nghia Mac - Le-nin," *TCCS*, 3, 3–7.

Lich Su Dang Cong San I. *Lich su Dang cong san Viet Nam, tap I, 1920–1954. Chuong trinh cao cap*. Hoc vien Nguyen Ai Quoc, Khoa lich su Dang. Ha Noi: Nha xuat ban tuyen huan 1988.

Lich Su Dang Cong San IV. *Lich su Dang cong san Viet Nam, tap IV, nhung bai hoc kinh nghiem. Chuong trinh cao cap*. Hoc vien Nguyen Ai Quoc, Khoa lich su Dang. Ha Noi: Nha xuat ban tuyen huan 1988.

Lien-xo–tru cot (1982) "Lien-xo–tru cot cua hoa binh va cho dua dang tin cay cua cach mang the gioi," *TCCS*, 3, 56–60.

Luu Van Loi (1986) "Suy nghi ve chinh sach bien trong chien luoc kinh te va quoc phong cua nuoc ta," *TCCS*, 4, 56–61, 55.

Mot giai doan phat trien. "Mot giai doan phat trien quan trong cua quan he huu nghi, hop tac Viet –Xo," (Xa luan bao Nhan Dan, 4.11.1978), *Tap Chi Quan Doi Nhan Dan*, 11, 5–7.

Mot tac pham soi sang (1970) "Mot tac pham soi sang con duong cach mang cua nhan dan ta," *Hoc Tap*, 3, 16–27.

Nguyen Co Thach (1989) "Tat ca vi hoa binh, doc lap dan toc va phat trien," *TCCS*, 8, 1–8.

Nguyen Duy Trinh (1974) "Kien quyet dau tranh de giu vung hoa binh, thi hanh nghiem chinh Hiep dinh Pa-ri ve Viet-nam," *Hoc Tap*, 1, 4–16.

Nguyen Duy Trinh (1975) "30 nam dau tranh ngoai giao vi doc lap, tu do cua to quoc va xay dung chu nghia xa hoi," *Hoc Tap*, 10, 5–19, 28.

Nguyen Duy Trinh (1977) "Problems of Foreign Relations," *VNC*, No. 57, February, 4–7.

Nguyen Duy Trinh (1979) *Mat tran ngoai giao thoi ky chong My cuu nuoc (1965–1975)*. Ha Noi: Nha xuat ban Su that.

Nguyen Giao Hien (1976) "Dong-Nam A 'Sau Viet-Nam'," *Hoc Tap*, 2, 61–69, 78.

Nguyen Hong Phong (1977) "Cach mang thang Muoi va su nghiep xay dung con nguoi moi xa hoi chu nghia," Uy ban Khoa hoc xa hoi Viet Nam, Vien su hoc: *Cach mang thang Muoi va Cach mang Viet Nam*. Ha Noi: Nha xuat ban khoa hoc xa hoi, 211–281.

Nguyen Huy Hong (1983) "Ve quan he giua ASEAN va Dong Duong (1975–1983)," Pham Nguyen Long va Dang Bich Ha (chu bien), *Ve lich su–van hoa ba nuoc Dong Duong*. Ha Noi: Vien Dong Nam A xuat ban, 257–288.

Nguyen Manh Cam (1993) "Tren duong trien khai chinh sach doi ngoai theo dinh huong moi," *TCCS*, 4, 11–15.

Nguyen Ngoc Minh (1979) "Bon banh truong va ba quyen nuoc lon Trung Quoc pham toi ac xam luoc, toi ac chong hoa binh va an ninh quoc te," Pham Nhu

Cuong (chu bien), *Phe phan chu nghia banh truong va ba quyen nuoc lon cua gioi cam quyen phan dong Bac Kinh*. Uy ban Khoa hoc xa hoi Viet Nam. Ha Noi: Nha xuat ban Khoa hoc xa hoi, 124–146.

Nguyen Nhu Lien (1975) "Buoc phat trien moi cua phong trao cac nuoc khong lien ket," *Hoc Tap*, 9, 86–89.

Nguyen Thanh Le (1986) "Nhung tong ket sau sac ve tinh hinh quoc te," *TCCS*, 6, 90–96.

Nguyen Tho Chan (1986) "May van de cap bach trong phong trao thi dua yeu nuoc xa hoi chu nghia," *TCCS*, 6, 29–34.

Nguyen Trong Thu (1991) "Ve trat tu quoc te moi," *TCCS*, 5, 60–62.

Nguyen Van Duc (1992) "Mot trat tu the gioi moi hay la mot hinh thai dau tranh moi?" *Tap Chi Quoc Phong Toan Dan*, 1, 57–61.

Nguyen Van Linh (1989) "Phat bieu cua dong chi tong bi thu Nguyen Van Linh. Be mac hoi nghi 7 cua BCHTUD," *TCCS*, 9, 5–12.

Pham Binh (1984) "Thuc chat tinh hinh hien nay o Dong Nam chau A," *TCCS*, 6, 82–88.

Pham Huy Chau (1979) "Ban chat khong thay doi cua gioi lanh dao Trung Quoc la chu nghia dan toc phan dong," Pham Nhu Cuong (chu bien), *Phe phan chu nghia banh truong va ba quyen nuoc lon cua gioi cam quyen phan dong Bac Kinh*. Uy ban Khoa hoc xa hoi Viet Nam. Ha Noi: Nha xuat ban Khoa hoc xa hoi, 86–123.

Pham Nhu Cuong (1979a) "Nhan Dan Viet Nam mai mai giuong cao ngon co vi dai cua chu nghia Le-nin bach chien bach thang," *TCTH*, 2 (25), 6, 3–12.

Pham Nhu Cuong (1979b) "Bon phan dong Trung Quoc xam luoc va chu nghia banh truong dai dan toc, ba quyen nuoc lon cua chung nhat dinh se tha bai tham hai," Pham Nhu Cuong (chu bien), *Phe phan chu nghia banh truong va ba quyen nuoc lon cua gioi cam quyen phan dong Bac Kinh*. Uy ban Khoa hoc xa hoi Viet Nam. Ha Noi: Nha xuat ban Khoa hoc xa hoi, 7–31.

Pham Nhu Cuong (1984) "Phan dau nang cao chat luong cua cong tac giang day nghien cuu ly luan Mac - Le-nin theo tinh than cua nghi quyet dai hoi Dang lan thu V," Truong Dang Cao Cap Nguyen Ai Quoc, Khoa triet hoc: *Quan triet nghi quyet dai hoi lan thu V cua Dang. Vao giang day va nghien cuu triet hoc*. Ha Noi: Nha xuat ban sach giao khoa Mac - Le-nin, 44–60.

Pham Van Dong (1958) "The Foreign Policy of the Democratic Republic of Vietnam," *International Affairs* (Moscow), July, 19–22.

Pham Van Dong (1978) "Build and Defend Our Socialist Fatherland," *VNC*, No. 77, October, 4–9.

Pham Van Dong (1983) "For Peace, National Independence and a New International Economic Order. A speech delivered at the plenary meeting of the Seventh Summit Conference of Non-Aligned Countries in New Delhi on March 8, 1983," *VNC*, No. 4, 7–11.

Pham Xuan Nam (1977) "Cach mang thang Muoi va su hinh thanh, phat trien the tien cong cua cach mang Viet Nam trong thoi dai moi," Uy ban Khoa hoc xa hoi Viet Nam, Vien su hoc: *Cach mang thang Muoi va Cach mang Viet Nam*. Ha Noi: Nha xuat ban khoa hoc xa hoi, 151–210.

Phan Doan (1986) "Nhin lai tinh hinh the gioi nam 1985," *TCCS*, 1, 103–106, 93.

Phan Doan Nam (1988) "Mot vai suy nghi ve doi moi tu duy doi ngoai," *TCCS*, 2, 50–54, 79.

Phan Doan Nam (1991a) "Van de phoi hop giua an ninh, quoc phong va ngoai giao trong giai doan cach mang moi," *TCCS*, 3, 29–31.

Phan Doan Nam (1991b) "Phuong phap nhan biet dac diem cua cuc dien the gioi hien nay," *TCCS*, 9, 55–59.

Phuc Cuong (1980) "Ba muoi lam nam dau tranh cua nhan dan ta tren mat tran quoc te," *TCCS*, 6, 35–48, 57.

Phuc Cuong (1981) "Con duong dan den hoa binh, doc lap, huu nghi va hop tac cua cac dan toc Dong Nam A," *TCCS*, 6, 20–34.

Quoc Tuy (1989) "Doi moi tu duy doi ngoai va nhung nguyen tac co ban cua Le-nin ve chinh sach doi ngoai," *TCCS*, 12, 12–16.

Quyet Thang (1978) "Mot lien minh 'ma quy'," *Tap Chi Quan Doi Nhan Dan*, 8, 18–27.

Song Tung (1992) "Vi sao chu nghia xa hoi hien thuc o Dong Au va Lien xo sup do?" *TCCS*, 2, 10–13, 17.

Ta Ngoc Lien (1979) "Chu nghia banh truong dai dan toc cua de quoc Trung Hoa phong kien va chu nghia banh truong dai dan toc cua bon cam quyen phan dong Bac Kinh ngay nay," Pham Nhu Cuong (chu bien), *Phe phan chu nghia banh truong va ba quyen nuoc lon cua gioi cam quyen phan dong Bac Kinh*. Uy ban Khoa hoc xa hoi Viet Nam. Ha Noi: Nha xuat ban Khoa hoc xa hoi, 160–180.

"Thang loi vi dai cua cach mang Lao," *Hoc Tap*, 12, 7–13.

Thanh Tin (1974) "'Thoi ky sau Viet-nam', thoi ky khung hoang tram trong nhat cua chien luoc My," *Hoc Tap*, 7, 71–79.

Third National Congress. *Third National Congress of the Viet Nam Workers' Party, Volume I and III*. Hanoi: FLPH 1960.

Thong bao (1992) "Thong bao. Hoi nghi lan thu ba ban chap hanh trung uong dang (khoa VII)," *TCCS*, 7, 3–5.

"Tinh hinh the gioi dau thap ky 80," *TCCS*, 2, 1981, 65–70.

Tinh nghia Viet-Lao mai mai vung ben hon nui hon song. Ha Noi: Nha xuat ban Su that 1978.

To nghien cuu lich su chien tranh (1972a) To nghien cuu lich su chien tranh, Hoc vien quan su: "Tai thao luoc kiet xuat cua ong cha ta," *Hoc Tap*, 11, 20–34.

To nghien cuu lich su chien tranh (1972b) To nghien cuu lich su chien tranh, Hoc vien quan su: "Tai thao luoc kiet xuat cua ong cha ta," *Hoc Tap*, 12, 41–53.

Tran Ba Khoa (1993) "Canh giac voi am muu dien bien hoa binh cua cac the luc thu dich," *TCCS*, 1, 18–20.

Tran Con (1983) "Nhan thuc ve van de dau tranh giai cap, dau tranh giua hai con duong o nuoc ta hien nay," *TCTH*, 1 (40), 3, 43–65.

Tran Con (1984) "Suy nghi ve cuoc dau tranh giai cap, dau tranh giua hai con duong hien nay," Truong Dang Cao Cap Nguyen Ai Quoc, Khoa triet hoc: *Quan triet nghi quyet dai hoi lan thu V cua Dang. Vao giang day va nghien cuu triet hoc*. Ha Noi: Nha xuat ban sach giao khoa Mac - Le-nin, 123–134.

Tran Quynh (1983) "Chu nghia quoc te xa hoi chu nghia trong hanh dong," *TCCS*, 11, 27–32.

Tran Trong Thin (1991) "Can can quan su dang thay doi chien luoc gi cho ngay mai?" *TCCS*, 4, 58–59, 56.

Triet Hoc Mac - Le-nin (1978) *Triet Hoc Mac-Le-nin. Trich tac pham kinh dien. Chuong trinh trung cap*. Vu bien soan, Ban tuyen huan Trung Uong. Ha Noi: Nha xuat ban sach giao khoa Mac-Le-nin.

Truc Xuyen (1979) "Bac-kinh cau ket voi chu nghia de quoc va cac loai phan dong chong ba trao luu cach mang the gioi," *TCCS*, 3, 44–52.

Truong Chinh (1972) "Ve cong tac mat tran hien nay," *Hoc Tap*, 3, 8–30.

Truong Chinh (SW) *Selected Writings*. Hanoi: FLPH 1977.

Truong Khue Bich (1979) "Bon banh truong ba quyen nuoc lon Bac kinh di theo vet xe do cua bon banh truong phong kien nha Tong," *TCTH*, 4 (27), 12, 65–80.

Tu dien triet hoc. M Rodentan va P Iudin (chu bien). Ha Noi: Nha xuat ban Su that 1976.

"Tuyen bo chung Viet-nam - Lao," *Tinh nghia Viet–Lao mai mai vung ben hon nui hon song*. Ha Noi: Nha xuat ban Su that 1978, 77–93.

Van Hien (1978) "Ve xu the doc lap, hoa binh, trung lap o khu vuc Dong Nam A," *TCCS*, 7, 98–105.

Van Tao (1980) "Nhung net khac nhau giua cach mang Viet Nam va cach mang Trung Quoc," *NCLS*, 1, 1–8.

Van Tao (1988) "Van de hoa binh trong su chuyen hoa cua cac mau thuan co ban cua thoi dai," *TCCS*, 1, 69–74..

Van Tien Dung (1977) *Our Great Spring Victory*. New York and London: Monthly Review Press.

Van Trong (1979) "Vai manh gom Trung-hoa co khong thay doi duoc chu quyen cua Viet-nam o quan dao Hoang-sa," *TCCS*, 6, 50–59.

Vietnam Social Sciences 1/1984.

Vo Nguyen Giap (1961) *People's War, People's Army*. Hanoi: FLPH.

Vo Nguyen Giap (1971) *National Liberation War in Viet Nam*. Hanoi: FLPH.

Vo Nguyen Giap (1974) "Suc manh vo dich cua chien tranh nhan dan Viet-Nam trong thoi dai moi," *Hoc Tap*, 12, 11–43.

Vo Nguyen Giap (1975) *Unforgettable Days*. Hanoi: FLPH.

Vo Nguyen Giap (1979) *Ca nuoc mot long, bao ve vung chac to quoc Viet Nam xa hoi chu nghia*. Ha Noi: Nha xuat ban Su that.

Vu Hien (1983) "Mot buoc tien moi cua phong trao khong lien ket," *TCCS*, 5, 67–70.

Vu Khoan (1993) "Chau A – Thai Binh Duong – mot huong lon trong chinh sach doi ngoai cua nha nuoc ta," *TCCS*, 7, 57–58.

Vu Tien (1982) "Tinh hinh the gioi va chinh sach doi ngoai cua dang va nha nuoc ta," *TCCS*, 5, 85–93.

Yen Van (1976) "Quyen tu quyet cua nhan dan Dong Ti-mo phai duoc ton trong," *Hoc Tap*, 1, 75–78.

DOCUMENTS SERIES AND RADIO MONITORING SERVICES

ADS. *ASEAN Documents Series 1967–1986. Compiled by the ASEAN Secretariat. Second (revised) Edition*, Jakarta 1986.

The Belgrade Conference. *The Conference of Heads of State or Government of Non-Aligned Countries, Belgrade, September 1–6, 1961*. Publicisticko-Izdavacki Zavod "Jugoslavija", Beograd 1961.

CDNAC. *The Third World without Superpowers. The Collected Documents of the Non-Aligned Countries I – VI*. Edited by Odette Jankowitch and Karl P. Sauvant. New York, Dobbs Ferry: Oceana Publications, Inc 1978.

The Colombo Conference. *5th Conference of Heads of State or Government of Non-Aligned Countries. Colombo 16–19 August 1976.* Sri Lanka 1977.

DKP. *Documents on the Kampuchean Problem 1979–1985.* Department of Political Affairs, Ministry of Foreign Affairs, Bangkok, Thailand. Thai Watana Panich Press Co., Ltd.

DLN. *Departemen Luar Negeri. Departemen Luar Negeri R.I. Jakarta.* Ministry of Foreign Affairs, Indonesia.

FAB. *Foreign Affairs Bulletin.* Information Department, Ministry of Foreign Affairs. Bangkok, Thailand.

FAM. *Foreign Affairs Malaysia.* Ministry of Foreign Affairs, Malaysia.

FBIS-APA. *Foreign Broadcasts Information Service, Asia-Pacific.*

Havana Addresses. *Addresses Delivered at the Sixth Conference of Heads of State or Government of Non-Aligned Countries. Havana 3–9 September 1979.* La Habanna: Editoral de ciencias sociales 1980.

Interaction for progress (1991). *Report of an International Symposium on Interaction for Progress – Vietnam's new course and ASEAN experiences.* Organised by National Center For Social Sciences, Vietnam and Central Institute For Economic Management Information and Resource Center, Singapore. Vietnam Commentary 3, Nov–Dec.

JPRS-SEA. *Joint Press Research Service, Southeast Asia.*

The Non-Aligned in Havanna. *The Non-Aligned in Havanna. Documents of the Sixth Summit Conference and an Analysis of their Significance for the Global Political System.* Edited by Peter Willets. London: Frances Pinter (Publishers) 1981.

RIA. *Review of International Affairs* (Belgrade).

Singapore Bulletin. Publicity Division, Ministry of Culture, Singapore.

Speeches. A Selection of Ministerial Speeches. Publ. by the Information Division, Ministry of Culture, Singapore.

SWB FE. *British Broadcasting Corporation. Summary of World Broadcasts, The Far East.*

The United Nations' Documents
A/ United Nations, *Official Records of the General Assembly* (UNGA).
A/no/PV UNGA, *Plenary Meetings.*
A/C.4/no/SR UNGA, *Fourth Committee.*
A/S-10 Official Records of the General Assembly. *Tenth Special Session, Plenary Meetings. Verbatim Records of the Meeting. (Tenth Special Session for Disarmament 23 May – 30 June 1978).*

NEWSPAPERS AND WEEKLIES

Asiaweek.
FEER. *Far Eastern Economic Review.*
New Nation (Singapore).
New Straits Times (Kuala Lumpur)
NT. *New Times* (Moscow).
The Straits Times (Singapore).

OTHER LITERATURE

Allison, Roy (1988) *The Soviet Union and the Strategy of Non-Alignment in the Third World.* Cambridge: Cambridge University Press.
Amer, Ramses (1989) *The General Assembly and the Kampuchean Issues. Intervention, Regime Recognition and the World Community 1979 to 1987.* Department of Peace and Conflict Research. Uppsala: Uppsala University.
Amer, Ramses (1990) "The United Nations and Kampuchea: The Issue of Representation and Its Implications." *Bulletin of Concerned Asian Scholars*, Vol. 22, No. 3, July–Sept.
Amer, Ramses (1991) *The Ethnic Chinese in Vietnam and Sino-Vietnamese Relations.* Kuala Lumpur: Forum.
Amer, Ramses (1992) *The United Nations and Foreign Military Interventions. A Comparative Study of the Application of the Charter. Second edition.* Department of Peace and Conflict Research.Upsala: Upsala University.
Arendt, Hannah (1953) "Ideology and Terror: A Novel Form of Government," *Review of Politics*, July.
Arendt, Hannah (1967) *The Originis of Totalitarianism.* George Allen and Unwin Ltd.
Barilli, Renato (1989) *Rhetoric.* Theory and History of Literature, Volume 63. Minneapolis: University of Minnesota Press.
Bekaert, Jacques (1983) "Kampuchea. The Year of the Nationalists?" In Pushpa Thambipillai (ed.), *Southeast Asian Affairs 1983.* Aldershot, Hampshire: Gower Publishing Company Limited.
Bernstein, Basil (1971) *Class, Codes and Control. Vol. 1.* Theoretical Studies towards a Sociology of Language. London: Routledge & Kegan Paul.
Berry, Peter (1972) *Sovjetunionens Officielle Utrikespolitiska Doktrin*, Stockholm: Utrikespolitiska institutet, forskningsrapport.
Bondarevsky, G. and Sofinsky V. (1976) "The Non-aligned Movement and International Relations," *International Affairs* (Moscow) 7.
Brodin, Katarina (1977) *Studiet av Utrikespolitiska Doktriner. Teori och två empiriska tillämpningar.* Stockholm: Departementens offsetcentral.
Broms, H. and Gahmberg, H. (1983) "Communication to Self in Organizations and Cultures," *Administrative Science Quarterly*, 28, September.
Broms, Henri (1988) "Autocommunication – a way to induce visions to the organization," in H. Broms and R. Kaufman (eds.), *Semiotics of Culture.* Helsinki: Arator Inc, Publishers.
Brown, M. and Zasloff J.J. (1986) *Apprentice Revolutionaries. The Communist Movement in Laos, 1930–1985.* Stanford, California: Hoover Institution Press.
Brown, MacAlister (1988) "The Indochinese Federation Idea: Learning from History," in Joseph J. Zasloff (ed.), *Postwar Indochina, Old Enemies and New Allies.* Department of State Publication 9657, Foreign Service Institute, Center for the Study of Foreign Affairs.
Bui Tin (1995) *Following Ho Chi Minh. Memoirs of a North Vietnamese Colonel.* London: Hurst & Company.
Buszynski, Leszel (1984) "Vietnam's ASEAN Diplomacy, Incentives for Change," *The World Today*, January.
Butler, Wiliam E. (1989) "International Law, Foreign Policy and the Gorbachev Style," *Journal of International Affairs*, Vol. 42, No. 2, Spring 1989.

Carney, Timothy (1989) "The Unexpected Victory," in Karl D. Jackson (ed.), *Cambodia 1975–1978: Rendezvous with Death*. Princeton, New Jersey: Princeton University Press.

Chan, Stephen (1994) "Revolution, culture and the foreign policy of China," in Stephen Chan and Andrew J. Williams (ed.), *Renagade States. The evolution of revolutionary foreign policy*. Manchester and New York: Manchester University Press.

Chanda, Nayan (1986) *Brother Enemy. The War after the War. A History of Indochina since the Fall of Saigon*. Orlando, Florida: Harcourt Brace Jovanovich, Publishers.

Chandler, David P. (1976) "The Constitution of Democratic Kampuchea (Cambodia): The Semantics of Revolutionary Change," *Pasific Affairs*, Vol. 49, No. 3, Fall.

Chang, C.Y. (1983) "The Sino-Vietnam Rift: Political Impact on China's Relations with Southeast Asia," *Contemporary Southeast Asia*, Vol. 4, March.

Chen, King C. (ed.) (1979) *China and the Three Worlds. A Foreign Policy Reader*. Ann Arbor, Michigan: Macmillan.

Chen, King C. (1987) *China's War with Vietnam. Issues, Decisions, and Implications*. Stanford, California: Hoover Institution Press.

Chouldry, Golam W. (1982) *China in World Affairs. The Foreign Policy of the PRC Since 1970*. Boulder, Colorado: Westview Press.

Daniels, Robert V. (1980) "Doctrine and Foreign Policy," in Erik P. Hoffman & Frederic J. Fleron Jr. (ed.) *The Conduct of Soviet Foreign Policy*. New York: Aldine Publishing Company.

Donnell J.C. and Gurtov M. (1968) *North Vietnam: Left of Moscow, Right of Peking*. The Rand Corporation.

Duiker, William J. (1986) *China and Vietnam: The Roots of Conflict*. Berkeley: Institute of East Asian Studies, University of California.

Duiker, William J. (1988) "China and Vietnam and the Struggle for Indochina," in Zasloff, Joseph J. (ed.), *Postwar Indochina. Old Enemies and New Allies*. Department of State Publication 9657, Foreign Service Institute, Center for the Study of Foreign Affairs.

Duncan W.R. and Mcgiffert Ekedahl C. (1990) *Moscow and Third World under Gorbachev*. Boulder, San Francisco: Westview Press .

Duncanson, Dennis (1978) "'Limited sovereignty' in Indochina," *The World Today*, July.

Duong Quoc Thanh (1991) "Back to the World. Recent Changes in Vietnamese Domestic and Foreign Policy," *Bulletin of Peace Proposals*, Vol. 22 (1).

Eckstein, Harry (1988) "A Culturalist Theory of Political Change," *American Political Science Review*, Vol. 82, No. 3, September.

Eco, Umberto (1976) *A Theory of Semiotics*. Thetford, Norfolk: Macmilllan.

Editorial Department of "Renmin Ribao" (1977) "Chairman Mao's Theory of the Differentation of the Three Worlds is a Major Contribution to Marxism-Leninism," *Peking Review*, No. 45, November 4.

Edmondson, Ricca (1984) *Rhetoric in Sociology*. London and Basingstoke: Macmillan.

Evans, G. and Rowley, K. (1984) *Red Brotherhood at War. Indochina since the Fall of Saigon*. London: Verso.

Evans, Paul M. (1989) "Vietnam in the Changing System of Economic &

Security Relations in Eastern Asia," in R. Stubbs (ed.), *Vietnam: Facing the 1990s*. Asia Papers No. 1. Toronto: Joint Centre for Asia Pacific Studies.

Fitzgerald, Frances (1972) *Fire in the Lake. The Vietnamese and the Americans in Vietnam*. Boston: Little, Brown and Co.

Frost, Frank (1993) *Vietnam's Foreign Relations: Dynamics of Change*. Pacific Strategic Papers. Singapore: Institute of Southeast Asian Studies.

George, Alexander L. (1980) "The 'Operational Code': A Neglected Approach to the Study of Political Leaders and Decision-Making," in Erik P. Hoffman and Frederic J. Fleron Jr. (ed.) *The Conduct of Soviet Foreign Policy*. New York: Aldine Publishing Company.

Halliday, M.A.K. (1978) *Language as social semiotic. The social interpretation of language and meaning*. London: Edward Arnold (Publishers) Ltd.

Halliday, M.A.K. (1984) "Language as code and language as behaviour: a systemic-functional interpretation of the nature and ontogenesis of dialogue," in Robin P. Fawcett et al. (ed.), *Semiotics of Culture and Language, Vol. 1. Language as Social Semiotic*. London: Frances Pinter (Publishers).

Hänggi, Heiner (1991) *ASEAN and the ZOPFAN Concept*. Pacific Strategic Papers, Singapore: Institute of Southeast Asian Studies.

Heder, Stephen (1979) "Kampuchea's Armed Struggle. The Origins of an Independent Revolution," *Bulletin of Concerned Asia Scholars*, Vol. 11, No. 1.

Heder, Stephen (1981) "The Kampuchean-Vietnamese Conflict," in Elliot, David W.P. (ed.), *The Third Indochina Conflict*. Boulder, Colorado: Westview Press.

Heradsveit, D and Narvesen, O (1978) "Psychological Constraints on Decision-making. A Discussion of Cognitive Approaches: Operational Code and Cognitive Map," *Cooperation and Conflict*, Vol. XIII.

Hoang Anh Tuan (1993) "Why Hasn't Vietnam Gained ASEAN Membership?" *Contemporary Southeast Asia*, Vol. 15, No. 3, December.

Hoffman, E.P. and Fleron F.J. (1980) "Communist Ideology, Belief Systems, and Soviet Foreign policy," in Erik P. Hoffman and Frederic J. Fleron Jr. (ed.) *The Conduct of Soviet Foreign Policy*. New York: Aldine Publishing Company.

Holsti, K.J. (1977) *International Politics. A Framework for Analysis*. Englewood Cliffs, New Jersey: Prentice-Hall, Inc.

Horelick, Arnold L. (1974) "The Soviet Union's Asian Collective Security Proposal: A Club in Search of Members," *Pacific Affairs*, Vol. 47, No. 3, Fall.

Huxley, Tim (1985) *ASEAN and Indochina. A Study of Political Responses 1975–1981*. Canberra: Department of International Relations, the Australian National University.

Huynh Kim Khanh (1982) *Vietnamese Communism 1925–1945*. Ithaca and London: Cornell University Press.

Huynh Kim Khanh (1988) "Vietnam's Reforms: 'Renewal or Death'," *Indochina Issues*, No. 84, September.

Huynh Kim Khanh (1989) "Revolution at an Impasse: Impressions of Vietnamese Communism Circa 1990," in R. Stubbs (ed.), *Vietnam: Facing the 1990s*. Asia Papers No. 1. Toronto: Joint Centre for Asia Pacific Studies.

IMCWP. *International Meeting of Communist and Worker's Parties, Moscow 1969*. Prague: Peace and Socialism Publishers.

Ionescu, Ghita (1972) *Comparative Communist Politics*. Studies in Comparative

Politics. London and Basingstoke: Macmillan.

Irvine, Roger (1982) "The Formative Years of ASEAN: 1967–1975," in Alison Broinowski (ed.) *Understanding ASEAN*. London 1982: Macmillan.

Jakobson, Roman (1986) "Closing Statement: Linguistics and Poetics," in Robert E. Innis (ed.) *Semiotics. An introductory anthology*. London: Hutchinson & Co. (Originally published in Style in Language, edited by Thomas A Seabeok, the MIT Press, 1960).

Kautsky, John H. (1973) "Comparative Communism Versus Comparative Politics," *Studies in Comparative Communism*, Vol. VI, Nos. 1 and 2, Spring/Summer.

Kolko, Gabriel (1995) "Vietnam Since 1975: Winning a War and Losing the Peace," *Journal of Contemporary Asia*, Vol. 25, No 1.

Konstantinov F. (1968) "Internationalism and the World Socialist System," *International Affairs* (Moscow) 7.

Kroef, Justus van der (1981) "ASEAN, Hanoi, and the Kampuchean Conflict: Between 'Kuantan' and 'Third Alternative'," *Asian Survey*, Vol. XXI, No. 5, May.

Kroef, Justus van der (1983) "The Kampuchean Problem: Diplomatic Deadlock and Initiative," *Contemporary Southeast Asia*, Vol. 5, No. 3, December.

Kubálková V. and Cruickshank A.A. (1985) "Marxism and International Relations," Oxford: Clarendon Press.

Larrabee, F. Stephen (1976) "The Soviet Union and the Non-Aligned," *The World Today*. December, Vol. 32, No. 12.

Lefort, Claude (1978) *Les formes de l'histoire. Essais d'anthropologie politique*. Gallimard.

Lefort, Claude (1979) *Éléments d'une critique de la bureaucratic*. Gallimard.

Lefort, Claude (1988) *Democracy and Political Theory*. Polity Press.

Leifer, Michael (1993) "Indochina and ASEAN: Seeking a New Balance," *Contemporary Southeast Asia,* Vol. 15, No. 3, December.

Leites, Nathan (1953) *A Study of Bolshevism*. Glencoe, Illinois: The Free Press, Publishers.

Light, Margot (1988) *The Soviet Theory of International Relations*. Brighton, Sussex: Wheatsheaf Books Ltd.

Longmire, R. A. (1989) *Soviet Relations with South-East Asia. An Historical Survey*. London: Keagan Paul International Limited.

Lotman, Yuri M. (1990) *Universe of the Mind. A Semiotic Theory of Culture*. London: I.B. Tauris & Co. LTD Publishers.

Marcuse, Herbert (1969) *Soviet Marxism – A Critical Analysis*. London: Routledge & Keagan Paul.

Marr, David G. (1971) *Vietnamese Anticolonialism 1885–1925*. Berkeley: University of California Press.

Marr, David G. (1981) *Vietnamese Tradition on Trial, 1920–1945*. Berkeley: University of California Press.

Minogue, Kenneth (1985) *Alien Powers. The Pure Theory of Ideology*. London: Weidenfield and Nicolson.

Minogue, Kenneth (1989) "Nietzsche and the Ideological Project," in Noel O'Sullivan (ed.), *The Structure of Modern Ideology*. Aldershot Hants: Edward Elgar.

Mitchell, R. Judson (1972) "The Brezhnev Doctrine and Communist Ideology,"

The Review of Politics, Vol. 34, No. 2, April.

Mitchell, R. Judson (1982) *Ideology of a Superpower. Contemporary Soviet Doctrine on International Relations*. Stanford, California: Hoover Institution Press.

Mouritzen, Hans (1981) "Prediction on the Basis of Official Doctrines," *Cooperation and Conflict*, Vol. XVI.

Nagornyi, Alexander (1990) "Perestroika in the USSR and Reforms in China: Contrasts and Assessments of Their International Impacts," in Mel Gurtow (ed.), *The Transformation of Socialism. Perestroika and Reform in the Soviet Union and China*. Boulder, Colorado: Westview Press.

Nair, K.K. (1986) *Words and Bayonets; ASEAN and Indochina*. Kuala Lumpur: Federal Publications.

Nguyen Vu Tung (1993) "Vietnam-ASEAN Cooperation in Southeast Asia," *Security Dialogue*, Vol. 24 (1).

Orestov, O. (1976) "Anti-Imperialist Course Confirmed," *International Affairs* (Moscow) 11.

Palmujoki, Eero (1990) "Diplomacy over the Kampuchean Question," in Ng Chee Yuen and Chandran Jeshurun (eds.), *Southeast Asian Affairs 1990*. Singapore: Institute of Southeast Asian Studies.

Pao-min Chang (1982) *Beijing, Hanoi, and the Overseas Chinese*. China Research Monograph 24. Berkeley: Center for Chinese Studies, Institute of East Asian Studies, University of California.

Pao-min Chang (1985) *Kampuchea between China and Vietnam*. Singapore: Singapore University Press.

Pao-min Chang (1986) *The Sino-Vietnamese Territorial Dispute*. New York: Praeger Publishers.

Paribatra, Sukhumbhand (1987) *From Enmity to Alignment. Thailand's Evolving Relations with China*. ISIS Paper No. 1. Bangkok: Institute of Security and International Studies, Chulalongkorn University.

Perelman, C. and Obrechts-Tyteca, L. (1971) *The New Rhetoric. A Treatise on Argumentation*. Notre Dame, Indiana: University of Notre Dame Press.

Perelman Chaim (1982) The Realm of Rhetoric. Notre Dame, Indiana: University of Notre Dame Press.

Petkovic, Ranko (1979) "The Lessons and Impact of the Sixth Conference of Nonaligned Countries," *Review of International Affairs*, Vol. XXX, No. 708, 1979.

Pike, Douglas (1966) *Viet Cong. The Organization and Techniques of the National Liberation Front of South Vietnam*. Cambridge, Massachusetts, and London: The M.I.T. Press.

Pike, Douglas (1971) "Operational Code of the North Vietnamese Politburo," *Asia Quarterly*, No. 1.

Pike, Douglas (1987) *Vietnam and the Soviet Union. The Anatomy of an Alliance*. Boulder, Colorado: Westview Press.

Porter, Gareth (1981) "Vietnamese Policy and the Indochina Crises," in Elliot (ed.), *The Third Indochina Conflict*. Boulder, Colorado: Westview Press.

Porter, Gareth (1985) "Vietnam's Evolving Policy toward Thailand: Implications for the Future," in William S. Turley (ed.) *Confrontation or Coexistence. The Future of ASEAN-Vietnam Relations*. Bangkok: Institute of Security and International Studies, Chulalongkorn University.

Porter, Gareth (1990a) "The Transformation of Vietnam's World-view: From Two Camps to Interdependence," *Contemporary Southeast Asia*, Vol 12, No. 1, June.

Porter, Gareth (1990b) "The Politics of 'Renovation' in Vietnam," *Problems of Communism*, Vol. 39, No. 3, May–June.

Porter, Gareth (1993) *Vietnam. The Politics of Bureaucratic Socialism*. Ithaca: Cornell University Press.

Pye, L.W. and Verba, S. (eds.) (1965) *Political Culture and Political Development*. Princeton, New Jersey: Princeton University Press.

Pye, Lucian W. (1985) *Asian Power and Politics. The Cultural Dimensions of Authority*. The Belknap Press of Harvard University Press, Cambridge, Massachusetts and London 1985.

Pyykkö, Riitta (1992) "Gorbatsovin perestroikan keskeinen sanasto," *Politiikka* No. 1.

Rakowski, Mieczyslaw (1976) "Asia's Pressing Problem," *International Affairs* (Moscow) 4.

Ricoeur, Paul (1988) *Hermaneutics and Human Science*. Ed. John B. Thompson. New York: Cambridge University Press.

Romanov A. (1956) "The Unbreakable Ideological Unity of the Communist Parties;" *International Affairs* (Moscow) 11.

Rosenberg, S. W. and Wolsfeld, G. (1977) "International Conflict and the Problem of Attribution," *Journal of Conflict Resolution*, Vol. 21, No. 1, March.

Ross, Robert S. (1988) *The Indochina Triangle. China's Vietnam Policy 1975–1979*. New York: Columbia University Press.

Sakwa, Richard (1990) *Gorbachev and his Reforms 1985–1990*. Hertfordshire: Philip Allan.

Sanakoyev Sh. (1969) "The Leninist Methodology of Studying International Problems," *International Affairs* (Moscow) 9.

Saravanamutu, Johan (1984) "ASEAN Security for 1980s: The Case for a Revitalized ZOPFAN," *Contemporary Southeast Asia*, Vol. 6, No. 1.

Scalapino, R.A. and Dalchoong Kim (eds.) (1988) *Asian Communism. Continuity and Transition*. Korea Research Monograph, No. 15. Berkeley: Institute of East Asian Studies. University of California.

Shee Poon-Kim (1977) "A Decade of ASEAN 1967–1977," *Asian Survey*, Vol. XVII, No. 8, August.

Shevardnadze, Eduard (1990) "To 'International Affairs' Readers," *International Affairs* (Moscow) 1.

Singham, A.W. (1978) "Conclusion," in A.W. Singham (ed.), *The Nonaligned Movement in World Politics*. Westport, Connecticut: Lawrence Hill & CO.

Smyser, W.R. (1980) *The Independent Vietnamese: Vietnamese Communism Between Russia and China, 1956–1969*. Papers in International Studies, Southeast Asia, No. 55. Ohio University, Center for International Studies.

Starr, John Bryan (1973) *Ideology and Culture. An Introduction to the Dialectic of Contemporary Chinese Politics*. New York: Harper & Row cop.

Stern, Lewis M. (1985) "The Overseas Chinese in the Socialist Republic of Vietnam, 1979–82," *Asian Survey*, Vol. XXV, No. 5, May.

Stern, Lewis M. (1986) "Vietnamese Communist Policies towards the Overseas Chinese, 1930–60," *The Journal of Communist Studies*, Vol. 2. No. 1, March.

Stuart-Fox, Martin (1986) *Laos. Politics, Economics and Society.* London: Frances Pinter Publishers.

Suh, Mark B. (1984) "Political Cooperation among ASEAN Countries," in W. Pfennig and M.B. Suh (eds.) *Aspects of ASEAN.* Munchen: Weltforum Verlag,

Summa, Hilkka (1990) "Ethos, Pathos and Logos in Central Governmental Texts: Rhetoric as an Approach to Studying a Policy-Making Process," in S. Hänninen and K. Palonen (eds.) *Texts, Contexts, Concepts. Studies on Politics and Power in Language.* Jyväskylä: The Finnish Political Science Association.

Susiluoto, Ilmari (1982) "Kieli ja valta: näkökohtia kulttuurirelativismista totalitarismin kielitieteeseen," *Politiikka*, Vol. 24, No. 2.

Susiluoto, Ilmari (1990) "Deritualization of Political Language: The case of the Soviet Union," in S. Hänninen and K. Palonen (eds.) *Texts, Contexts, Concepts. Studies on Politics and Power in Language.* Jyväskylä: The Finnish Political Science Association.

Thai Quang Trung (1985) *Collective Leadership and Factionalism. An Essay on Ho Chi Minh's Legacy.* Singapore: Institute of Southeast Asian Studies.

Thakur, R. and Thayer, C.A. (1992) *Soviet Relations with India and Vietnam.* London: Macmillan.

Thayer, Carlyle A. (1983) "Vietnam's Two Strategic Tasks. Building Socialism and Defending the Fatherland," in Pushpa Thambipillai (ed.), *Southeast Asian Affairs 1983.* Aldershot, Hampshire: Gower Publishing Company Limited.

Thayer, Carlyle A. (1984) "Vietnamese Perspectives on International Security: Three Revolutionary Currents," in Donald Hugh McMillen (ed.) *Asian Perspectives on International Security.* Hong Kong: Macmillan.

Thayer, Carlyle A. (1985) "Vietnam: Ideology and the Lessons from Experience," in William S. Turley (ed.), *Confrontation or Coexistence. The Future of ASEAN-Vietnam Relations.* Bangkok: Institute of Security and International Studies, Chulalongkorn University.

Thayer, Carlyle A. (1989a) *War by Other Means. National Liberation and Revolution in Viet-Nam 1954–60.* Sydney: Allen & Unwin.

Thayer, Carlyle A. (1989b) "Vietnam and the Soviet Union: Perceptions and Policies," in Pushpa Thambipillai and Daniel C. Matuszewski (eds.), *The Soviet Union and the Asia-Pacific Region. Views from the Region.* New York: Praeger.

Thayer, Carlyle A. (1991) "Civil Society and the Soviet-Vietnamese Alliance," in Kukathas, Lovell and Maley (eds.), *The Transition from Socialism. State and Civil Society in the USSR.* Melbourne: Longman Chesire.

Thayer, Carlyle A. (1992a) "Political Reform in Vietnam: Doi Moi and the emergence of civil society," in Robert F. Miller (ed.), *The Developments of Civil Society in Communist Systems.* Sydney: Allen & Unwin.

Thayer, Carlyle A. (1992b) "Comrade Plus Brother: The New Sino-Vietnamese Relations," *The Pacific Review*, Vol. 5. No. 4.

Tilman Robert O. (1987) *Southeast Asia and the Enemy Beyond. ASEAN Perceptions of External Threats.* Boulder, Colorado: Westview Press.

Trinh Van Thao (1990) *Vietnam: Du confucianisme au communisme.* Paris: Edition's L'Harmattan.

Triska, J.F. and Finley, D. D. (1968) *Soviet Foreign Policy.* Toronto: Macmillan.

Tsapanov, V. (1972) "Proletarian Internationalism: The Basis of Relations among the Fraternal Parties and Countries," *International Affairs* (Moscow) 9.

Turley William S. (1980) "Political Participation and the Vietnamese Communist Party," in William S. Turley (ed.), *Vietnamese Communism in Comparative Perspective*. Boulder, Colorado: Westview Press.

Turner, Robert F. (1975) *Vietnamese Communism. Its Origins and Development*. Stanford, California: Hoover Institution Press.

Tønnesson, Stein (1992) "Vietnam as a Regional Great Power: a Study in Failure," in Iver B. Neumannn (ed.), *Regional Great Powers in International Politics*. London: Macmillan.

Ulam, Adam P. (1980) "Soviet Ideology and Soviet Foreign Policy," in E.P. Hoffman and F.J. Fleron Jr. (eds.), *The Conduct of Soviet Foreign Policy*. New York: Aldine Publishing Company.

The USSR Foreign Ministry (1989) "The Foreign Policy and Diplomatic Activity of the USSR (April 1985–October 1989). A Survey Prepared by the USSR Foreign Ministry," *International Affairs* (Moscow) 1.

Weatherbee, Donald E. (1985) "The Diplomacy of Stalemate," in D.E. Weatherbee (ed.), *Southeast Asia Divided*. Boulder and London: Westview Press.

White, Stephen et al. (1982) *Communist Political Systems: An Introduction*. New York: St. Martin's Press.

White, Stephen (1991) *Gorbachev and After*. Cambridge: Cambridge University Press.

Vickery, Michael (1986) *Kampuchea. Politics, Economics and Society*. London: Frances Pinter Publishers.

Willetts, Peter (1978) *The Non-Aligned Movement. The Origins of a Third World Alliance*. London: Frances Pinter Ltd.

Willets, Peter (1981) "Background to the Documents," in Willets (ed.), *The Non-Aligned in Havanna. Documents of the Sixth Summit Conference and an Analysis of Their Significance for the Global Political System*. London: Frances Pinter (Publishers).

Vo Nhan Tri (1990) *Vietnam's Economic Policy since 1975*. Singapore: Institute of Southeast Asian Studies.

Woodside, Alexander B. (1976) *Community and Revolution in Modern Vietnam*. Boston: Houghton Mifflin Company.

Wurfel, David (1989) "Perestroika, Vietnamese Style: Problems and Prospects," in R. Stubbs (ed.), *Vietnam: Facing the 1990s*. Asia Papers No. 1. Toronto: Joint Centre for Asia Pacific Studies.

Yan Sun (1994) "The Chinese and Soviet Reassessment of Socialism: The Theoretical Bases of Reform and Revolution in Communist Regimes," *Communist and Post-Communist Studies*, Vol. 27, No. 1.

Index

Truong Chinh, 22, 216, 218, 219, 220;
  on friend/enemy division, 23;
  on Kampuchea, 146;
  on traditional culture and Marxist ideology, 26
Truong Khue Bich, 223

United Nations, 7, 113, 120–127;
  and East Timor, 124–126;
  and Kampuchean question, 126, 129, 138, 146, 148–149, 152–157, 161, 163 168, 197–198;
  and Sino–Soviet rift, 120–121, 127;
  and US military bases, 122–124;
  and US war reparations, 122
United States, 42, 47;
  and China, 34, 41, 76, 128, 146, 150, 159, 166;
  and decline of global power, 46, 65, 67, 99, 187;
  and Kampuchean question, 153;
  new role of, 192, 193, 194;
  and Non-Aligned Movement, 118, 119–120;
  and Southeast Asia, 62, 68, 99, 103, 105, 106, 107, 108;
  and war reparations, 119–120, 122;
  and Vietnam, 1, 33, 35, 59, 125, 127, 129, 198;
  and World's revolutionary forces, 48, 49

Van Hien, 221, 228
Van Tao, 223, 235

Van Trong, 231
Vo Nguyen Giap, 22, 216, 218, 219, 223, 230;
  on China, 70, 133;
  disagreements with Party leadership, 132, 230;
  dismissal of, 131–132, 143, 222;
  on friend/enemy division, 23–24, 25, 133;
  on ideology and mobilization, 25, 26–27;
  pragmatism of, 34, 58, 132–134, 135, 191;
  on Soviet bloc, 133–134
World's revolutionary forces [luc luong cach mang the gioi], 42, 43, 45–50, 93, 135, 202
Vu Hien, 158, 159, 233
Vu Khoan, 237
Vu Tien, 221, 231

Yen Van, 229

ZOPFAN, 100, 198;
  and China, 101;
  and Colombo Conference, 104, 119;
  and Havana Conference, 152;
  and Kampuchean question, 153, 155–157;
  and Malaysia, 100, 110, 111, 156;
  and regional diplomacy, 162–163, 164, 165, 166, 167;
  and Soviet Union, 101;
  and Vietnam, 102–103, 104, 105, 107–108, 110–112, 139, 155–157, 197